AF693278

Microsoft Dynamics NAV 7 Programming Cookbook

Learn to customize, integrate and administer NAV 7 using practical, hands-on recipes

Rakesh Raul

[PACKT] enterprise
PUBLISHING
professional expertise distilled

BIRMINGHAM - MUMBAI

Microsoft Dynamics NAV 7 Programming Cookbook

First published: September 2013

Production Reference: 1170913

Published by Packt Publishing Ltd.
Livery Place
35 Livery Street
Birmingham B3 2PB, UK.

ISBN 978-1-84968-910-6

www.packtpub.com

Cover Image by Jarek Blaminsky (milak6@wp.pl)

Credits

Author
Rakesh Raul

Reviewers
Danilo Capuano
Neil Murray
Giancarlo Zavala

Acquisition Editor
James Jones

Lead Technical Editor
Anila Vincent

Technical Editors
Veena Pagare
Jinesh Kampani
Iram Malik
Sandeep Madnaik
Shashank Desai

Copy Editors
Tanvi Gaitonde
Sayanee Mukherjee
Kirti Pai
Alfida Paiva
Adhiti Shetty

Project Coordinator
Navu Dhillon

Proofreader
Bridget Braund

Indexer
Monica Ajmera

Graphics
Abhinash Sahu

Production Coordinator
Arvindkumar Gupta

Cover Work
Arvindkumar Gupta

About the Author

Rakesh Raul is from a small town in India, with a vision of doing something big in programming. He completed his first diploma in programming at the age of 16, and continued higher studies in computer software development.

He started his programming career with a small software development company in Mumbai. After 2 years of development in Visual Basic, he was introduced to Microsoft Dynamics NAV Version 3. For the first 2-3 years he worked as a Microsoft Dynamics NAV developer and at the same time he learned all the areas of the product and earned his first Microsoft Certification-Business Solutions Professional. He continues to stay updated with new releases of the product and is certified in multiple areas for versions 4.0, 5.0, 2009, and 2013. Apart from Microsoft Dynamics NAV, he also has good knowledge of Microsoft SQL Server and Business Intelligence.

His seven-year journey with Microsoft Dynamics NAV includes more than 30 implementations; one horizontal and two vertical solution designs and development.

Currently, he works in Tectura, India, as a Senior Technical Consultant. Tectura is a worldwide provider of business consulting services delivering innovative solutions.

I would like to thank my wife, Ashwini, for supporting and always standing by my side in good and bad days.

I would like to take this opportunity to thank all the mentors I was blessed with, who unconditionally shared their knowledge and inspired me.

Mibuso and all Microsoft Dynamics NAV related blogs are a great boon for all NAV consultants. I would like to thank all the contributors of these great sites.

Love you Aabha, my cute little princess!

About the Reviewers

Danilo Capuano is a Software Engineer with over seven years of industry experience. He lives in Naples, Italy, where he earned a degree in computer science. He currently works as a developer on Microsoft Dynamics NAV in an IT company where he also completed the MCTS certification. You can visit his website: `www.capuanodanilo.com` or his Twitter account: `@capuanodanilo`.

Neil Murray began his development career as a C++ and Visual Basic developer, qualifying as a Microsoft Certified Solution Developer on Visual Basic 6.0 in 1999. He has been a Microsoft Dynamics NAV developer since 2001, providing consulting, customization, and support to customers across sub-Saharan Africa. He currently works for a large multi-national IT organization, providing technical and business process support to dairy, manufacturing, and retail clients.

I would like to thank my wife, Justine, and lovely daughters, Ember and Danica, for their love and understanding while I have dedicated precious family time to conduct the technical review of this book.

Giancarlo Zavala is an all-round expert in Microsoft Dynamics NAV technologies specializing in Application Analysis, Design and Development, and ERP implementations. He began as a network administrator in 1999 and eventually transitioned into application management. He also has a strong background with more than 15 years on Microsoft Server and networking technologies, Database Administration and Server Infrastructure deployment.

He has worked on a wide range of implementations and development projects in his career; including working as lead technical and functional consulting roles, as well as project management roles. He earned his first Microsoft Certification in SQL Database Administration in 2003, and later studied the Microsoft Dynamics ERP and CRM technologies.

He has now been managing business applications for over 10 years. He has built a unique set of skills working on full end-to-end implementations and application rollouts in various industries. He has helped various mid- to large-scale organizations successfully implement Microsoft Dynamics NAV in multiple countries around the globe, including Europe and Latin America.

Recently, he spent a couple of years in Houston working on the Oil and Energy industry with one of the largest NAV application setups around the globe. He worked on dozens of implementations as lead consultant, getting extensive knowledge of methodologies, business workflows, and best operational practices including Manufacturing, Distribution, Servicing, Warehouse Management, Intercompany Operations, Cost Accounting, and Financial Reporting amongst others. During this time, he also transitioned into design and development for Microsoft Dynamics NAV. He has worked with many of Microsoft's top partners and other well-known software vendors on multiple projects.

His passion is to always learn new skills and technologies related to Microsoft Dynamics, to create business specific solutions and to pass on his knowledge by training companies and coaching other colleagues. He enjoys building and working with a good team and taking on challenging projects with mission critical operations.

Currently, he lives in Miami and works at Tectura, U.S. as a Senior Consultant. He works on leading implementations, doing system analysis and in program development. Tectura is one of Microsoft's leading worldwide gold partners, providing consulting services and innovative solutions for small to large businesses.

Outside of work he enjoys travelling, surfing, and painting.

Acknowledgements

I want to thank everyone who helped me so that I could have the time and opportunity to work on this book. I've taken time away from the people I love in order to be able to accomplish this task. I wouldn't have been successful without the support from my family and friends who have always been there for me; and from my colleagues who have given me endless help and motivation. A very special thank you to my loving wife, Carolina, for her unconditional support on this journey. While I spent many nights working away from my loved ones, she took care of our two beautiful daughters on her own and made it all possible. I would be nowhere without her and I can only hope that in time I can repay her for the time I took away from us.

I would like to give my gratitude to Rakesh Raul (the author of this book), and Anila Vincent (Lead Technical Editor) for giving me the opportunity to work on this cookbook project.

Big thanks to my grandfather who gave me strong roots and good moral values to live a positive life filled with love. Much love to my mom and dad who I wish could be here today to see this. Big thanks to my Brother and Tia Magaly for believing in me always and showing me the right path. Thanks again to all my friends and family who have been with us for so many years and to those who have supported me throughout the review of this book. Thanks to my friend, Chuck Luciano, for always giving me moral support; thanks to Jan Verleur, John Byrne, David Diaz, Steve Bloch, Stacy Racca, Sowmya Sridhar, Brett Boullion, Lurleen Cloud, Kim Parker, Craig Sanders, and Elizabeth Peña for teaching me, keeping faith in my abilities, and giving me some of the most important opportunities in the early years of my career.

For every night that I have not been able to kiss you goodnight, this work is dedicated to the two most beautiful and brightest lights in my world, Sofia and Valentina.

Live, Learn, Create, Teach, and Love.

www.PacktPub.com

Support files, eBooks, discount offers and more

You might want to visit www.PacktPub.com for support files and downloads related to your book.

Did you know that Packt offers eBook versions of every book published, with PDF and ePub files available? You can upgrade to the eBook version at www.PacktPub.com and as a print book customer, you are entitled to a discount on the eBook copy. Get in touch with us at service@packtpub.com for more details.

At www.PacktPub.com, you can also read a collection of free technical articles, sign up for a range of free newsletters and receive exclusive discounts and offers on Packt books and eBooks.

PACKTLIB™

http://PacktLib.PacktPub.com

Do you need instant solutions to your IT questions? PacktLib is Packt's online digital book library. Here, you can access, read and search across Packt's entire library of books.

Why Subscribe?

- Fully searchable across every book published by Packt
- Copy and paste, print and bookmark content
- On demand and accessible via web browser

Free Access for Packt account holders

If you have an account with Packt at www.PacktPub.com, you can use this to access PacktLib today and view nine entirely free books. Simply use your login credentials for immediate access.

Instant Updates on New Packt Books

Get notified! Find out when new books are published by following @PacktEnterprise on Twitter, or the *Packt Enterprise* Facebook page.

Table of Contents

Preface

Microsoft Dynamics NAV 7 is a product of the Microsoft Dynamics family. It's a business management solution that helps simplify and streamline business processes, such as finance, manufacturing, customer relationship management, supply chains, analytics, and electronic commerce for small and medium-sized enterprises. Microsoft Dynamics partners can have full access to the source code, which is very easy to customize. Learning NAV programming in NAV 7 will give a full inside view of the ERP system and open doors to many other exciting areas.

The Microsoft Dynamics NAV 7 Programming Cookbook will take you through interesting topics that span a wide range of areas, for example, integrating the NAV system with other software applications, such as Microsoft Office and creating reports to present information from multiple areas of the system. You will not only learn the basics of NAV programming, but you will also be exposed to the technologies that surround the NAV system, such as .NET programming, SQL Server, and NAV system administration.

The first half of the cookbook will help programmers using NAV for the first time by walking them through the building blocks of writing code and creating objects, such as tables, pages, and reports.

The second half focuses on using the technologies surrounding NAV to build better solutions and administration of the NAV service tier. You will learn how to write .NET code that works with the NAV system and how to integrate the system with other software applications, such as Microsoft Office or even custom programs.

What this book covers

Chapter 1, String, Dates, and Other Data Types, describes the method of working with the most common data types. You will learn how to use the functions related to data types. Every recipe includes actual NAV code with a brief explanation about code that will make the data type learning process very interesting.

Chapter 2, General Development, covers the C/AL development structure that includes loops, conditional statements, functions, and so on. You will find some recipes describing C/AL specific commands and functions.

Chapter 3, Working with Tables, Records, and Queries, focuses on the database structure and data retrieval. You will learn how to design a table using filters to retrieve specific data. This chapter will also discuss new object type Query.

Chapter 4, Designing Pages, focuses on data presentation using pages. You will learn how to develop different types of pages including Role Center, Queue, wizard, and many more.

Chapter 5, Report Design, explains how to design an RDLC report. You will find recipes describing the process of adding a request page, setting filters, linking two reports and many more interesting topics related to reports.

Chapter 6, Diagnosing Code Problems, explains how to use built-in tools to debug code problems. You will also learn about debugging the NAV application server.

Chapter 7, Roles and Security, focuses on NAV user security, which includes creating roles and assigning permissions to a role. It will also explain about security filters and filter groups.

Chapter 8, Leveraging Microsoft Office, describes different methods to integrate with the Microsoft Office suite, which includes Word, Excel, InfoPath, and Visio.

Chapter 9, OS Interaction, focuses on different ways to integrate with the Windows operating systems. You will learn how to search the filesystem as well as how to query the system registry.

Chapter 10, Integration, describes different ways of integrating NAV with other applications. You will learn how to exchange data using flat file and XMLport. You will find a recipe describing how to use ADO to access data stored in other databases.

Chapter 11, Working with the SQL Server, provides an introduction to the SQL Server environment. You will learn about writing queries, configuring automated backups, and maintaining SQL logfiles. There is a recipe that will help you to understand the Sum Index Field Technology.

Chapter 12, NAV Server Administration, will help you to learn and understand the NAV service tier. It will also explain about creating a user and maintaining a NAV license.

What you need for this book

The following software are required for the recipes in this book:

- Microsoft Dynamics NAV 7 with developer license
- Microsoft SQL Server 2008 R2
- Microsoft Visual Studio 2010
- Microsoft Office 2010

Who this book is for

If you are an entry-level NAV developer, then the first half of the book is designed primarily for you. You may or may not have any experience in programming. It focuses on the basics of NAV programming. It would be best if you have already gone through a brief introduction to the NAV client.

If you are a mid-level NAV developer, you will find the second half more useful. These chapters explain how to think outside the NAV box when building solutions. Towards the end of the book, we will learn NAV server tier configuration.

Conventions

In this book, you will find a number of styles of text that distinguish between different kinds of information. Here are some examples of these styles, and an explanation of their meaning.

Code words in text are shown as follows: "The `sp_who` command returns a list of all connections to the server by querying the `sys.sysprocesses` system table."

A block of code is set as follows:

```
Customer.RESET;
IF Customer.FINDSET THEN
  REPEAT
  CustCount:=CustCount+1;
  UNTIL Customer.NEXT=0;
  MESSAGE('There are %1 customers in the database',
    CustCount);
```

Any command-line input or output is written as follows:

```
sn.exe -T "C:\Program Files (x86)\Microsoft Dynamics NAV\70\
RoleTailored Client\Add-ins\NAV_RSS.dll"
```

New terms and **important words** are shown in bold. Words that you see on the screen, in menus or dialog boxes for example, appear in the text like this: "From the Tools menu in the NAV client select **Debugger** | **Debug Session** (*Shift* + *Ctrl* + *F11*)".

> Warnings or important notes appear in a box like this.

> Tips and tricks appear like this.

Reader feedback

Feedback from our readers is always welcome. Let us know what you think about this book—what you liked or may have disliked. Reader feedback is important for us to develop titles that you really get the most out of.

To send us general feedback, simply send an e-mail to `feedback@packtpub.com`, and mention the book title via the subject of your message.

If there is a topic that you have expertise in and you are interested in either writing or contributing to a book, see our author guide on `www.packtpub.com/authors`.

Customer support

Now that you are the proud owner of a Packt book, we have a number of things to help you to get the most from your purchase.

Errata

Although we have taken every care to ensure the accuracy of our content, mistakes do happen. If you find a mistake in one of our books—maybe a mistake in the text or the code—we would be grateful if you would report this to us. By doing so, you can save other readers from frustration and help us improve subsequent versions of this book. If you find any errata, please report them by visiting `http://www.packtpub.com/submit-errata`, selecting your book, clicking on the **errata submission form** link, and entering the details of your errata. Once your errata are verified, your submission will be accepted and the errata will be uploaded on our website, or added to any list of existing errata, under the Errata section of that title. Any existing errata can be viewed by selecting your title from `http://www.packtpub.com/support`.

Piracy

Piracy of copyright material on the Internet is an ongoing problem across all media. At Packt, we take the protection of our copyright and licenses very seriously. If you come across any illegal copies of our works, in any form, on the Internet, please provide us with the location address or website name immediately so that we can pursue a remedy.

Please contact us at `copyright@packtpub.com` with a link to the suspected pirated material.

We appreciate your help in protecting our authors, and our ability to bring you valuable content.

Questions

You can contact us at `questions@packtpub.com` if you are having a problem with any aspect of the book, and we will do our best to address it.

1

String, Dates, and Other Data Types

In this chapter, we will cover the following recipes:

- Retrieving the system date and time
- Retrieving the work date
- Determining the day, month, and year from a given date
- Using the date formula to calculate dates
- Converting a value to a formatted string
- Creating an array
- Creating an option variable
- Converting a string to another data type
- Manipulating string contents

Introduction

Data types are the base component in **C/AL** (**Client/server Application Language**) programming. Most of the data types are equivalent to the data types used in other programming language. Boolean, integer, decimal, dates, and strings are the most used data types in C/AL programming.

As developers, our job is to build a business tool that will manipulate the data input by users and make sure that data stored in tables is meaningful. Most of this data will be of the decimal, string, and date data types. NAV is, after all, a financial system at heart. At its most basic level, it cares about three things: "How much money?" (decimal), "What was it used for?" (string), and "When was it used?" (date).

The recipes in this chapter are very basic, but they will help you to understand the basics of C/AL coding. All recipes are accompanied by actual C/AL code from NAV objects.

Retrieving the system date and time

Most times, we need to capture the system date and time of users' actions on NAV. This recipe will illustrate how to get the system date and time.

How to do it...

1. Let's create a new codeunit from **Object Designer**.
2. Now add the following code into the `OnRun` trigger of the codeunit:

   ```
   MESSAGE('Todays Date: %1\Current Time: %2', TODAY, TIME);
   ```

3. To complete the development of the codeunit, save and close it.
4. On executing the codeunit, you should see a window similar to the one in the following screenshot:

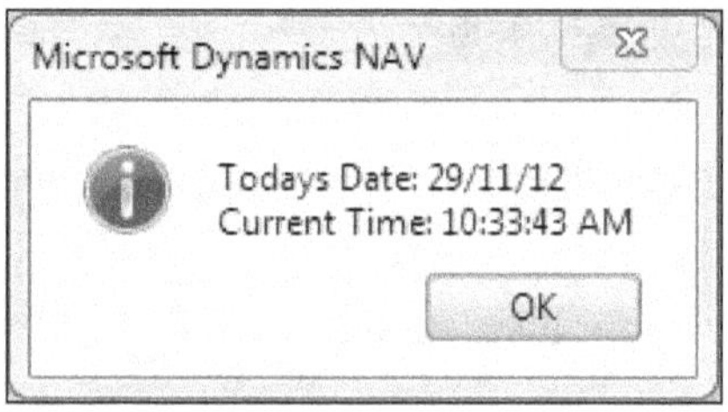

How it works...

The `TODAY` keyword returns the date and the `TIME` keyword returns the time from the NAV Server system.

In the case of the older version of the NAV client—specifically the classic client—the date and time are taken from the client computer, which allows users to manipulate the system clock as per their personal requirement.

You can also retrieve the system date and time all at once using the `CURRENTDATETIME` function. The date and time can be extracted using the `DT2DATE` and `DT2TIME` functions respectively.

> For a complete list of date functions, run a search for the `date` function and the `time` function in the **Developer and IT Pro Help** option in the **Help** menu of Microsoft NAV Development Environment

There's more...

The change log is a base NAV module that allows you to track changes to specific fields in tables. The following code can be found in the `423, Change Log Management` codeunit in the `InsertLogEntry()` method:

```
ChangeLogEntry.INIT;
ChangeLogEntry."Date and Time" := CURRENTDATETIME;
ChangeLogEntry.Time := DT2TIME(ChangeLogEntry."Date and Time");
```

Here, instead of using the `WORKDATE` function, we use the `CURRENTDATETIME` function and then extract the time using the `DT2TIME` function. The system designers can just do the following setup:

```
ChangeLogEntry.Date := TODAY;
ChangeLogEntry.Time := TIME;
```

The advantage of using `CURRENTDATETIME` over `TODAY` and `TIME` is minimal. `CURRENTDATETIME` makes one request to the system while the second method makes two. It is possible that another operation or thread on the client machine could take over between retrieving the date and time from the computer; however, this is very unlikely. The operations could also take place right before and after midnight, generating some very strange data. The requirements for your modification will determine which method is best suited, but generally `CURRENTDATETIME` is the correct method to use.

See also

- *Retrieving the work date*
- *Determining the day, month, and year from a given date*
- *Converting a value to a formatted string*

Retrieving the work date

To perform tasks such as completing transactions for a date that is not the current date, you may have to temporarily change the work date. This recipe will show you how to determine what that actual work date is as well as when and where you should use it.

Getting ready

1. Navigate to **Application Menu** | **Set Work Date** or select the date in the status bar at the bottom of Microsoft Dynamics NAV.
2. Input the work date in the **Work Date** field or select it from the calendar.

How to do it...

1. Let's get started by creating a new codeunit from **Object Designer**.
2. Then add the following code into the `OnRun` trigger of the codeunit:

```
MESSAGE('Work Date: %1\Todays Date: %2\Current Time: %3',WORKDATE,
TODAY, TIME);
```

3. To complete the task, save and close the codeunit.
4. On executing the codeunit, you should see a window similar to the following screenshot:

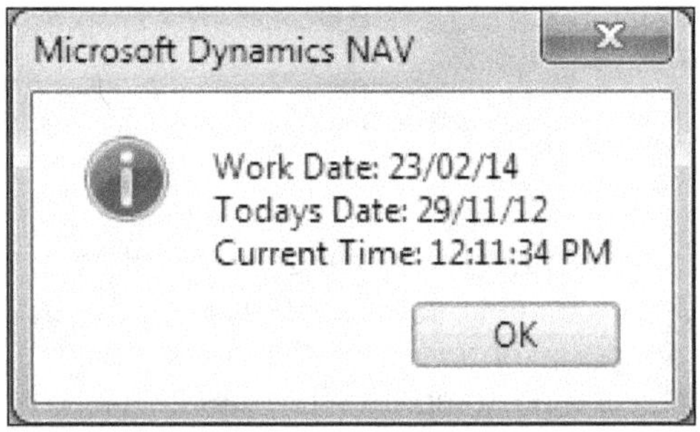

How it works...

To understand `WORKDATE`, we have used two more keywords in this recipe. The work date is a date internal to the NAV system. This date is returned using the `WORKDATE` keyword. It can be changed at any time by the user. The next date is `TODAY`; it's a keyword to retrieve the present date that provides the date from the system. In the end, we used the `TIME` keyword, which provides current time information from the system clock.

> It is important to understand the difference between the NAV work date and the computer system date; they should be used in specific circumstances. When performing general work in the system, you should almost always use the `WORKDATE` keyword. In cases where you need to log information and the exact date or time when an action occurred, you should use `TODAY` or `TIME`, or `CURRENTDATETIME`.

There's more...

The following code can be found in the `38, Purchase Header` table, in the `UpdateCurrencyFactor()` method:

```
IF "Posting Date" <> 0D THEN
CurrencyDate := "Posting Date"
ELSE
CurrencyDate := WORKDATE;
```

Looking at this code snippet, we can see that if a user has not provided any specific posting date, the system will assign the value `WORKDATE` as the default value for the posting date.

See also

- *Determining the day, month, and year from a given date*
- *Converting a value to a formatted string*
- The *Checking for conditions using an IF statement* recipe in *Chapter 2, General Development*
- The *Using the CASE statement to test multiple conditions* recipe in *Chapter 2, General Development*

Determining the day, month, and year from a given date

Sometimes it is necessary to retrieve only part of a date. NAV has built-in functions to do just that. We will show you how to use them in this recipe.

How to do it...

1. Let's create a new codeunit from **Object Designer**.
2. Then add the following global variables by navigating to **View** | **C/AL Globals** (*Alt* + *V* + *B*):

Name	Type
`Day`	Integer
`Month`	Integer
`Year`	Integer

3. Write the following code into the `OnRun` trigger of the codeunit:

```
Day := DATE2DMY(TODAY, 1);
Month := DATE2DMY(TODAY, 2);
Year := DATE2DMY(TODAY, 3);
MESSAGE('Day: %1\Month: %2\Year: %3', Day, Month, Year);
```

4. To complete the task, save and close the codeunit.
5. On executing the codeunit, you should see a window similar to the following screenshot:

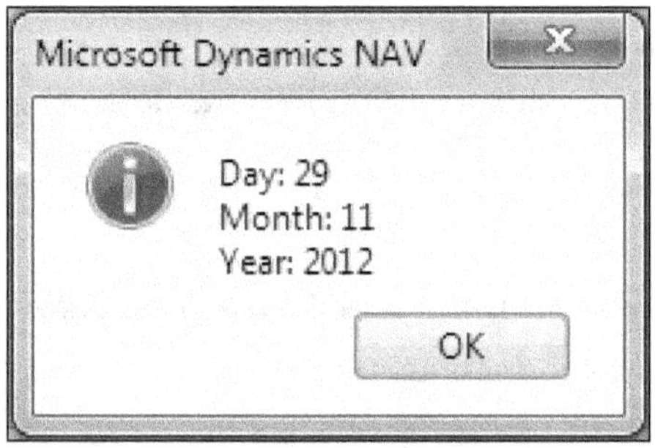

How it works...

The `Date2DMY` function is a basic feature of NAV. The first parameter is a date variable. This parameter can be retrieved from the system using `TODAY` or `WORKDATE`. Additionally, a hardcoded date such as `01312010D` or a field from a table, such as `Sales Header` or `Order Date` can be used as a first parameter. The second parameter is an integer that tells the function which part of the date to return. This number can be 1, 2, or 3, and corresponds to the day, month, and year (DMY) respectively.

> NAV has a similar function called `Date2DWY`. It will return the week of the year instead of the month if `2` is passed as the second parameter.

There's more...

The following code can be found in the `485, Business Chart Buffer` table in the `UpdateCurrencyFactor()` method of the `GetNumberOfYears()` function:

```
EXIT(DATE2DMY(ToDate,3) - DATE2DMY(FromDate,3));
```

This function has two parameters of type date and it returns the value in integer. The basic usage of this function is to calculate the duration between two dates in terms of years.

See also

- *Retrieving the system date and time*
- *Retrieving the work date*
- The *Repeating code using a loop* recipe in *Chapter 2, General Development*
- The *Checking for conditions using an IF statement* recipe in *Chapter 2, General Development*

Using the date formula to calculate dates

The date formula allows us to determine a new date based on a reference date. This recipe will show you how to use the built-in `CALCDATE` NAV function for date calculations.

How to do it...

1. Let's start by creating a new codeunit from **Object Designer**.
2. Add the following global variable by navigating to **View** | **C/AL Globals** (*Alt* + *V* + *B*):

Name	Type
`CalculatedDate`	Date

3. Write the following code into the `OnRun` trigger of the codeunit:

```
CalculatedDate := CALCDATE('CM+1D', 010110D);
MESSAGE('Calculated Date: %1', CalculatedDate);
```

4. Now save and close the codeunit.
5. On executing the codeunit, you should see a window similar to the following screenshot:

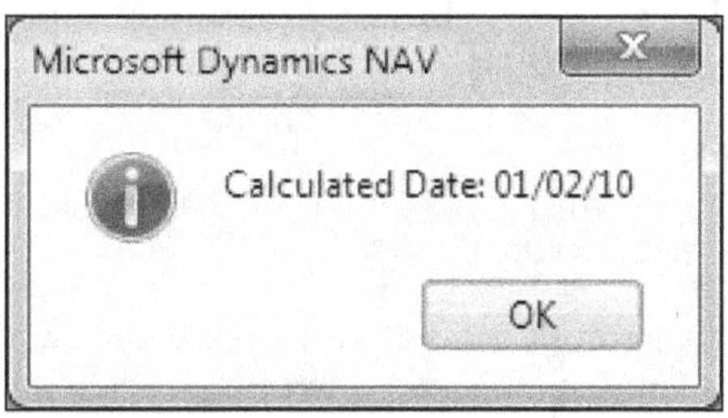

How it works...

The `CALCDATE()` function takes in two parameters: a calculation formula and a starting date. The calculation formula is a string that tells the function how to calculate the new date. The second parameter tells the function which date it should start with. A new date is returned by this function, so the value must be assigned to a variable.

The following units can be used in the calculation formula:

Unit	Description
D	Day
WD	Weekday
W	Week
M	Month
Q	Quarter
Y	Year

These units may be different depending on what language version NAV is running under.

You have two options to place the number before the unit. It can either be a standard number ranging between 1 and 9 or the letter C, which stands for current. These units can be added and subtracted to determine a new date based on any starting date.

Calculation formulas can become very complex. The best way to fully understand them is to write your own formulas to see the results. Start out with basic formulas such as *1M + 2W - 1D* and move on to more complex ones, such as *-CY + 2Q - 1W*.

There's more...

The following code is part of the `CalcNumberOfPeriods()` function of the `485, Business Chart Buffer` table:

```
"Period Length"::Week:
  NumberOfPeriods := (CALCDATE('<-CW>',ToDate)-
    CALCDATE('<CW>',FromDate)) DIV 7;
```

The preceding code snippet will return the difference between two dates in terms of weeks. `<-CW>` will provide a week start date of `ToDate` whereas `<CW>` will provide a week end day of `FromDate`. The difference between the calculated days will be divided by 7 to get the total number of weeks.

For more details on `CALCDATE`, visit the following URL:

`http://msdn.microsoft.com/en-us/library/dd301368(v=nav.70).aspx`

See also

- *Retrieving the system date and time*
- *Retrieving the work date*
- *Determining the day, month, and year from a given date*
- The *Checking for conditions using an IF statement* recipe in *Chapter 2, General Development*

Converting a value to a formatted string

There will be many occasions when you will need to display information in a certain way or multiple variable types on a single line. The `FORMAT` function will help you change almost any data type into a string that can be manipulated in any way you see fit.

How to do it...

1. Let's get started by creating a new codeunit from **Object Designer**.
2. Then add the following global variable:

Name	Type	Length
`FormattedDate`	Text	30

3. Now write the following code into the `OnRun` trigger of the codeunit:

```
FormattedDate := FORMAT(TODAY, 0, '<Month Text> <Day,2>,<Year4>');
MESSAGE('Today is %1', FormattedDate);
```

4. To complete the task, save and close the codeunit.
5. On executing the codeunit, you should see a window similar to the following screenshot:

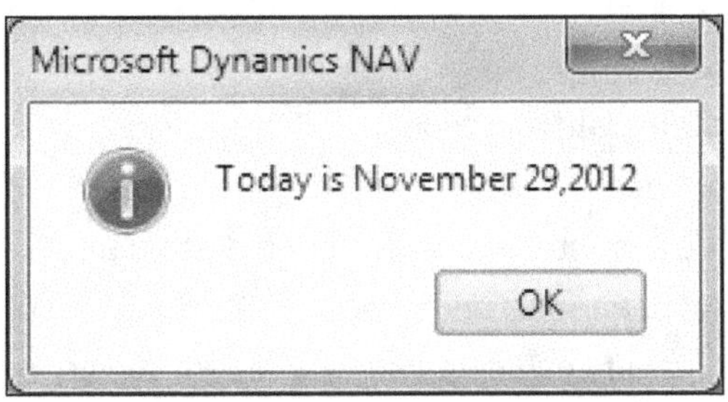

How it works...

The FORMAT function takes one to three parameters. The first parameter is required and can be of almost any type: date, time, integer, decimal, and so on. This parameter is returned as a string.

The second parameter is the length of the string to be returned. The default, zero, means that the entire string will be returned, a positive number tells the function to return a string of exactly that length, and a negative number returns a string not larger than that length.

There are two options for the third, and final, parameter. One is a number, representing a predefined format you want to use for the string, and the other is a literal string. In the example, we used the actual format string. The text contained in the angular brackets (< >) will be parsed and replaced with the data in the first parameter.

> There are many predefined formats for dates. Run a search for Format Property in the **Developer and IT Pro Help** option in the **Help** menu of Microsoft NAV Development Environment or visit the following URL:
>
> http://msdn.microsoft.com/en-us/library/dd301059(v=nav.70).aspx

There's more...

The following code can be found on the OnValidate() trigger of the Starting Date field from the 50, Accounting Period table:

```
Name := FORMAT("Starting Date",0,Text000);
```

In the preceding code, Text000 is a text constant and carries the <Month Text> value. This code will return month of "Starting Date" in text format.

See also

- *Retrieving the system date and time*
- *Retrieving the work date*
- *Determining the day, month, and year from a given date*
- *Converting a string to another data type*
- The *Checking for conditions using an IF statement* recipe in *Chapter 2, General Development*
- The *Advanced filtering* recipe in *Chapter 3, Working with Tables, Records, and Queries*
- The *Retrieving data using the FIND and GET statements* recipe in *Chapter 3, Working with Tables, Records, and Queries*

Creating an array

Creating multiple variables to store related information can be time consuming. It leads to more code and more work. Using an array to store related and similar types of information can speed up development and lead to much more manageable code. This recipe will show you how to create and access array elements.

How to do it...

1. Let's create a new codeunit from **Object Designer**.
2. Add the following global variables by navigating to **View** | **C/AL Globals** (*Alt* + *V* + *B*):

Name	Type
`i`	Integer
`IntArray`	Integer

3. Now, with the cursor on the `IntArray` variable, navigate to **View** | **Properties** (*Shift* + *F4*).
4. In the **Property** window, set the following property:

Property	Value
Dimensions	`10`

5. Write the following code into the `OnRun` trigger of the codeunit:

```
FOR i := 1 TO ARRAYLEN(IntArray) DO BEGIN
  IntArray[i] := i;
  MESSAGE('IntArray[%1] = %2', i, IntArray[i]);
END;
```

6. To complete the task, save and close the codeunit.
7. On executing the codeunit, you should see a window similar to the following screenshot:

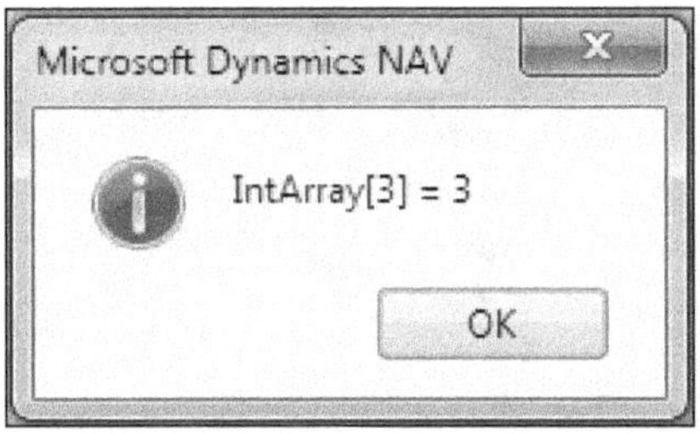

How it works...

An array is a single variable that holds multiple values. The values are accessed using an integer index. The index is passed within square brackets ([ ]).

> NAV provides several functions to work with arrays. For instance, `ARRAYLEN` returns the number of dimensions of the array and `COPYARRAY` will copy all of the values from one array into a new array variable. You can find a complete list of the array functions in the **Developer and IT Pro Help** option in the **Help** menu of Microsoft NAV Development Environment.

There's more...

Open the `365, Format Address` codeunit. Notice that the first function, `FormatAddr`, has a parameter that is an array. This is the basic function that all of the address formats use. It is rather long, so we will discuss only a few parts of it here.

This first section determines how the address should be presented based on the country of the user. Variables are initialized depending on which line of the address should carry certain information. These variables will be the indexes of our array.

```
CASE Country."Contact Address Format" OF
  Country."Contact Address Format"::First:
    BEGIN
      NameLineNo := 2;
      Name2LineNo := 3;
      ContLineNo := 1;
      AddrLineNo := 4;
      Addr2LineNo := 5;
      PostCodeCityLineNo := 6;
      CountyLineNo := 7;
      CountryLineNo := 8;
    END;
```

Then we will fill in the array values in the following manner:

```
AddrArray[NameLineNo] := Name;
AddrArray[Name2LineNo] := Name2;
AddrArray[AddrLineNo] := Addr;
AddrArray[Addr2LineNo] := Addr2;
```

Scroll down and take a look at all of the other functions. You'll see that they all take in an array as the first parameter. It is always a text array of length `90` with eight dimensions. These are the functions you will call when you want to format an address. To use this codeunit correctly, we will need to create an empty array with the specifications listed before and pass it to the correct function. Our array will be populated with the appropriately formatted address data.

See also

- *Manipulating string contents*
- The *Using the CASE statement to test multiple conditions* recipe in *Chapter 2, General Development*

Creating an option variable

If you need to force the user to select a value from a predefined list, an **option** is the way to go. This recipe explains how to create an `Option` variable and access each of its values.

How to do it...

1. Let's create a new codeunit from **Object Designer**.
2. Then add the following global variable:

Name	Type
`ColorOption`	Option

3. With the cursor on the `ColorOption` variable, navigate to **View** | **Properties** or (*Shift + F4*).
4. In the **Property** window, set the following property:

Property	Value
OptionString	None,Red,Green,Blue

5. Now write the following code into the `OnRun` trigger of the codeunit:

```
ColorOption := ColorOption::Green;
CASE ColorOption OF
  ColorOption::None: MESSAGE('No Color Selected');
  ColorOption::Red: MESSAGE('Red');
  ColorOption::Green: MESSAGE('Green');
  ColorOption::Blue: MESSAGE('Blue');
END;
```

6. Save and close the codeunit.

7. On executing the codeunit, you should see a window similar to the one shown in the following screenshot:

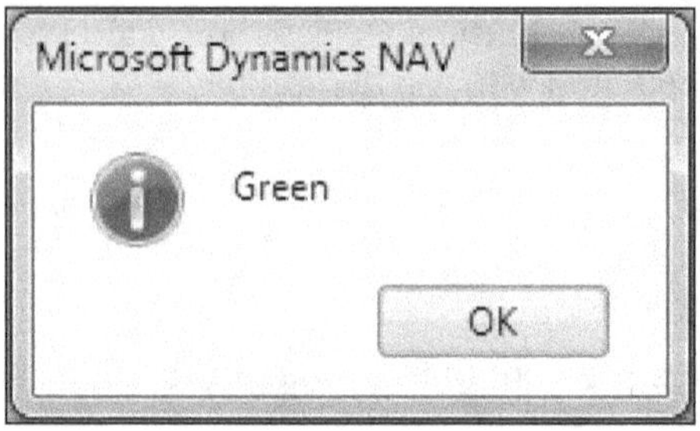

How it works...

An `Option` is a field or variable that stores one value from a selectable list. In a form, this list will appear as a dropdown from which the user can select a value. The list of options is stored as a comma-separated string in the `OptionString` property. If we query such stored values from a SQL database, we will receive an integer value representing each option. In our current example, the integer value has been mapped with options, where `None` = `0`, `Red` = `1`, `Green` = `2`, and `Blue` = `3`.

These values are accessed using the `variable_name::option_name` syntax. The first line of the example assigns one of the possible values (`Green`) to the variable. Then we use a `CASE` statement to determine which of the values were selected.

> There are many predefined formats for dates. Run a search for `Format Property` in the **Developer and IT Pro Help** option in the **Help** menu of Microsoft NAV Development Environment.

There's more...

The `Option` fields are prevalent throughout the NAV system, but most commonly on documents. In NAV, many documents share the same table. For example, sales quotes, orders, invoices, and return orders are all based on the `Sales Header` table. In order to distinguish between the types, there is an `Option` field called `Document Type`. Design the `36, Sales Header` table to see the available options for this field.

Now design the `80, Sales-Post` codeunit. Examine the `OnRun` trigger. At the start of the function, you will see the following code:

```
CASE "Document Type" OF
"Document Type"::Order:
  Receive := FALSE;
"Document Type"::Invoice:
```

```
    BEGIN
      Ship := TRUE;
      Invoice := TRUE;
      Receive := FALSE;
    END;
  "Document Type"::"Return Order":
    Ship := FALSE;
  "Document Type"::"Credit Memo":
    BEGIN
      Ship := FALSE;
      Invoice := TRUE;
      Receive := TRUE;
    END;
  END;
```

This is a common example of how options are used in NAV. You can scroll through the codeunit to find more examples.

See also

- The *Using the CASE statement to test multiple conditions* recipe in *Chapter 2, General Development*

Converting a string to another data type

Sometimes, a string representation isn't enough. In order to perform certain actions, you need your data to be in a certain format. For example, we are reading data from a text file, so our entire data is simple text, which needs to be converted into an appropriate data type to use it in NAV. This recipe will show you how to change that data into a format that you can use.

How to do it...

1. Let's start by creating a new codeunit from **Object Designer**.
2. Now add the following global variables:

Name	Type	Length
DateText	Text	30
DateValue	Date	

3. Write the following code into the `OnRun` trigger of the codeunit:

```
DateText := '01/10/2012';
EVALUATE(DateValue, DateText);
MESSAGE('Microsoft Dynamics NAV 2013 launch date is %1',
  DateValue);
```

4. To complete the development, save and close the codeunit.
5. On executing the codeunit, you should see a window similar to the one shown in the following screenshot:

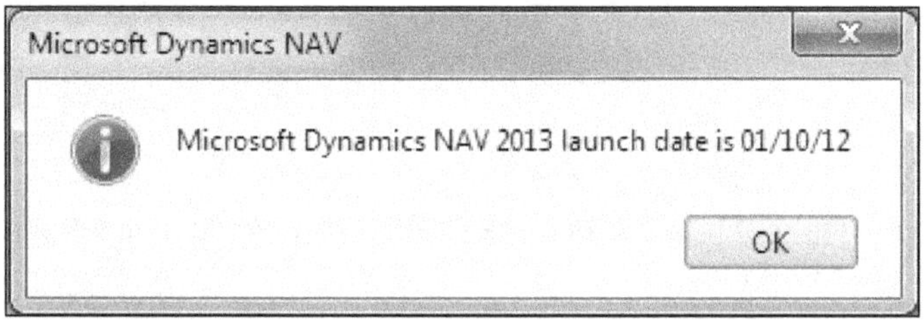

How it works...

The `EVALUATE()` function takes in two parameters. The first is a variable of the type that we want our value to be converted into. This could be date, time, Boolean, integer, or any other simple data type. This parameter is passed by reference, meaning that the result of the function is stored in that variable. There is no need to do a manual assignment to get a return value.

The second parameter is the string that you need to convert. This text is usually stored in a field or variable, but can also be hardcoded.

> `EVALUATE()` returns a Boolean value when executed. If the conversion is successful, it returns `TRUE` or `1`; otherwise, it returns `FALSE` or `0`. If the function returns `FALSE`, an error will be generated.

There's more...

The `EVALUATE()` function is widely used in NAV C/AL code. The following code snippet is taken from the `CheckCreditCardData()` function of the `825, Do Payment Mgt` codeunit:

```
EVALUATE (IntValue1,FORMAT(TODAY,0,'<Year>'));
EVALUATE (IntValue2,COPYSTR(DOPaymentCreditCard."Expiry Date",3,2));
IF IntValue1 > IntValue2 THEN
  ERROR (Text006, CreditCardNo,
    DOPaymentCreditCard.FIELDCAPTION ("No."));
```

Before completing a transaction, the credit card's validity period needs to be checked. The preceding code extracts the year from the current date provided by the `TODAY` function and the expiry date of the credit card. Both the values are evaluated using the relational operator. If the card has expired, the system will execute a predefined error message in text constant `Text006`.

See also

- *Converting a value to a formatted string*
- The *Checking for conditions using an IF statement* recipe in *Chapter 2, General Development*
- The *Passing parameters by reference* recipe in *Chapter 2, General Development*

Manipulating string contents

It can be very useful to parse a string and retrieve certain values. This recipe will show you how to examine the contents of a string and manipulate that data.

How to do it...

1. Let's create a new codeunit from **Object Designer**.
2. Add a function called `RemoveNonNumeric`. It should return a text variable called `NewString`.
3. Add the following parameters for the same function:

Name	Type	Length
String	Text	30

4. Now add the following global variables:

Name	Type	Length
OldPhoneNumber	Text	30
NewPhoneNumber	Text	30
I	Integer	

5. Write the following code to the `RemoveNonNumeric` function:

```
FOR i := 1 TO STRLEN(String) DO BEGIN
IF String[i] IN ['0', '1', '2', '3', '4', '5', '6', '7','8','9']
THEN
  NewString := NewString + FORMAT(String[i]);
END;
```

6. Write the following code into the `OnRun` trigger of the codeunit:

```
OldPhoneNumber := '(230) 299-876';
NewPhoneNumber := RemoveNonNumeric(OldPhoneNumber);
MESSAGE('Old Phone Number: %1\New Phone Number: %2',
OldPhoneNumber, NewPhoneNumber);
```

7. To complete the task, save and close the codeunit.
8. On executing the codeunit, you should see a window similar to the one shown in the following screenshot:

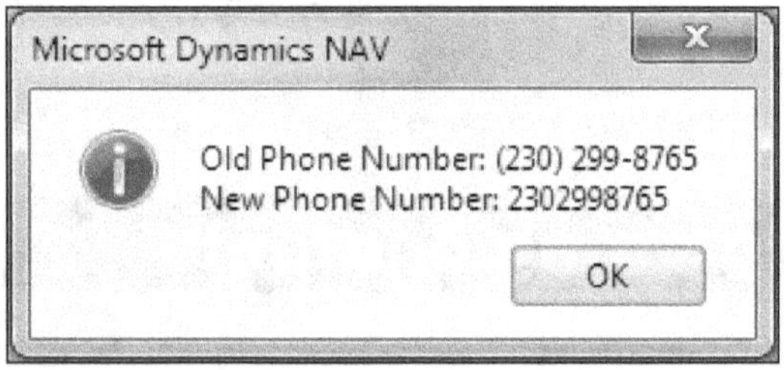

How it works...

A string is actually an array of characters. The same array syntax will be used to access the individual characters of the string.

We start with a `FOR` loop that begins at the first character, with index `1`, and goes on until we reach the end of our string. This is determined using the `STRLEN()` function, which stands for string length. As the first index is `1`, the last index will be `N` or the number of characters in the string.

Next, we access the character at that index using square brackets. If the character is a number, meaning we want to keep it because it is a numeric value, we add it to our resulting string.

> NAV comes with plenty of built-in string manipulation functions to remove characters, return substrings, find characters within strings, and many more. A search in the **Developer and IT Pro Help** option of the **Help** menu of Microsoft NAV Development Environment for string functions will give you a complete list.

There's more...

The `CheckIBAN` function of the `79, Company Information` table is a simple example of string manipulation to validate **IBAN** (**International Bank Account Number**). IBAN is internationally agreed on and adopted. It consists of up to 34 alphanumeric characters: the first two letters are the country code, then two `check digits`, and finally a country-specific Basic Bank Account Number. The same is validated by manipulating the input string using various functions. The following code gives you an example for the same:

```
IF IBANCode = '' THEN
  EXIT;
IBANCode := DELCHR(IBANCode);
Modulus97 := 97;
IF (STRLEN(IBANCode) <= 5) OR (STRLEN(IBANCode) > 34) THEN
  IBANError;
ConvertIBAN(IBANCode);
WHILE STRLEN(IBANCode) > 6 DO
  IBANCode := CalcModulus(COPYSTR(IBANCode,1,6),Modulus97) +
    COPYSTR(IBANCode,7);
EVALUATE(I,IBANCode);
IF (I MOD Modulus97) <> 1 THEN
  IBANError;
```

There are a few more functions used to validate the string; such as `ConvertIBAN`, `CalcModulus`, and `ConvertLetter`. These functions can give you a basic idea to write your own code.

For more complex examples, please follow the `DecomposeRowID()` function in the `6500, Item Tracking Management` codeunit. The code evaluates the value stored in the `Source RowId` field of the `6508, Value Entry Relation` table.

See also

- *Converting a value to a formatted string*
- *Creating an array*
- The *Repeating code using a loop* recipe in *Chapter 2, General Development*
- The *Checking for conditions using an IF statement* recipe in *Chapter 2, General Development*

2

General Development

In this chapter, we will learn the following:

- Displaying the progress bar and data in process
- Repeating code using a loop
- Checking for conditions using an `IF` statement
- Using the `CASE` statement to test multiple conditions
- Rounding decimal values
- Creating functions
- Passing parameters by reference
- Referencing dynamic tables and fields
- Using recursion

Introduction

C/AL (**Client/server Application Language**) is a programming language used in **Client/server Integrated Development Environment** (**C/SIDE**). Using C/AL, we can create business rules to ensure that the data stored in the database is consistent and meaningful. The main purpose of using C/AL is to manipulate data. Besides handling data, C/AL helps to manage execution of C/SIDE objects (such as a table, page, report, codeunit, query, and XMLport).

This chapter consists of recipes that will make understanding of C/AL very easy.

Displaying the progress bar and data in process

During the execution of a big batch job or reports, if the system is not displaying any progress information it can be frustrating and confusing. To avoid this for our customers, we should always display the progress bar and/or data in progress.

How to do it...

1. Let's get started by creating a new codeunit from **Object Designer**.
2. Add the following global variables:

Name	Type
ProgressBar	Dialog
AmountProcessed	Integer
AmountToProcess	Integer
PercentCompleted	Integer

3. Now let's add the following code to the `OnRun` trigger of the codeunit:

```
AmountToProcess := 500000;
ProgressBar.OPEN('@1@@@@@@@@@@@\#2###########');
REPEAT
  AmountProcessed += 1;
  PercentComplete := ROUND(AmountProcessed / AmountToProcess
*10000, 1);
  ProgressBar.UPDATE(1, PercentComplete);
  ProgressBar.UPDATE(2, PercentComplete);

UNTIL AmountProcessed = AmountToProcess;
```

4. Save and close the codeunit.
5. On execution of the codeunit, you should see a window similar to the following screenshot:

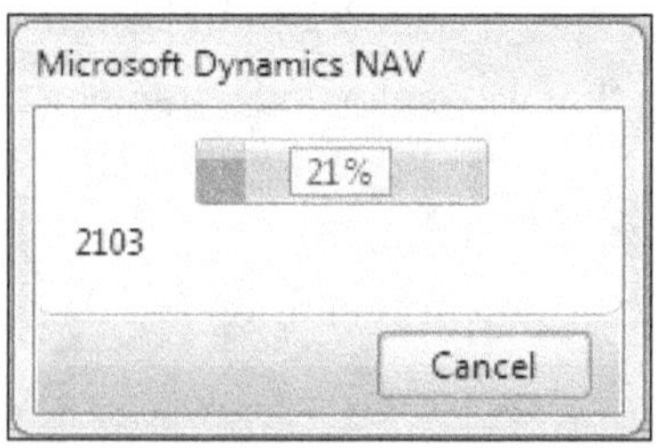

How it works...

In order to track the progress of something, we need to know two things: how much we have to do and how much we have already done. We create two variables for this data, `AmountToProcess` and `AmountProcessed`. In our code shown in step 3, we have set the `AmountToProcess` value equal to `500000`. Depending on the speed of the computer, this may make the progress bar advance either too quickly or too slowly.

Basic information such as this is displayed to the user using what is called a **dialog**. A string as an input parameter is given to the dialog. The `@` sign tells the dialog to display the information as a progress indicator, and `1` identifies the indicator for later updates. The rest of the `@` signs specify the length of the progress bar, whereas the `#` sign tells it to display the information as a data string, and `2` identifies the indicator for later updates. The rest of the `#` signs specify the length of the string to display.

The minimum and maximum values for the progress bar are not `0` and `100` as you might expect. Instead, they are `0` and `10000` respectively. This is why we multiply `ROUND(AmountProcessed / AmountToProcess)` by `10000` when we are calculating our `PercentComplete` value. As the `PercentComplete` variable is an integer value, we must also round up our result to the nearest digit.

There's more...

As I mentioned in the *Introduction* section, we should display the progress information on the batch job activities; a common way to process a large amount of data is to create a "processing only" report. In this situation, our `AmountToProcess` variable would be the number of records in the table. This would be calculated in the `OnPreDataItem` trigger. We would also open the dialog here. In the `OnAfterGetRecord` trigger, we would update our `AmountProcessed` variable and update the progress bar as necessary.

Some examples of the "processing only" reports in the base system are `296 (Batch Post Sales Orders)` and `299 (Delete Invoiced Sales Orders)`.

See also

- *Checking for conditions using an IF statement*
- *Creating a report to process data*

Repeating code using a loop

Looping is an essential part of any data manipulation. Same as the other programming languages, C/AL offers a variety of looping methods. The following recipe will help you understand how to use the `FOR` loop in C/AL code.

How to do it...

1. Let's start by creating a new codeunit from **Object Designer**.
2. Then add the following global variables:

Name	Type
n	Integer
i	Integer
Factorial	Integer

3. Now write the following code in the `OnRun` trigger of the codeunit:

```
Factorial := 1;
n := 4;
FOR i := 1 TO n DO BEGIN
  Factorial := Factorial * i;
  MESSAGE('Factorial of %1 = %2', n, Factorial);
END;
```

4. To complete the task, save and close the codeunit.
5. On execution of the codeunit, you should see a window similar to the following screenshot:

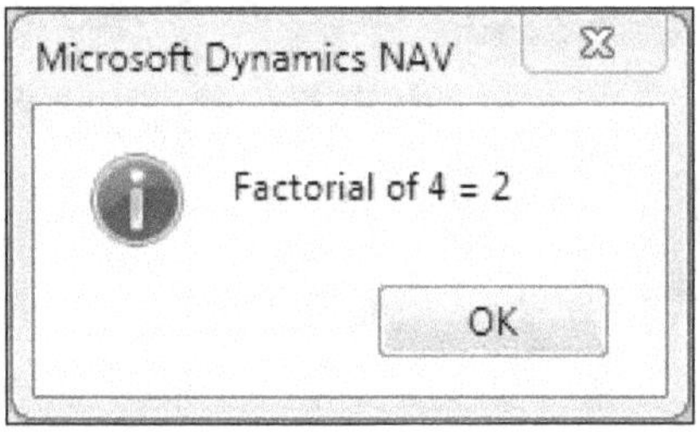

How it works...

A FOR loop has four parts: a counter, a starting value, the step to be taken, and an ending value. In this code, our counter variable is i. The starting value is 1 and the ending value is n, which in this case has been assigned the value 4.

On execution of the previous code, we will get four messages with values 1, 2, 6, and 24. Each time the loop iterates, the value of i is increased by one (the step). The code indented under the FOR loop will be executed four times. It is exactly the same as:

```
Factorial := Factorial * 1;
Factorial := Factorial * 2;
Factorial := Factorial * 3;
Factorial := Factorial * 4;
```

> If we want to use a step other than 1 or -1, we need to use a WHILE loop or a REPEAT..UNTIL loop.

There's more...

You can also use a FOR loop by decreasing the counter. To do this, instead of TO, use DOWNTO. The structure for this type of loop is as follows:

```
Factorial := 1;
n := 4;
FOR i := n DOWNTO 1 DO
Factorial := Factorial * i;
MESSAGE('Factorial of %1 = %2', n, Factorial);
```

Using a WHILE loop

A WHILE loop is similar to a FOR loop; the main difference is that you have to take control of the counter, as shown in the following code:

```
Factorial := 1;
n := 4;
i := 1;
WHILE i <= n DO BEGIN
Factorial := Factorial * i;
i += 1;
END;
MESSAGE('Factorial of %1 = %2', n, Factorial);
```

The following is what happens in the WHILE loop:

1. First we have to initialize our starting value, which is accomplished by the third line `i := 1`.
2. Then in the `WHILE` line, we have to give a stop condition. As long as `i <= n (4)` holds true, we want the statements to execute.
3. Finally, we have added the `i += 1;` command to the code inside our loop. A `FOR` loop does this behind the scenes, but a `WHILE` loop doesn't. Here, we can increment our counter by any value we want. This basic line is perhaps most important. Without it, we will never reach our stop condition, and will be stuck in an infinite loop.

Using a REPEAT..UNTIL loop

The difference between this type of loop and a standard `WHILE` loop is that the code is guaranteed to execute at least once; we will use this type of loop often to access records through tables. The following is the structure of a `REPEAT..UNTIL` loop:

```
Factorial := 1;
n := 4;
i := 1;
REPEAT
Factorial := Factorial * i;
i += 1;
UNTIL i > n;
MESSAGE('Factorial of %1 = %2', n, Factorial);
```

See also

- *Checking for conditions using an IF statement*
- The *Creating reports to process data* recipe in *Chapter 5, Report Design*

Checking for conditions using an IF statement

Sometimes, we want to execute a section of code on a specific condition; this recipe will help to explain the syntax for the same.

How to do it...

1. Let's create a new codeunit from **Object Designer**.
2. Add the following global variables:

Name	Type	SubType
`SalesHeader`	Record	Sales header
`RecordsProcessed`	Integer	

3. Now write the following code in the `OnRun` trigger of the codeunit:

```
IF SalesHeader.FINDSET THEN BEGIN
  REPEAT
    RecordsProcessed += 1;
  UNTIL SalesHeader.NEXT = 0;
  MESSAGE('Processed %1 records.', RecordsProcessed);
END ELSE
  MESSAGE('No records to process.');
```

4. Save and close the codeunit to complete the task.
5. On execution of the codeunit, you should see a window similar to the following screenshot:

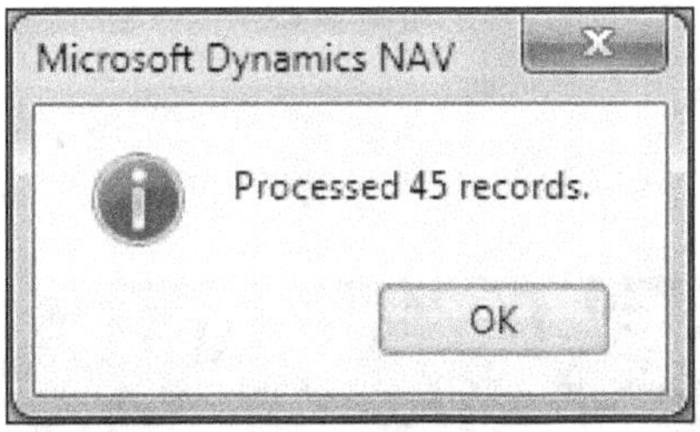

How it works...

In order to execute the code that processes the records, there must be records in the table. That's exactly what the first line of the previous code does. It tells the code that *if* you find some records, *then* it should do these actions. In this case, the action is to count the records in the table and display a message to the user.

When the condition in the `IF` statement does not evaluate to true, the control falls to the next `ELSE` statement. So if we find some records, then the code must do something, otherwise (`ELSE`) it should do something else. Our "something else" is to inform the user that no records were found. The `ELSE` part is not required, but we should always consider what should happen if the condition is false.

There's more...

You can also use the nested IF statement.

The nested IF statement

The following is the code for a nested IF statement:

```
IF DATE2DMY(WORKDATE,1) = 1 THEN
  MESSAGE('Monday')
ELSE IF DATE2DMY(WORKDATE,1) = 2 THEN
  MESSAGE('Tuesday')
ELSE IF DATE2DMY(WORKDATE,1) = 3 THEN
  MESSAGE('Wednesday')
ELSE IF DATE2DMY(WORKDATE,1) = 4 THEN
  MESSAGE('Thursday')
ELSE IF DATE2DMY(WORKDATE,1) = 5 THEN
  MESSAGE('Friday')
ELSE
  MESSAGE('Its the weekend!');
```

We can combine the operators (AND, OR, and NOT) to form complex conditionals, and test as many conditions as necessary.

See also

- *Using the CASE statement to test multiple conditions*

Using the CASE statement to test multiple conditions

When we have more than two conditions to test, it will be beneficial to use a CASE statement for better code readability.

How to do it...

1. Create a new codeunit from **Object Designer**.
2. Let's add the following global variables:

Name	Type
i	Integer

3. Now write the following code in the `OnRun` trigger of the codeunit:

```
i := 2;
CASE i OF
  1:
    MESSAGE('Your number is %1.', i);
  2:
    MESSAGE('Your number is %1.', i);
  ELSE
    MESSAGE('Your number is not 1 or 2.');
END;
```

4. It's time to save and close the codeunit.
5. On execution of the codeunit, you should see a window similar to the following screenshot:

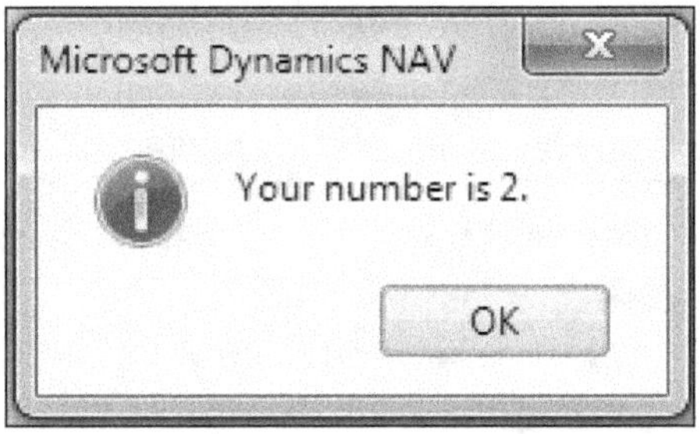

How it works...

A `CASE` statement compares the value given, in this case `i`, to various conditions contained within that statement. Each condition other than the default `ELSE` condition is followed by a colon. The same logic can be written using the `IF` statement:

```
IF i = 1 THEN
  MESSAGE('Your number is %1.', i)
ELSE IF i = 2 THEN
  MESSAGE('Your number is %1.', i)
ELSE
  MESSAGE('Your number is not 1 or 2.');
```

See also

- *Checking for conditions using an IF statement*

Rounding decimal values

As Navision is a financial system, it's obvious that most of the time we need to handle decimal values, and rounding decimals is a very important part of it. When we are converting high-value currency to low-value currency, a small decimal can make a big difference.

How to do it...

1. Let's get started by creating a new codeunit from **Object Designer**.
2. Add the following global variables:

Name	Type
AmountToRound	Decimal
RoundToNearest	Decimal
RoundToUp	Decimal
RoundToDown	Decimal

3. Now write the following code in the `OnRun` trigger of the codeunit:

```
AmountToRound:=345.8689999999;
RoundToNearest:=ROUND(AmountToRound,0.01,'=');
RoundToUp:=ROUND(AmountToRound,0.01,'>');
RoundToDown:=ROUND(AmountToRound,0.01,'<');

MESSAGE('Amount Before Rounding = %1 \\Rounded to nearest value =
%2'+'\Rounded to upper value = %3\Rounded to lower value = %4',Amo
untToRound,RoundToNearest,RoundToUp,RoundToDown);
```

4. It's time to save and close the codeunit.
5. On execution of the codeunit, you should see a window similar to the following screenshot:

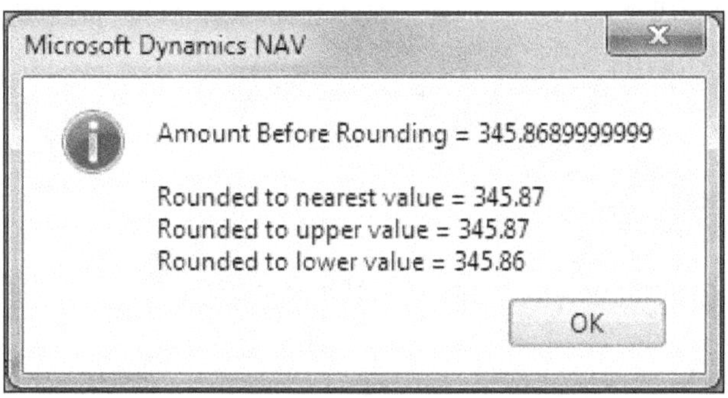

How it works...

For a `Round` function, we need to specify three parameters, that is, a number to round, the precision, and the direction. The precision parameter determines the precision used when rounding off. The default value of the precision parameter is `0.01`. The direction parameter details how to round. The default value for direction is =, which will round our number to the nearest value; > will round to the greater value, whereas < will round to a lesser value.

> For more rounding examples, search for a `Round Function` in the **Developer and IT Pro Help** menu in **Help** of the **Microsoft NAV Development Environment** page or visit the following URL:
>
> `http://msdn.microsoft.com/en-us/library/dd301418(v=nav.70).aspx`

See also

- The *Retrieving data from a database with different FIND statements* recipe in *Chapter 3, Working with Tables, Records, and Queries*

Creating functions

Most programs will need to execute code from different NAV objects. This code is contained in functions. This recipe will show you how to create a function and explain in more detail what functions are.

How to do it...

1. To start, let's create a new codeunit from **Object Designer**.
2. Add a function called `CountToN` that takes an integer parameter `n`.
3. Now add the following global variables:

Name	Type
i	Integer

4. Write the following code in the function:

```
FOR i := 1 TO n DO
  MESSAGE('%1', i);
```

5. Write the following code in the `OnRun` trigger of the codeunit:

```
CountToN(3);
```

6. It's time to save and close the codeunit.

7. On execution of the codeunit, you should see a window similar to the following screenshot:

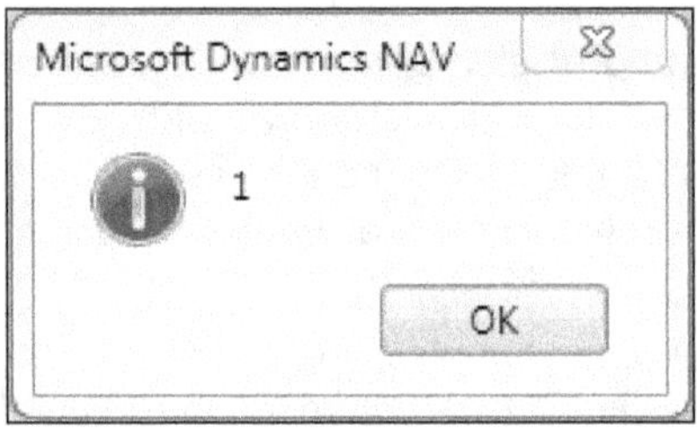

How it works...

By creating a function, we can reference multiple lines of code using one easy-to-understand name. Our function is called `CountToN`, and it takes an integer `n` as a parameter. This function will display a message box for every number ranging between one and the number that is passed to the function.

There's more...

Proper use of functions is essential to good software development. You will have difficulty finding any objects in NAV that don't contain even a single function.

The main use of functions is to divide complex tasks into manageable chunks of code. This makes debugging a lot easier. Other developers who may add content to our code later will be able to understand better what we were trying to accomplish. By encapsulating code in functions, you also reduce the number of places where changes need to be made when you find faulty business logic.

Once written, these functions can then be called from other objects. A better practice is to keep a codeunit with common utility functions in it. We can load this codeunit into any database we happen to be working on, and have instant access to our code from any object in the system.

Creating local or private functions

By default, all functions are created as global functions, which means that they can be accessed from any object in the system. Sometimes, though, you may only want a function to be accessed from within the object in which it resides.

It may seem counterintuitive, but you still define these functions in the same way you define global functions. If you view the properties of the function (*Shift* + *F4* or navigate to **View** | **Properties** from the menu), you will see one called **Local**. Set this property to **Yes**, and it will only be available in the current object.

See also

- *Passing parameters by reference*

Passing parameters by reference

Sometimes, we may want our function to modify multiple values. As we can't return more than one value from a function (unless we use an array), it can be beneficial to pass our parameters by reference to the function.

How to do it...

1. Let's get started by creating a new codeunit from **Object Designer**.
2. Add the following global variables:

Name	Type	SubType	Length
`CustomerRec`	Record	Customer	
`OldName`	Text		50
`NewName`	Text		50

3. Then add a function called `ChangeCustomerName`.
4. The function should take the following parameter:

Name	Type	SubType
`Customer`	Rec	Customer

5. Let's write the following code in the `ChangeCustomerName` function:

```
Customer.Name := 'Changed Name';
```

6. Add another function called `ChangeCustomerNameRef`.
7. The function should take the following parameter:

Name	Type	SubType
`Customer`	Rec	Customer

8. Place a check mark in the `Var` column for the parameter.
9. Write the following code in the `ChangeCustomerNameRef` function:

```
Customer.Name := 'Changed Name';
```

10. Write the following code in the OnRun trigger of the codeunit:

```
IF CustomerRec.FINDFIRST THEN BEGIN
  OldName := CustomerRec.Name;
  ChangeCustomerName(CustomerRec);
  NewName := CustomerRec.Name;
  MESSAGE('Pass by value:\Old Name: %1\New Name: %2', OldName,
             NewName);
  OldName := CustomerRec.Name;
  ChangeCustomerNameRef(CustomerRec);
  NewName := CustomerRec.Name;
  MESSAGE('Pass by reference:\Old Name: %1\New Name: %2',
          OldName, NewName);
END;
```

11. It's time to save and close the codeunit.
12. On execution of the codeunit, you should see a window similar to the following screenshot:

How it works...

The first function, ChangeCustomerName, passes the parameter by value, which means that a copy of the variable is created and the function uses that copy. So, even though the customer name is changed in the function, only its copy is changed. The original stays the same.

The second function, ChangeCustomerNameRef, passes the parameter by reference. When you pass a parameter by reference, the parameter refers to the same location in memory that the actual variable is stored in. No copy is made. Any changes made to the parameter will be reflected in the original variable.

There's more...

Reference parameters are common throughout NAV, especially in codeunits. Codeunits such as `12 (General Journal Lines)`, `80 (Sales)`, and `90 (Purchases)` are all written to work with a specific type of record. This is defined under the `TableNo` property in the codeunit's properties. When you set a value here, the `OnRun` trigger will automatically have a reference parameter named `Rec` added to it. Any changes made to the `Rec` variable will change the actual value in that record. Also, if you only pass a record by value to a function, you do not get any of the filters applied to the record set.

See also

- *Creating functions*

Referencing dynamic tables and fields

On occasions, we may need to retrieve data from the system, but not know in advance where that data should come from. NAV accommodates this by allowing you to reference tables and fields dynamically.

How to do it...

1. Let's start by creating a new codeunit from **Object Designer**.
2. Add a global function, `GetFirstRecord`:
3. The function should take the following parameter:

Name	Type
`TableNo`	Integer

4. Now add the following local variables:

Name	Type
`RecRef`	`RecordRef`
`FieldRef`	`FieldRef`

5. With the cursor on the `FieldRef` variable, navigate to **View** | **Properties** or press *Shift + F4*.
6. Let's set the following property:

Property	Value
`Dimensions`	`2`

7. Write the following code in the `GetFirstRecord` function:

```
RecRef.OPEN(TableNo);
IF RecRef.FINDFIRST THEN BEGIN
  IF RecRef.FIELDEXIST(1) THEN
    FieldRef[1] := RecRef.FIELDINDEX(1);

  IF RecRef.FIELDEXIST(2) THEN
    FieldRef[2] := RecRef.FIELDINDEX(2);

  IF FieldRef[1].ACTIVE AND FieldRef[2].ACTIVE THEN
    MESSAGE('Table: %1\%2: %3\%4: %5', RecRef.NAME,

  FieldRef[1].NAME, FieldRef[1].VALUE,
  FieldRef[2].NAME, FieldRef[2].VALUE)
ELSE
  MESSAGE('You cannot retrieve an inactive field.');
END ELSE
  MESSAGE('No records found!');
```

8. Write the following code in the `OnRun` trigger of the codeunit:

```
GetFirstRecord(DATABASE::Customer);
GetFirstRecord(DATABASE::Vendor);
```

9. It's time to save and close the codeunit.
10. On execution of the codeunit, you should see a window similar to the following screenshot:

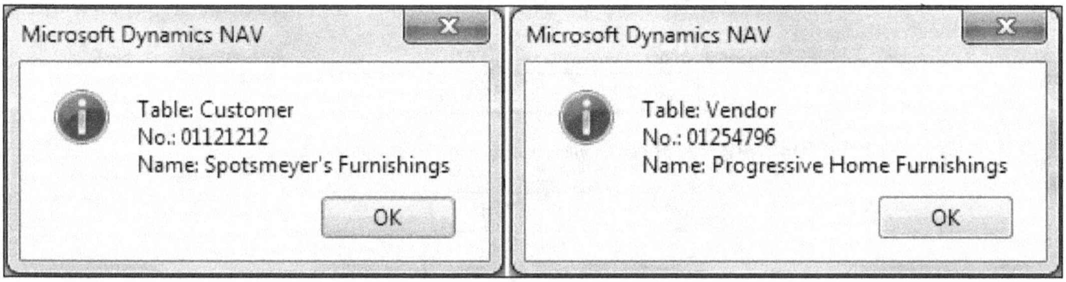

How it works...

We are creating a function, `GetFirstRecord`, which will return information about the first record found in an unknown table. The `TableNo` parameter will tell the function which table in the database to find the data in.

When you don't know the table until runtime, you must use a `RecordRef` variable, which stands for record reference, and can refer to any record/table in the database. To point it to the right table, you use the `OPEN` command. Here, we tell the `RecordRef` variable to open any table we pass into the function. If a record is found in that table, we continue on, otherwise we display the message **No records found!**.

To store references to the fields, we have created an array of the `FieldRef` variables called `FieldRef`. In this function, we have hardcoded a lookup for fields `1` and `2`. We can even pass another parameter with the `ID` value of the field we need. If that field exists, we assign its value into our `FieldRef` variable to an appropriate index.

Finally, we have to determine whether the fields are active or in use and available for use by the system. If they were not, we would not have been able to retrieve their values, and would instead display a message to the user. But if they are active, we display the name and value of each field using the properties of the same name.

The code in the `OnRun` trigger runs the function with two different tables. The `DATABASE::"Table Name"` syntax resolves to an integer. You could also pass the actual ID of the tables.

There's more...

Record references act just like their record counterparts. We can use them to insert, modify, or delete records. We can set filters on them and use them to find records. For a complete list of functions and properties, use the **Symbol** menu and investigate in the **Developer and IT Pro Help** menu from **Help** of the **Microsoft NAV Development Environment** page.

The data migration codeunits in NAV are full of functions that use record and field references. I recommend you to start with the functions in codeunit `8611` (`Config. Package Management`). This is a great place to see real examples of how this type of code can be used.

See also

- *Checking for conditions using an IF statement*
- *Passing parameters by reference*

Using recursion

Recursion is not used often in NAV, but the option is available, and can shorten your code. Recursion is the process by which a function calls itself.

How to do it...

1. Let's create a new codeunit from **Object Designer**.
2. Then add a global function called `Fibonacci` that returns an integer with no name.
3. Provide the following parameters for the function:

Name	Type
`i`	Integer

4. Now write the following code to the `Fibonacci` function:

```
IF (i <= 2) THEN
  EXIT(1);

EXIT ( Fibonacci(i-1) + Fibonacci(i-2) );
```

5. Write the following code in the `OnRun` trigger of the codeunit:

```
MESSAGE('Fibonacci(%1) = %2', 4, Fibonacci(4));
```

6. It's time to save and close the codeunit.
7. On execution of the codeunit, you should see a window similar to the following screenshot:

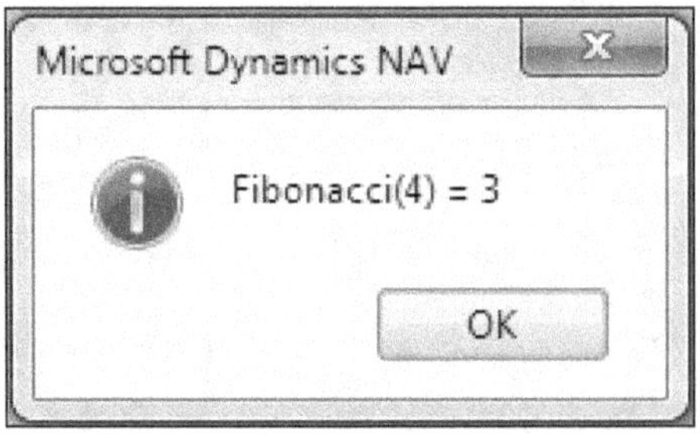

How it works...

The `Fibonacci` sequence is a series of numbers, where the value in a certain position is the sum of the number in the previous two positions, that is, 1, 1, 2, 3, 5, 8, 13, 21, 34, 55, and so on.

A recursive function has two parts. The first is a stopping condition. In our `Fibonacci` function, the stopping condition is when the variable `i` is less than or equal to `2`. In that case, the function will return `1` as the output.

The second part is where the function calls itself with a different parameter. Recursion can be confusing, so let's go through the code to get a better understanding. We'll use the following diagram to explain this more clearly:

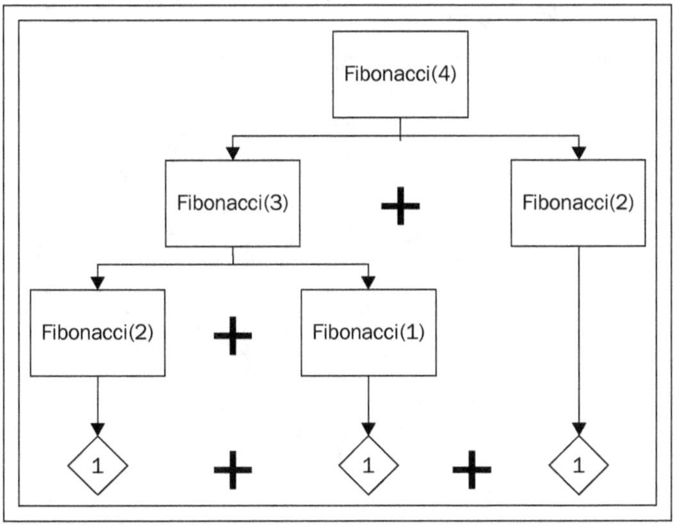

There's more...

We start by passing the number `4` as a parameter to our function, which means that the variable `i` is equal to `4`. As `4` is not less than or equal to `2`, we move to the last line of the function. The function will exit the loop with the `value Fibonacci(4 - 1) + Fibonacci(4 - 2)` expression, but we don't know what those values are. Now we evaluate each of those function calls separately.

`Fibonacci(3)` has a parameter that is also not less than `2`. Again, we move to the last line of the function and exit with `Fibonacci(3 - 1) + Fibonacci(3 - 2)`. This time, it gets easier.

`Fibonacci(2)` exits with the value `1`. `Fibonacci(1)` also exits with the value `1`, hence `Fibonacci(2) = 1` and `Fibonacci(1) = 1`. Substituting them back in, we get `Fibonacci(3) = Fibonacci(2) + Fibonacci(1) = 1 + 1 = 2.`

But we're not done. We still have the original `Fibonacci(4 - 2)` expression to evaluate:

```
Fibonacci(2) = 1. So let's sum it all up.

Fibonacci(4) =[ Fibonacci(3) ] + [ Fibonacci(2) ] =

[ Fibonacci(2) + Fibonacci(1) ] + [ Fibonacci(2) ] =[1 + 1] + [1] = 3.
```

See also

- *Repeating code using a loop*
- *Sharing information through XMLports*

3

Working with Tables, Records, and Queries

In this chapter, we will cover:

- Creating a table
- Adding a key to a table
- Retrieving data using the FIND and GET statements
- Advanced filtering
- Adding a FlowField
- Creating a SumIndexField
- Retrieving data from FlowField and SumIndexField
- Using a temporary table
- Retrieving data from other companies
- Using a query to extract data
- Creating a query to link three tables
- Working with queries in C/AL

Introduction

Microsoft Dynamics NAV systems store business information (data) in tables. Tables may be visualized as two-dimensional matrices consisting of columns and rows. Data stored in a table can be viewed by clicking on **Run** in **Object Designer**. Each row is the record and each column is the field, as shown in the following screenshot:

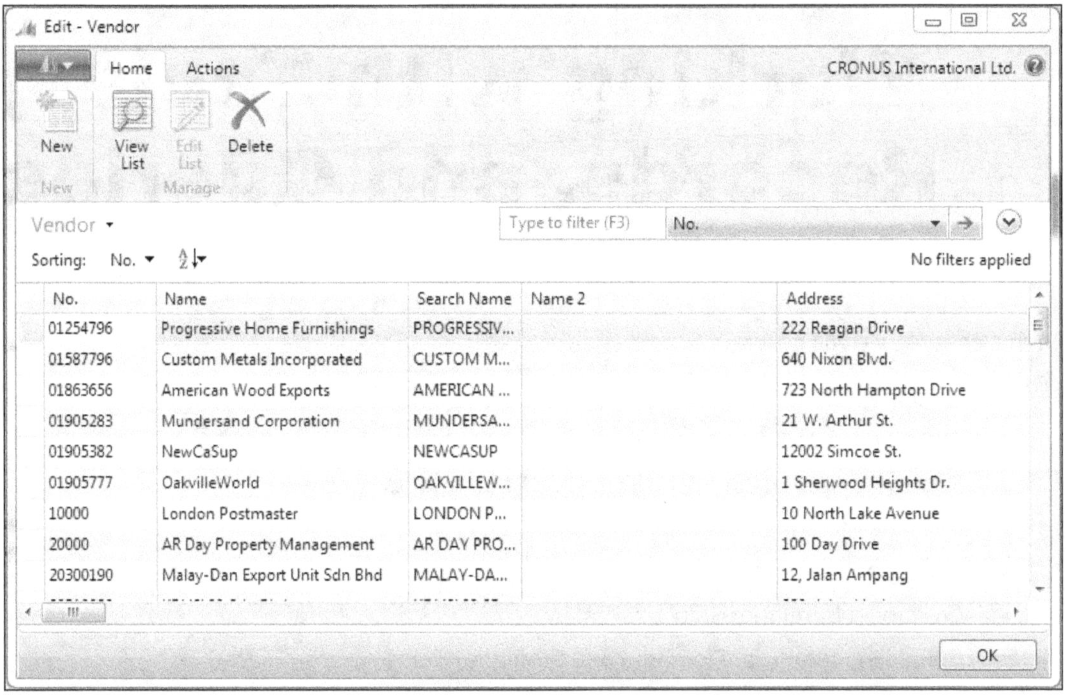

> NAV 2013 displays table data in the RTC client, so it is necessary to have NAV Server and Microsoft SQL Server (which is holding the NAV database) configured and running even for viewing data from NAV Developer Environment. Be careful! It is easy to accidently change something while executing the table with **Object Designer**.

A table can be divided into two parts: table data and table design. Table design comprises properties, triggers, fields, and keys. The following diagram can help to understand how all these are related to each other:

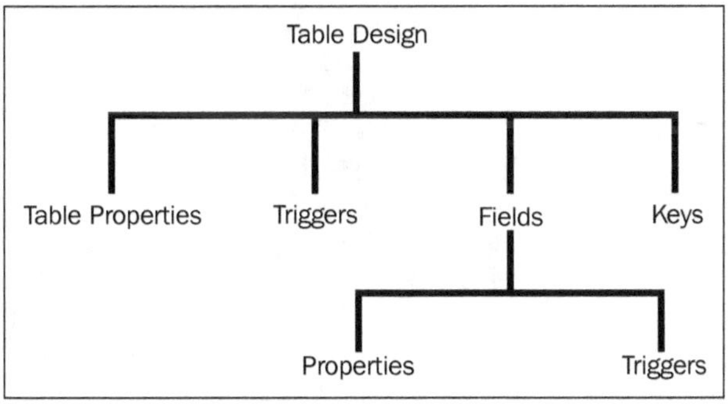

Microsoft Dynamics NAV 2013 introduced a new object named **Query**; it helps you retrieve data from one or more tables as a single dataset. This chapter will help you understand how to create and use tables and queries. Detailed information on tables and queries can be found in the **Developer and IT Pro Help** menu from **Help** of **Microsoft NAV Development Environment**.

Creating a table

Tables are the building blocks for all other Dynamics NAV objects. They store the data that the business needs to access. This recipe will show you how to create a basic table and save it in the system.

How to do it...

1. Create a new table object with **Object Designer**.
2. Add the following fields in the table designer window:

Field No.	Field Name	Data Type	Length
1	`Entry No.`	`Integer`	
2	`Document No.`	`Code`	20
3	`Description`	`Text`	30
4	`Value`	`Decimal`	
5	`Posting Date`	`Date`	

It should look like the window shown in the following screenshot:

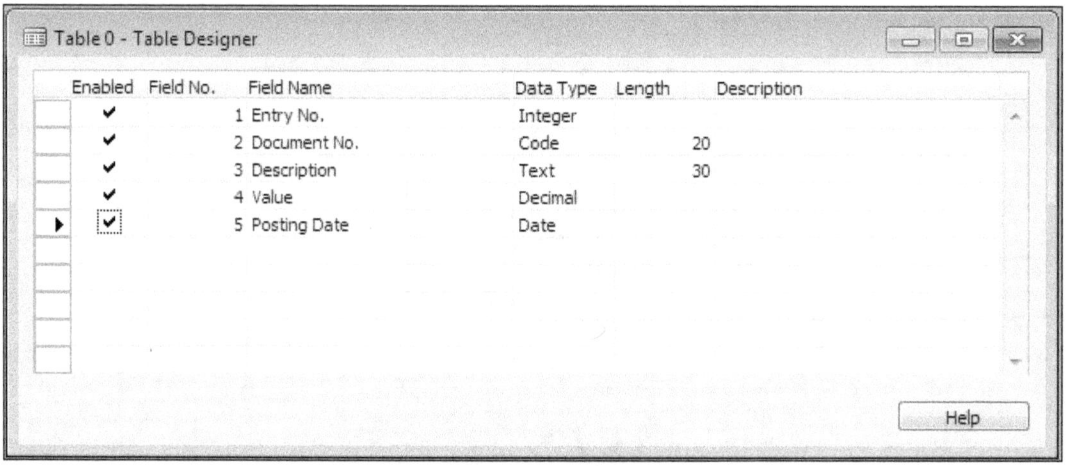

3. To save the table, go to **File** | **Save** (or press *Ctrl* + S).

In the **Save As** window, provide values to the **ID** and **Name** fields and keep the **Compiled** checkbox selected to save the table.

How it works...

Each field is just like a variable. These variables, however, are grouped together to form a new type of variable called a **record**. The field definitions provide the structure for all of the tables, as well as the data in them, inside the system. The data type of your fields can be almost anything. In this example, we have created five fields of the most common types.

There's more...

After completing the initial draft of your object, it is good practice to add a few notes, such as your initials and a date or a version number in the **Description** column, whenever you add a new field. This allows future developers to know precisely when the change was made and also what other modifications were made. An example description could be `XX 01/01/2013 MOD001`.

To maintain consistency and enable multilevel development, Microsoft has restricted designing of table and fields depending on their IDs. Visit the following URL for more detailed information on object numbering conventions:

`http://msdn.microsoft.com/en-us/library/ee414238(v=nav.70).aspx`

See also

- *Adding a key to a table*
- *Adding a FlowField*
- *Creating a SumIndexField*
- *Using a query to extract data*

Adding a key to a table

Keys are used to make sure that every record in the table is unique. They are often also referred to as indexes and are used to sort your data in ways that are most beneficial to the user. If you do not specify a key manually, the field you have placed in `Field No.` with the value `1` will act as the primary key for your table.

How to do it...

1. Follow the steps from the *Creating a table* recipe to create a table.
2. Navigate to **Design** in **Object Designer** to open the **Table Designer** page for that table.
3. Navigate to **Key** in **View** (*Alt + V + K*).
4. On the empty line, add a new key for **Document No., Posting date**.
5. Our key should look like the window shown in the following screenshot:

How it works...

Keys allow you to sort data in a way that will increase your application's performance. There is a trade-off, though; increased application performance later, costs you some effort earlier.

When we insert data into a table, it is automatically sorted based on the primary key of that table, but what about the other keys? The database engine doesn't just magically know how records should be sorted. For every key, the database keeps some sort of information about how the data will be ordered. More keys means it will take more time to insert and track all of that information. This increase in time is usually not noticeable to users, but you should be aware that there is a trade-off. One common technique for database optimization is to remove the keys that are not being used, especially on tables that have a high volume of transactions, such as `Item Ledger Entry` or `G/L Entry`.

There's more...

Tables can hold up to 40 active keys, out of which the first key will be the primary key and all the rest are secondary keys. For more details on keys, visit the following URL:

`http://msdn.microsoft.com/en-us/library/dd338755(v=nav.70).aspx`

See also

- *Adding a key to a table*
- *Adding a FlowField*
- *Creating a SumIndexField*
- *Retrieving data from FlowField and SumIndexField*

Retrieving data using the FIND and GET statements

The `FIND` and `GET` statements are two of the most commonly used functions in NAV programming. When it comes to retrieving data, we need to select the right `FIND/GET` function as it has a significant effect on the performance of the system. This recipe will help you understand how to use the `FIND` and `GET` functions.

How to do it...

1. Create a new codeunit with **Object Designer**.
2. Add the following local variables into the `run` trigger:

Name	Type	Subtype
Customer	Record	Customer
CustCount	Integer	

3. Add the following code into the `OnRun` trigger of the codeunit:

```
//FINDFIRST
Customer.RESET;
IF Customer.FINDFIRST THEN
  MESSAGE('The first customer in the database is:\No.:%1\Name:%2',
          Customer."No.", Customer.Name);

//FINDLAST
Customer.RESET;
IF Customer.FINDLAST THEN
  MESSAGE('The last customer in the database is:\No.: %1\Name:%2',
          Customer."No.", Customer.Name);

//FINDSET
Customer.RESET;
IF Customer.FINDSET THEN
REPEAT
  CustCount:=CustCount+1;
UNTIL Customer.NEXT=0;

MESSAGE('There are %1 customers in the database',
      CustCount);

//GET
IF Customer.GET('20000') THEN
  MESSAGE('Record Found!')
ELSE
  MESSAGE('Record NOT Found!');
```

4. Save and close the codeunit.

5. On executing the codeunit, you should see windows similar to those shown in the following screenshot:

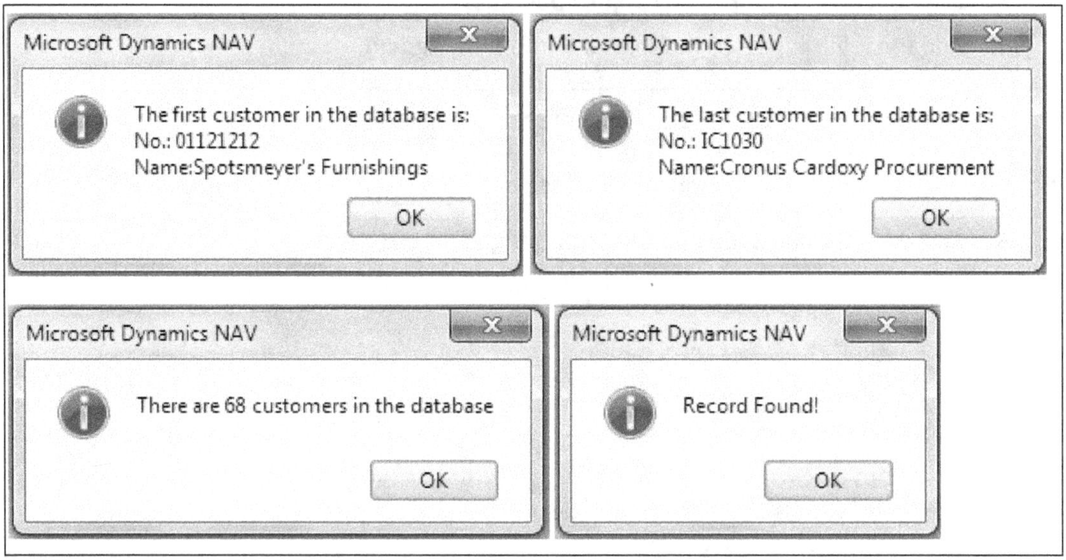

How it works...

There are three types of FIND functions, each of which will be discussed. The first two types are self-explanatory. FINDFIRST returns the first record in the dataset while FINDLAST returns the last record. These functions should only be used when we want to retrieve a single record from the database. For retrieving more than one record, we should use the FINDSET function in combination with the function REPEAT..UNTIL.

> FINDSET can retrieve records only in ascending order. If you want to loop from the bottom up, you should use FIND('+').

The GET function always uses the primary key already associated with the table. It ignores any filters that are set, except for the security filters. As No. is the primary key for the Customer table, we provided the value 20000. A value can be replaced by a variable as well.

There's more...

These functions were not introduced until Version 5.0 of NAV. In earlier versions, we would use FIND('-') for FINDFIRST and FIND('+') for FINDLAST.

See also

- The *Checking for conditions using an IF statement* recipe in *Chapter 2, General Development*
- *Advanced filtering*

Advanced filtering

Storing and retrieving data are the two main activities in Dynamics NAV. While retrieving data, most times we are looking for a specific set of data. To choose our desired data, the system needs to handle large datasets; in this situation, filtering plays a very important role. In this recipe, we will look at the advanced filtering of datasets in the C/AL code.

How to do it...

1. Create a new codeunit with **Object Designer**.
2. Add the following local variable into the `OnRun` trigger:

Name	Type	Subtype
`GLEntry`	`Record`	`G/L Entry`

3. Add the following code into the `OnRun` trigger of the codeunit:

```
GLEntry.RESET;
GLEntry.SETCURRENTKEY("Document No.","Posting Date");
GLEntry.SETRANGE("Posting Date",010113D,310113D);
GLEntry.SETRANGE("Document Type",GLEntry."Document
Type"::Invoice);
GLEntry.SETFILTER(Amount,'>%1',25000);
IF GLEntry.FINDFIRST THEN
  MESSAGE('Found!\Document No.: %1\Amount: %2', GLEntry."Document
  No.",
           GLEntry.Amount)
ELSE
  MESSAGE('Not Found!');
```

4. Save and close the codeunit.

5. On executing the codeunit, you should see a window similar to that shown in the following screenshot:

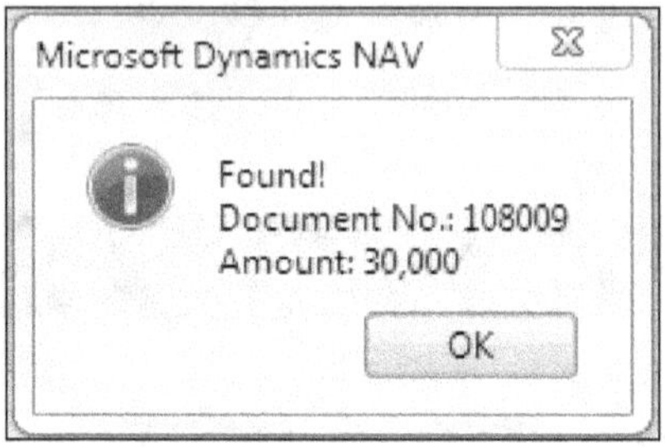

How it works...

In this recipe, we are filtering the G/L Entry table to retrieve a specific record set and selecting the first record out of the filtered record set. The RESET function will remove all filters and change the current key to the primary key. SETCURRENTKEY is used to select a key for a record and set the order of sorting. The key selected by us will sort data by Document No. and then by Posting Date.

SETRANGE removes any filters that were set previously and replaces them with the "from-value" and "to-value" parameters. While providing Date as a parameter, we need to remove date separators and add D at the end of the Date value. In the filter, when we provide the Date value, we need to consider the current system's data format. In this recipe, the data format used is dd/mm/yyyy. If you are following the US date format, the value should be 013113D, and if it is the UK date format, the value should be 310113D. Our filter will provide data between 01/01/2013 and 31/01/2013.

In the next SETRANGE filter, we provide only one value ("from-value"). In this system, we will set the "to-value" to the same as the "from-value".

SETFILTER provides functionalities to use multiple operators to filter data. We selected the Amount field and provided the relational operator > (greater than) with a placeholder. Finally, we set the value 25000 for the placeholder. If you are not sure about the exact filter value, you can use operators such as * and @ to provide an approximate or nearby value.

After applying filters, we used the FINDFIRST function to choose the first record out of the filtered record set. If your database does not have any value for a given filter, you will receive the **Not Found!** message.

There's more...

There are many ways to filter your data; for more detailed information, run a search for the help topic titled `Field Filters and Table Filters` in the **Developer and IT Pro Help** menu in the **Help** menu of **Microsoft NAV Development Environment**. Microsoft provides wonderful examples of all of the available filtering options, both individually and combined.

See also

- The *Creating functions* recipe in *Chapter 2, General Development*
- The *Passing parameters by reference* recipe in *Chapter 2, General Development*
- *Retrieving a single record from the database*
- *Retrieving data using the FIND and GET statements*

Adding a FlowField

FlowFields are fields that are not actually stored in the database. They are calculated fields that the user can call instead of performing the calculations themselves. This recipe will show you how to add a FlowField to your tables.

How to do it...

1. Follow the steps from the *Creating a table* recipe to create a table.
2. Add the following field to the table:

Field no.	Field name	Data type	Length
`10`	`Sell-to Customer No.`	`Code`	`20`

3. View the properties for this field (*Shift* + *F4*).
4. Set the following properties:

Property	Value
`FieldClass`	`Flowfield`
`CalcFormula`	`Lookup("Sales Invoice Header"."Sell-to Customer No." WHERE (No.=FIELD(Document No.)))`
`Editable`	`No`

5. Close the **Properties** window.
6. Save and close the table.

How it works...

To start, we create a field like any other field. It should have an ID number, name, and type. In order to make it a FlowField, we have to change the property named `FieldClass`. This property tells the system whether or not this is an actual field to be stored in the database (normal) or a field that should be calculated or used to calculate a value on the fly (FlowField or FlowFilter).

When defining a FlowField, you must tell the database how to calculate its value. This is done with the `CalcFormula` property. Our field is a lookup, meaning we just want to pull a value from another table that matches any given criteria. We also have to tell the database which table to pull its value from and which filters should be used to determine the value.

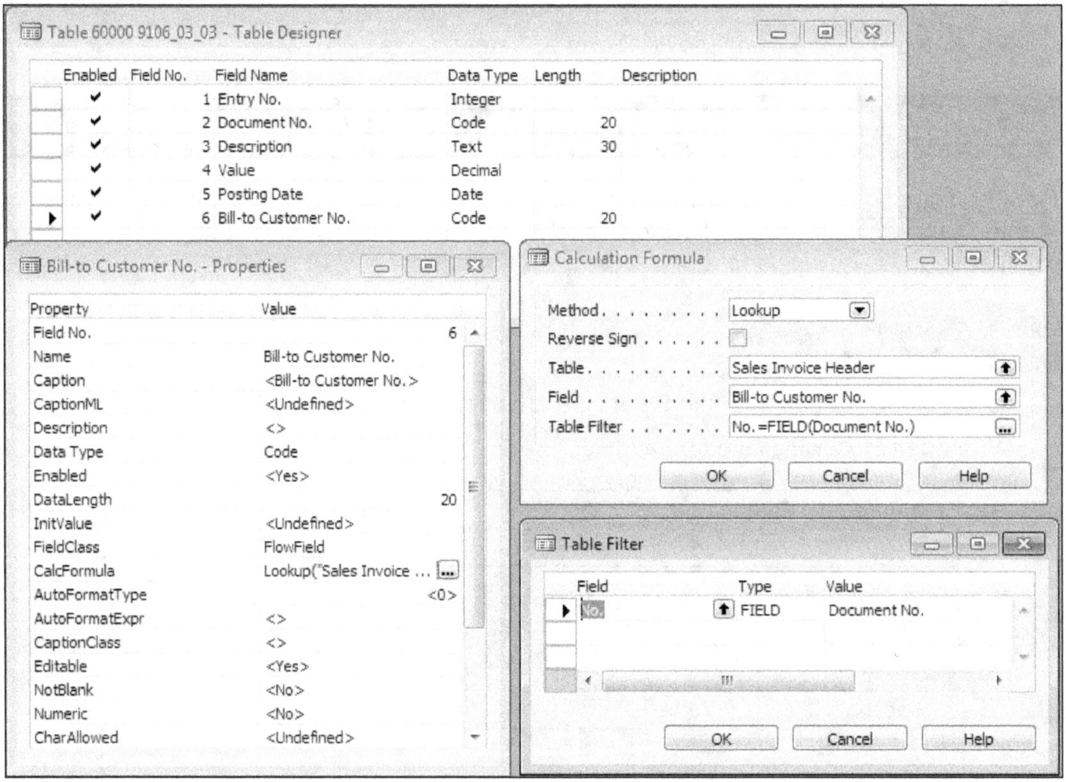

There's more...

A FlowField is not actually stored in the database, which means it can't be used outside the NAV client in other applications. It can't even be used in a SQL procedure. So what exactly is its use?

FlowFields can be used to display related information more easily. A great example is the `Cost` fields from the `Item Ledger Entry` table. The actual cost of an item is the sum of 67all of the associated records from the `Value Entry` table. You wouldn't want to manually check its value every time you require that information. You also wouldn't want to calculate them using code (this method of calculating and storing in a global variable does not allow you to filter the values). That's where the FlowField comes in. Not only does it allow you to compile information about related entries, but also the database keeps a track of it all for you, allowing for faster reporting and viewing of data.

See also

- *Creating a table*
- *Adding a key to a table*
- *Creating a SumIndexField*
- *Retrieving data from FlowField and SumIndexField*

Creating a SumIndexField

A SumIndexField is like a running total of certain fields in your table. Instead of calculating these sums manually, you can tell NAV to do it for you. Here, we'll tell you how to add a SumIndexField to your table and show you how to use it.

How to do it...

1. Follow the steps from the *Creating a table* recipe to create a table.
2. View the key by clicking on **Keys** in the **View** menu.
3. Add a key for the `Posting Date` field with a `SumIndexField` value.
4. Close the **Keys** window.
5. Save and close your table.

How it works...

This recipe, unlike a few others, is very straightforward. By adding fields to list in the `SumIndexFields` column of a key, you tell the database to keep a track of the totals for those fields for every combination of filters in the key, as shown in the following screenshot:

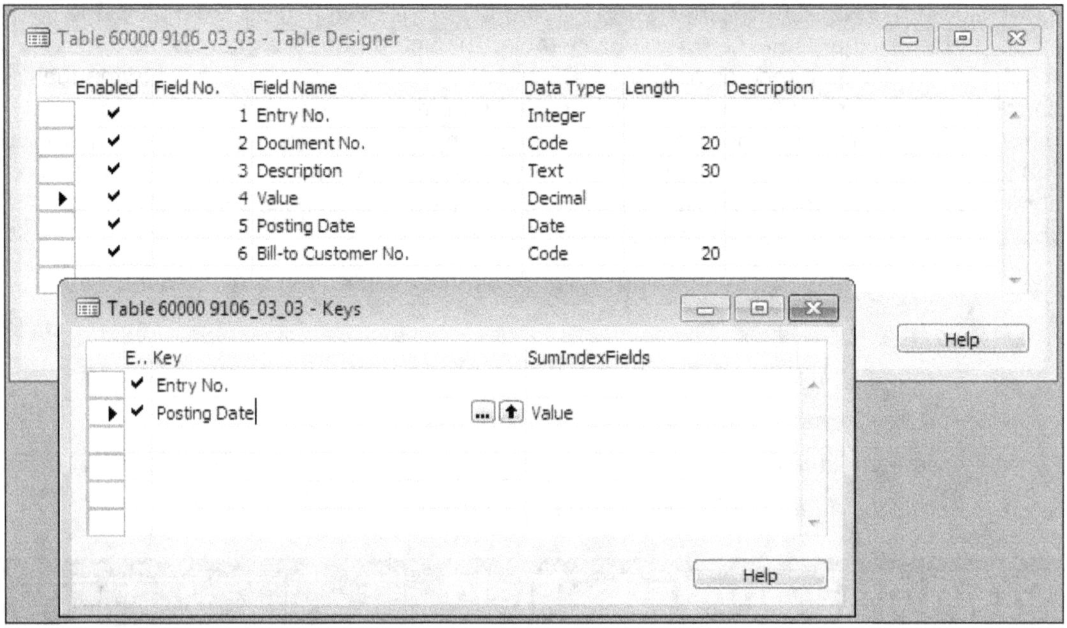

There's more...

Why use SumIndexFields? Why not just calculate these totals manually? The answer is that it is much faster to let the database do it. We won't get into the details behind the scenes regarding SumIndexFields, but will demonstrate how it works using a short example shown in the following screenshot:

Entry No.	Value	Total
1	10	10
2	20	30
3	30	60
4	40	100
5	50	150
6	60	210
7	70	280
8	80	360
9	90	450
10	100	550

In the background, NAV keeps a running total or sum of the values defined as SumIndexFields. If you were to calculate the total manually, you would have to sum up all ten entries individually.

With **SIFT** (**Sum Index Field Technology**), NAV can sum up the entires with only two entries. Let's try and find the sum of the entries `4` through `8`. By manually adding up these five entries, we have the total `300`. From the database, SIFT will take the sum of the values up until our first entry (so, the total of entries `1` through `3`; that is, `60`) and subtract that from the total of our last entry, the number `8` entry that is equal to `360`. *360 - 60 = 300* gives us the same result.

See also

- *Creating a table*
- *Adding a key to a table*
- *Creating a FlowField*
- *Retrieving data from Flowfield and SumIndexField*

Retrieving data from FlowField and SumIndexField

We have seen how to add FlowFields and SumIndexField; in this recipe, we will see how to calculate these fields using C/AL code.

How to do it...

1. Create a new codeunit with **Object Designer**.
2. Add the following local variables into the `OnRun` trigger:

Name	Type	Subtype
`GLAccount`	`Record`	`G/L Account`
`GLEntry`	`Record`	`G/L Entry`

3. Add the following code into the `OnRun` trigger of the codeunit:

```
GLAccount.GET('8410');
GLAccount.SETRANGE("Date Filter",0D,TODAY);
GLAccount.CALCFIELDS("Balance at Date");

GLEntry.SETCURRENTKEY("G/L Account No.","Posting Date");
GLEntry.SETRANGE("G/L Account No.",'8410');
GLEntry.SETRANGE("Posting Date",0D,TODAY);
```

```
GLEntry.CALCSUMS(Amount);

MESSAGE ('G/L Account 8410 Balance at %1\By FlowField : %2 \By
SumIndex Field : %3' , TODAY,GLAccount."Balance at Date", GLEntry.
Amount)
```

4. Save and close the codeunit.
5. On executing the codeunit, you should see a window similar to the one shown in the following screenshot:

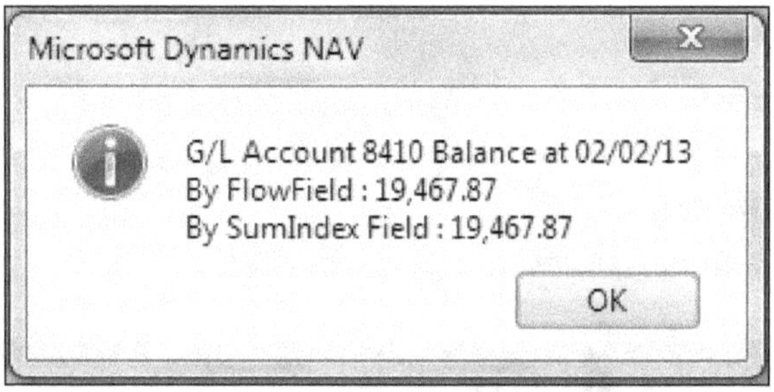

How it works...

FlowFields are automatically updated when they are the direct source expressions of controls, but when they are part of a more complex expression, the calculations must be performed explicitly. First, we filtered the GL account for the A/C number `8410` and then the filters applied on the `date` filter limited the data for the dates given in the database. The `Date Filter` field is a virtual field of the type FlowFilter. FlowFilter fields are generally used to limit the scope of FlowField data; in other words, they are used to apply filters to the FlowFields. Filters applied to these fields are passed to the source table of the FlowField. Finally, the `CALCFIELD` function will update the `Balance at Date` field. In the `G/L Account` table, the `Balance at Date` field represents the `Amount` field from the `G/L Entry` table. So basically, the `Balance at Date` data is fetched from the `G/L Entry` table.

There's more...

With NAV 2013, Microsoft introduced a new function, `SETAUTOCALCFIELDS`. This function will update the FlowFields before we retrieve the record and improve performance as we need not call `CALCFIELD` for every record.

For detailed information, search for the help topic titled **FlowFields and SumIndex fields** in the **Developer and IT Pro Help** menu in the **Help** menu of **Microsoft NAV Development Environment**.

See also

- *Creating a table*
- *Adding a key to a table*
- *Creating a FlowField*
- *Retrieving data from Flowfield and SumIndexField*

Using a temporary table

Temporary tables can be useful when you need to insert data into a table to perform calculations but don't want it saved to the database. This recipe will show you how to mark your records as temporary and what to watch out for when you do so.

How to do it...

1. Create a new codeunit with **Object Designer**.
2. Add the following global variables:

Name	Type	Subtype
`Customer`	`Record`	`Customer`
`TempCustomer`	`Record`	`Customer`

3. With the cursor hovering over the `Tempcustomer` variable, click on **Properties** in the **View** menu or press *Shift* + *F4*.
4. Set the following property:

Property	Value
`Temporary`	`Yes`

5. Write the following code into the `OnRun` trigger of the codeunit:

```
MESSAGE('Customer Count: %1\TempCustomer Count: %2',
                      Customer.COUNT, TempCustomer.COUNT);
```

6. Save and close the codeunit.

7. On executing the codeunit, you should see a window similar to the one in the following screenshot:

How it works...

Declaring a record variable as temporary is as easy as setting the `Temporary` property to `Yes`. But what is the purpose of setting a temporary table? A temporary table has all the code and properties of a normal table. They function in exactly the same way. The only difference is that when you perform a transaction, such as insert, modify, delete, or rename with a temporary table the data is not stored in the database. Instead, it is held in memory, just like any other variable.

There's more...

It may sound obvious, but when planning to work with a temporary table, don't forget to mark it as `Temporary`! There's nothing worse than running `TempGLEntry.DELETEALL` and realizing that all of your real data is gone. This is a perfect example of why you should always perform your development in a test system and have a recent backup of your data before performing any changes. Also, if you run a `DELETEALL(TRUE)` command on a temporary record variable, the code that is called in the `OnDelete` trigger will run with variables that are *not* temporary, which means that the actual data will be deleted. Again, be careful!

Storing records to be processed

Just as you can mark records that have to be processed using the `MARK` function, you can also create a temporary table to store them. Instead of `MARK`, the following code can be used:

```
TempCustomer := Customer;
TempCustomer.INSERT;
```

You assign the value of the actual data to a temporary record and then insert it into the temporary table. The data will be stored in memory, but not in the database, and you can use it for later operations.

See also

- *Creating a table*

Retrieving data from other companies

NAV can hold data for many companies under your corporate umbrella. Often, users will request consolidated reports that show them the data from all of the companies in the system. This recipe will show you how to retrieve that data from anywhere in the system.

Getting ready...

Make sure you have at least two companies in your database.

How to do it...

1. Create a new codeunit with **Object Designer**.
2. Add the following global variables:

Name	Type	Subtype
`Customer`	`Record`	`Customer`
`Company`	`Record`	`Company`

3. Write the following code into the `OnRun` trigger of the codeunit:

```
IF Company.FINDSET THEN
REPEAT
  Customer.CHANGECOMPANY(Company.Name);
 MESSAGE('Company Name: %1\Customer Count: %2',
 Company.Name,Customer.COUNT);
UNTIL Company.NEXT = 0;
```

4. Save and close the codeunit.

5. On executing the codeunit, you should see a window similar to the one in the following screenshot; the number of message screens displayed depends on the number of companies available in the database:

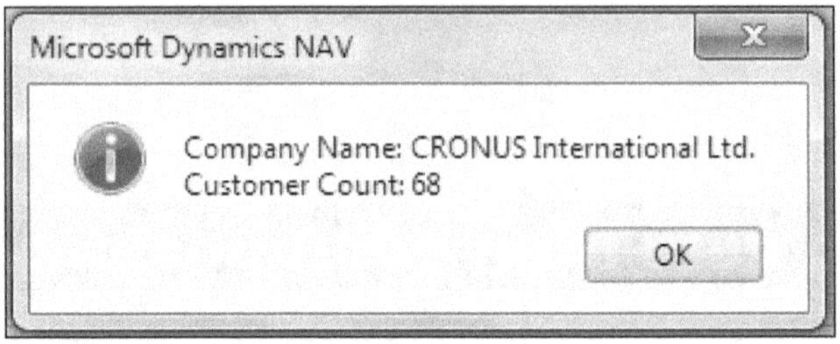

How it works...

In order to get data from another company within NAV, we have to tell it which company we want access to. Records have a built-in function called `CHANGECOMPANY`. This function takes in a text value that represents the name of the company as a parameter.

In our example, we are going to show the number of customers in every company in NAV. That's why we have the `Record` variable for `Company`. Looping through each record in the dataset, we pass the name of the company through the `CHANGECOMPANY` command and display the customer count. We could just as easily have stored our other company name in a text constant and passed that value instead. In most cases though it is good to store the name of the company you want to access in a setup table. This way if the company is renamed, your code will not break.

See also

- *Retrieving data using the FIND and GET Statements*

Using a query to extract data

Microsoft Dynamics NAV 2013 introduced a new object type called **query**. We can use a query to retrieve data from one or multiple tables. A query can be configured with specific filters, joins, and totaling methods. The following recipe will help to build a simple query to retrieve data from one table.

How to do it...

1. Create a new query with **Object Designer**.
2. In **Query Designer**, leave the default value of the column `Type` as it is; that is, `DataItem`.

3. Select `Customer` as `Data Source` from the table list.
4. In the next row, select `Column` as `Type` and `No.` as `Data Source`. Keep the method `None` as it is.
5. Add another two columns, `Name` and `Balance`, with the `Method Type` value `None`.
6. With the cursor hovering over the `Balance` row, click on **Properties** in the **View** menu or press *Shift* + *F4*.
7. In `ColumnFilter`, select the assist edit button to apply the following filter:

Column	Type	Value
Balance	Filter	<>0

You should see the following screenshot:

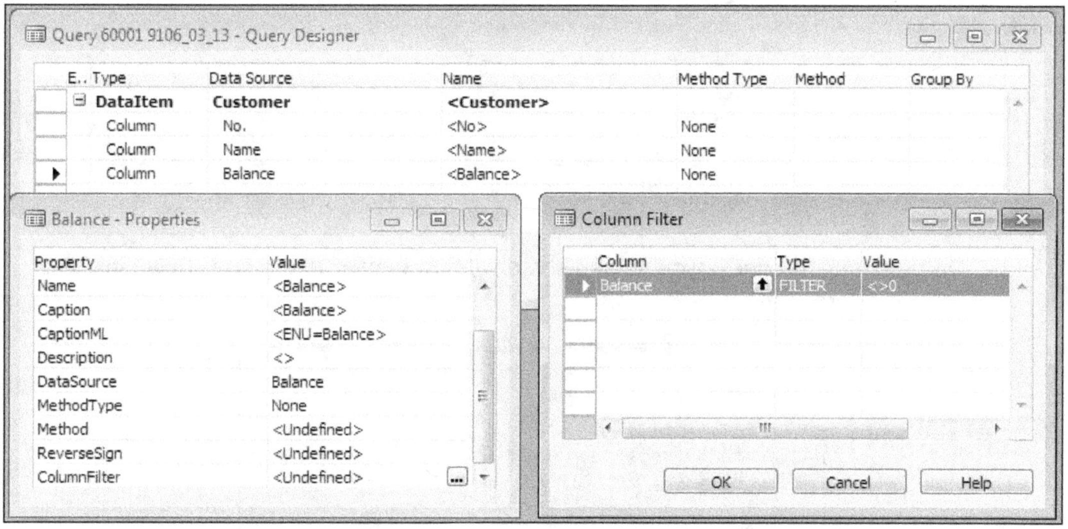

8. Select the blank row and click on **Properties** from the **View** menu, or press *Shift* + *F4*, to select the query properties.
9. In `OrderBy`, select the assist edit button and select the following fields:

Column	Direction
Name	Ascending

10. You should be able to see a window similar to the one shown in the following screenshot:

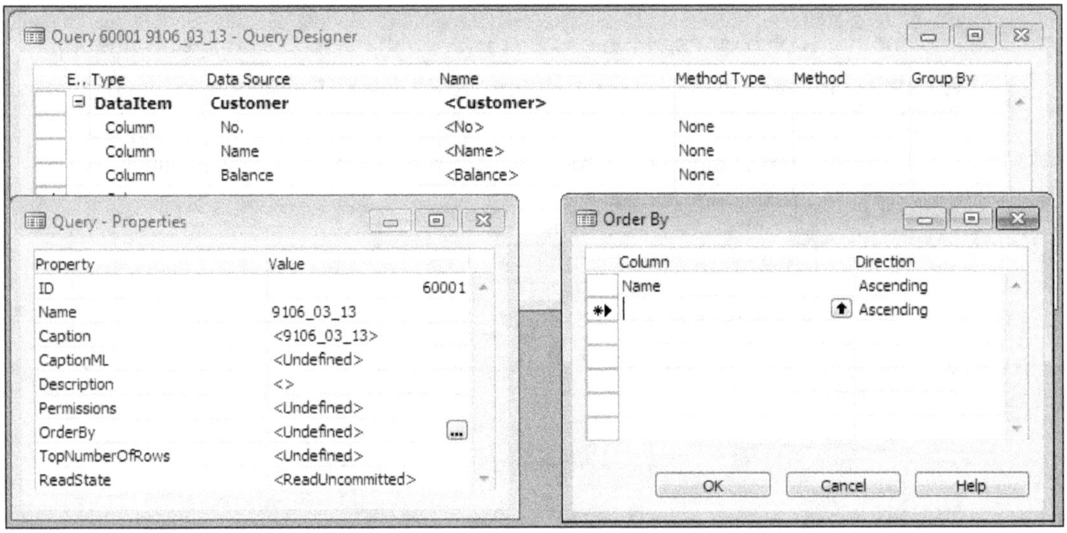

11. Save and close the query.

12. On executing the query, you should see a window similar to the one shown in the following screenshot:

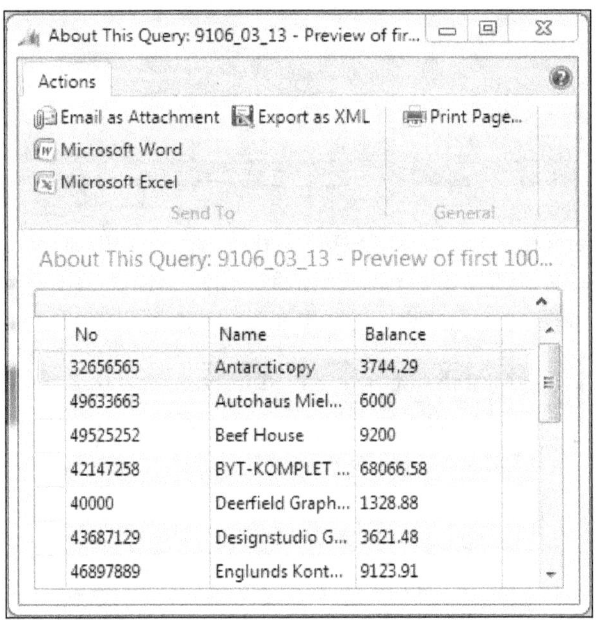

How it works...

In **Query Designer**, `DataItem` refers to the table whereas `Column` refers to a table field. Our query is retrieving data from the `Customer` table for the `No.`, `Name`, and `Balance` fields. Query autocalculated FlowField; that's why we have not selected any method to calculate the value of the `Balance` fields. To avoid data with zero balances, we have added a filter on the `Balance` field. At the end of the query, we added the sorting order based on the `Name` field. As an output of our query, we see a window with multiple data export options.

There's more...

A query can be used to generate charts, export data (XML or CSV format), or expose the data as an OData web service.

See also

- *Creating a table*
- *Creating a query to link three tables*

Creating a query to link three tables

Most times, we need to extract data from multiple tables; so, it's very important to understand how to join multiple tables. In this recipe, we will see how to join three tables, set up the method to calculate totals, and add filters to limit the result.

How to do it...

1. Create a new query object with **Object Designer**.
2. In **Query Designer**, choose `DataItem` from the drop-down list in the `Type` column.
3. Select `Currency` as a `Data Source` value from the table list.
4. In next row, select `Column` as `Type` and `Code` as `Data Source`. Keep the method `None` as it is.
5. In the next row, select `DataItem` in the `Type` column and `Sales Invoice Header` in the `Data Source` column.
6. In the next row, select `DataItem` in the `Type` column and `Sales Invoice Line` in the `Data Source` column.
7. Add one more row with `Column` as `Type` and `Amount` as `Data Source`. For this row, change `Method Type` to `Totals` and `Method` to `Sum`.

8. Maintain the indentation of all rows as shown in the following screenshot:

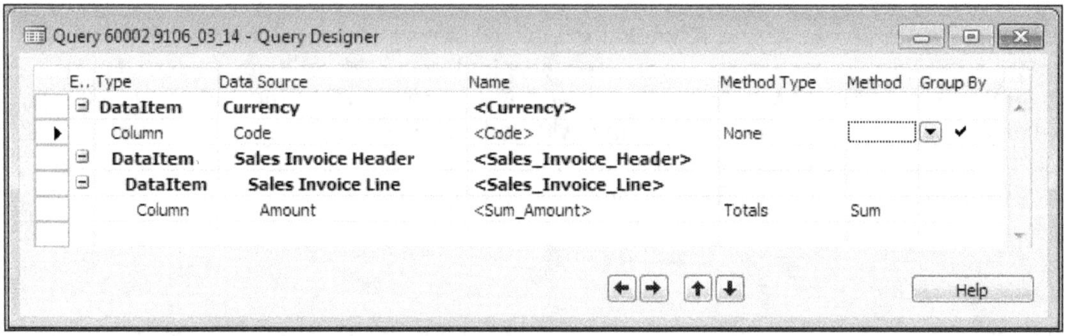

9. To set up a relation between the `Currency` and `Sales Invoice Header` table, hold the cursor over the `Sales Invoice Header` row and click on **Properties** in the **View** menu, or press *Shift* + *F4*.
10. In `DataItemLink`, select the assist edit button to apply the following filter:

Field	Reference DataItem	Reference Field
`Currency Code`	`Currency`	`Code`

11. You should see a window similar to the one shown in the following screenshot:

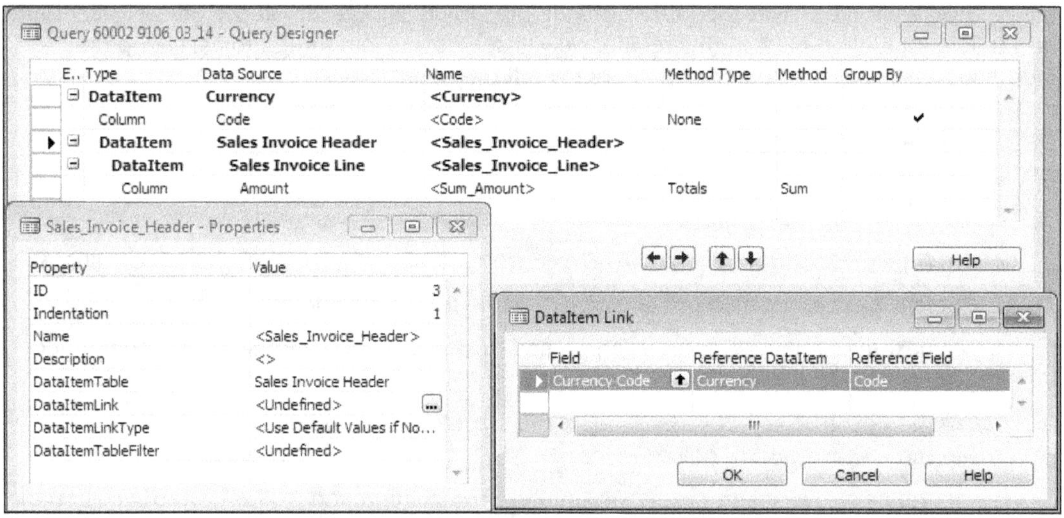

12. Next, to set up a relation between the `Sales Invoice Header` and `Sales Invoice Line` tables, hold the cursor over the `Sales Invoice Line` row and click on **Properties** in the **View** menu, or press *Shift* + *F4*.

13. In `DataItemLink`, select the assist edit button to apply the following filter:

Field	Reference data item	Reference field
`Document No.`	`Sales_Invoice_Header`	`No.`

14. Select `Exclude Row If No Match` as `DataItemLinkType`.
15. Save and close the query.
16. On executing the query, you should see a window similar to the one shown in the following screenshot:

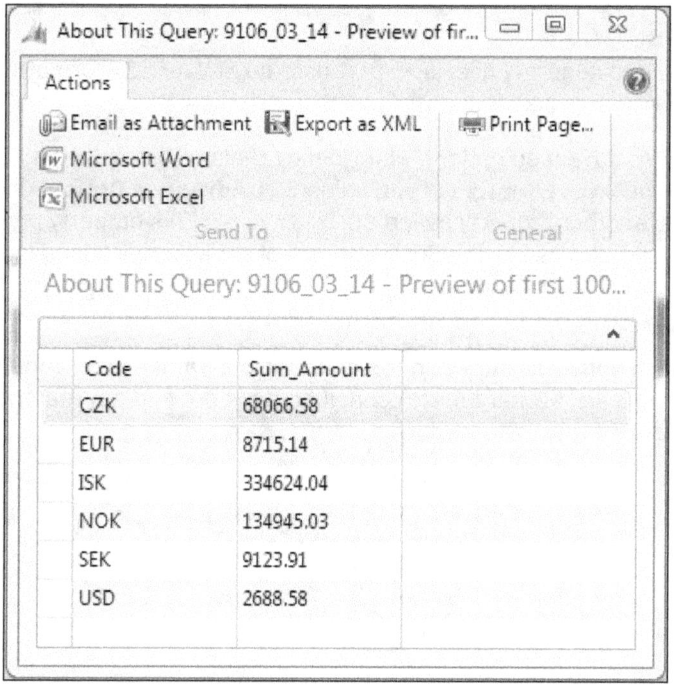

How it works...

As a result of the previous steps, we need to find total sales by each currency. To achieve this, we are building a new query. As we want the final result per currency, we will take the `Currency` table as the base table and add the `Code` field in the query. NAV saves the sales history data in the `Sales Invoice Header` and `Sales Invoice Line` tables. The sales value for each transaction is recorded in the `Amount` field of the `Sales Invoice Line` table. To get the desired output, we added these two tables and the `Amount` field in our query.

To get the sum of amounts, we selected `Method Type` as `Totals` and `Method` as `Sum`. You may have noticed that the system automatically selected `Currency Code` as a `Group By` column. This will consolidate all values as per the currency code.

After selecting all tables and fields, we need to set up a relation between all the tables. In the **Property** window of the child table we need to set up `DataItemLink`. The relation of the `Currency` and `Sales Invoice Header` tables is based on `Currency Code`, whereas the `Sales Invoice Header` and `Line` tables' relation is based on `Document No`.

If we execute a query with the previous setup, we will get an output with all of the currency codes and their respective sales values. To filter out currency with a zero amount value, we selected `DataItemLinkType` of the `Sales Invoice Line` table as `Exclude Row If No Match`. As the output of our query, we receive a window with multiple data export options.

There's more...

A query can be used to generate charts, export data (in XML or CSV format), or expose the data as an OData web service.

A NAV query provides advanced options while joining tables. To access the advanced options, we need to select the `DataItemLinkType` value **SQL Advanced Option**. On selecting this option, we activate another property called `SQLJoinType`. This property provides multiple options of join that we can use in the SQL queries. Let's take a quick look at these options.

Left outer join

The result for table `A` and `B` (as shown in the following diagram) always contains all records of the left/upper table (`A`), even if the join condition does not find any matching record in the right/lower table (`B`):

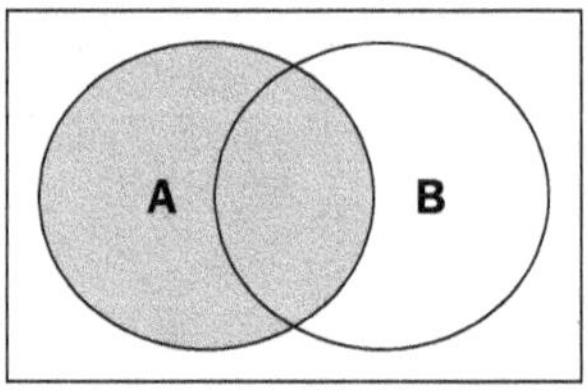

Inner join

An inner join creates a new result table, as shown in the following diagram, by combining the column values of two tables (`A` and `B`) based on the value of the linked column:

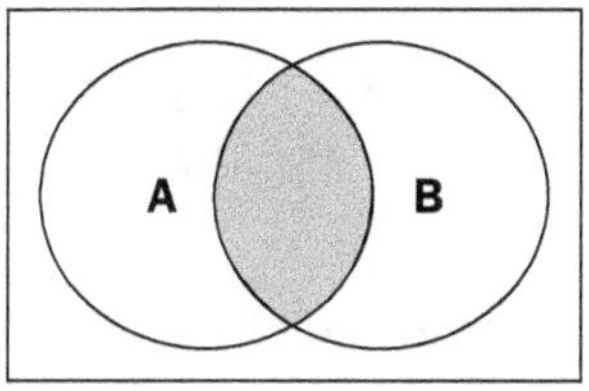

Right outer join

The result for tables `A` and `B`, as shown in the following diagram, always contains all records of the right/lower table (`B`), even if the join condition does not find any matching record in the left/upper table (`A`):

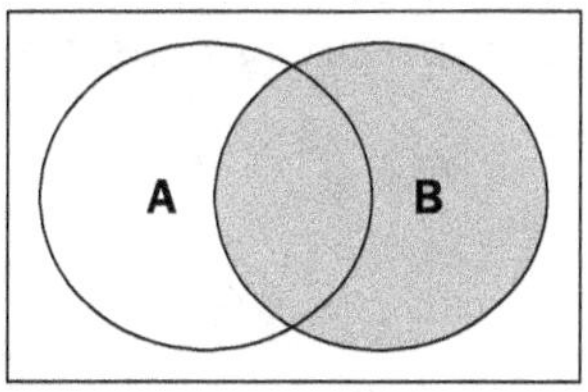

Full outer join

The result contains all records from the left/upper table (`A`) and the right/lower table (`B`), as shown in the following diagram, including records that do not have matching values for columns that are linked by the `DataItemLink` property:

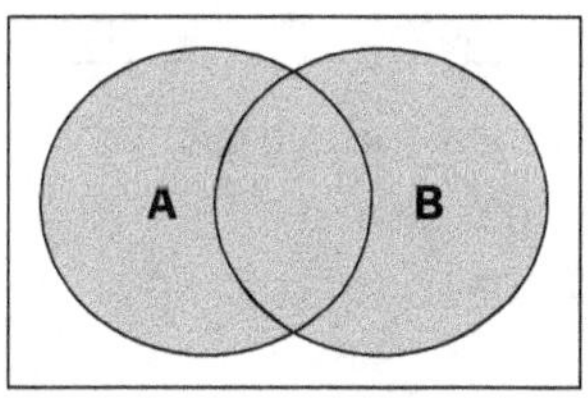

Cross join

A cross join contains rows that combine each row from the left/upper table (`A`) with each row from a right/lower table (`B`). Cross joins are also called **Cartesian products**. A cross join does not apply any comparisons between columns of data items, so the `DataItemLink` property is left blank.

See also

- *Creating a table*
- *Using a query to extract data*
- *Working with queries in C/AL*

Working with queries in C/AL

We can run a query and retrieve data using the C/AL code. To achieve this, NAV provides several functions. This recipe will demonstrate a simple example of executing a query using C/AL code.

How to do it...

1. Follow the steps from the *Using a query to extract data* recipe to create a query and save it as `Customer Balance`.
2. Create a new codeunit with **Object Designer**.
3. Add the following local variable to the `run` trigger:

Name	Type	Subtype
CustBalance	Query	Customer Balance

4. Add the following code into the `OnRun` trigger of the codeunit:

```
CustBalance.TOPNUMBEROFROWS(2);
CustBalance.SETFILTER(Balance, '>10000');
CustBalance.OPEN;
WHILE CustBalance.READ DO
BEGIN
MESSAGE('Customer Name : %1 \Balance : %2',   CustBalance.
Name,CustBalance.Balance);
END;
CustBalance.CLOSE;
```

5. Save and close the codeunit.

6. On executing the codeunit, you should see a window similar to the one shown in the following screenshot:

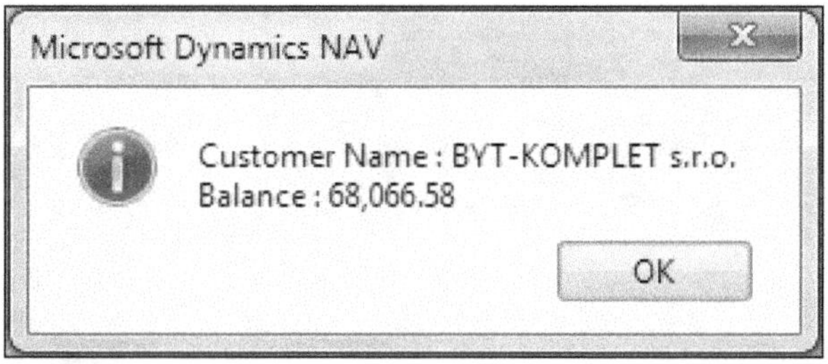

How it works...

We use the dataset provided by the `Customer Balance` query by setting it up as the `CustBalance` variable. The function `TOPNUMBEROFROWS` helps to filter the desired number of records from the result set. NAV provides functionality to filter the query objects using the `SETRANGE` and `SETFILTER` functions. Using the `SETFILTER` function, we are filtering the result dataset for amounts greater than `1000`.

Open the function, run the query and provide the dataset. Read the function retrieve row provided by the `Open` function. The values of columns in the row can be accessed by calling `Query.ColumnName`.

There's more...

We can use the `SAVEASCSV` or `SAVEASXML` function to generate the query output in a file.

See also

- *Creating a table*
- *Using a query to extract data*
- *Creating a query to link three tables*

4

Designing Pages

In this chapter, we will cover the following recipes:

- Creating a page using a wizard
- Using multiple options to run the page
- Applying filters on the lookup page
- Updating the subform page from a parent page
- Creating a FactBox page
- Creating a Queue page
- Creating a Role Center page
- Creating a wizard page
- Displaying a .NET add-in on a page
- Adding a chart to the page

Introduction

Microsoft announced a three-tier **RoleTailored client** (**RTC**) with Version 2009. As from Version 2013, Microsoft offers only three-tier RTC with NAV. In RTC, the object of type "FORM" is replaced by "PAGE". Pages provide the core way to interact with an NAV RoleTailored `client`. The business logic called by the page is executed on the NAV Server tier, whereas previously, the form was used by the client system to execute the business logic.

A page and form share lots of similarities in terms of properties, triggers, and controls. Some controls and features are reintroduced with a new presentation style and name. For example, "buttons" become "actions", "Tab Control" becomes "FastTabs", and "Zoom" is known as "About this Page". The following screenshot will help you to understand new naming conventions of page controls:

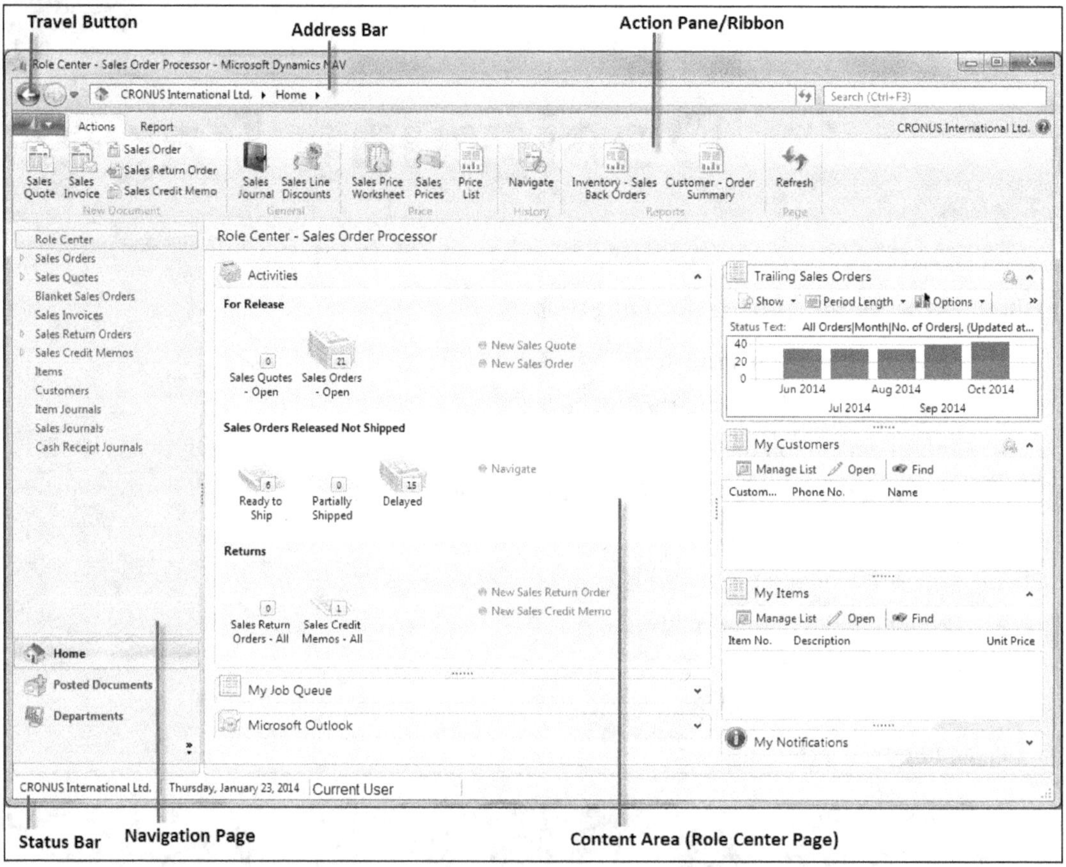

The preceding screenshot is of the **Role Center** page for the **Sales Order Processor** profile. With NAV 2013, we received 21 profiles and 21 Role Center pages, designed considering each profile work area. The following screenshot also gives additional information about the same profile:

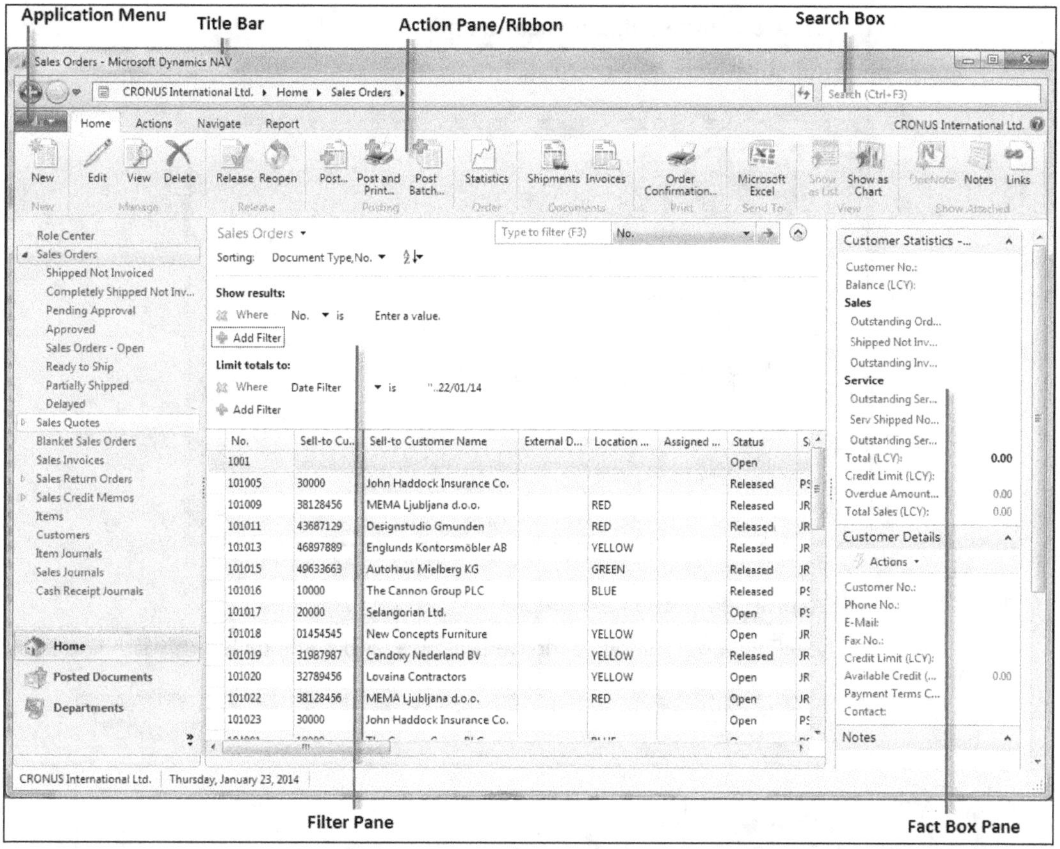

Creating a page using a wizard

Microsoft Dynamics NAV provides an option of a wizard to generate a page quickly. The page wizard presents a user with a sequence of dialog boxes that leads the user through well-defined steps. The next recipe will demonstrate the page wizard.

How to do it...

1. To start, create a new page from **Object Designer**.
2. Then select or type `Customer` in the **Table** selection.
3. Choose the **Create a page using a wizard:** option.
4. From the list of page types select **Card**.

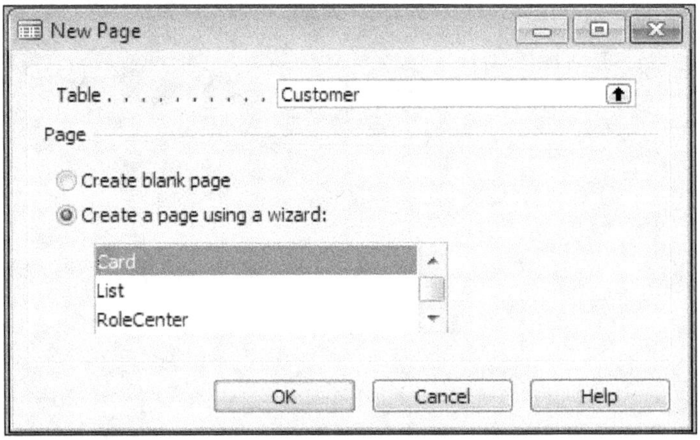

5. Click on **OK** to proceed to the next step.
6. To create a new FastTab addition to the default one, add a line called `Communication`.

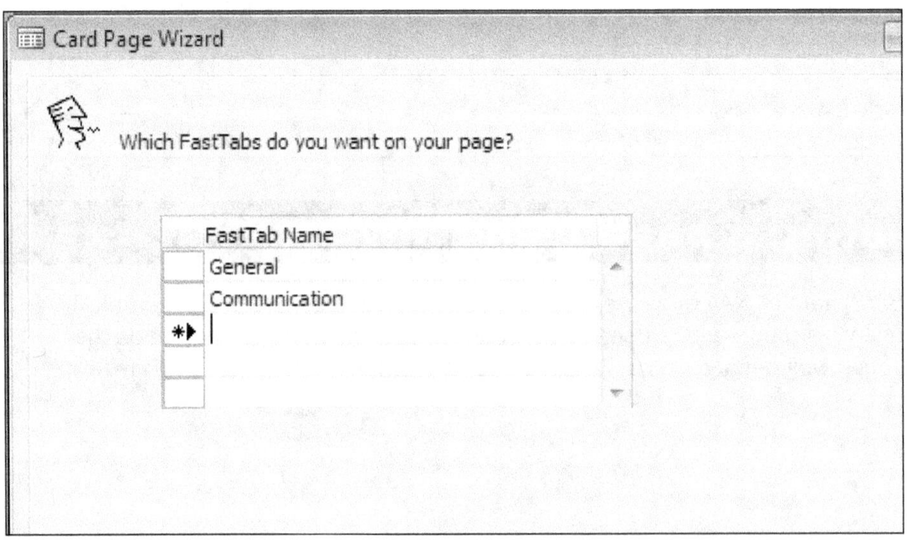

7. Click on **Next >** to complete the current step.
8. Let's add some fields to our page. Add the **No.**, **Name**, **Address**, **City**, and **County** fields to the **General** tab.
9. Add the **Phone No.** and **E-Mail** fields to the `Communication` tab.

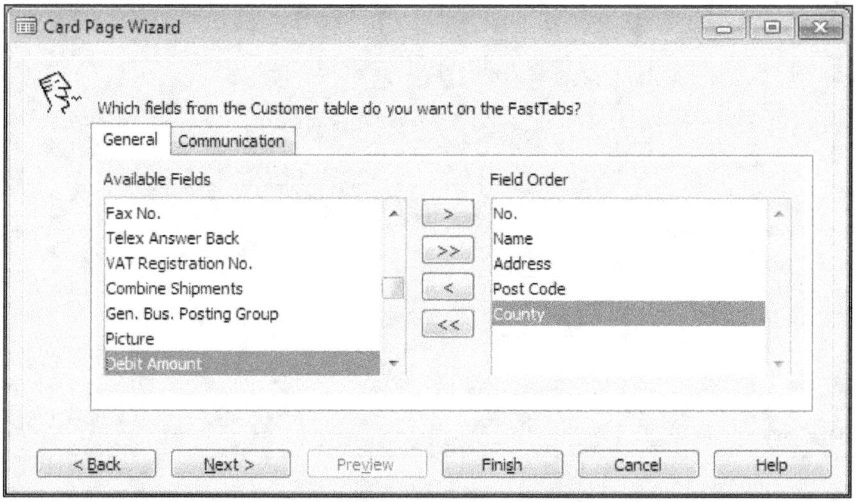

10. Click on the **Finish** button.
11. The page design generated by the wizard will look similar to the following screenshot:

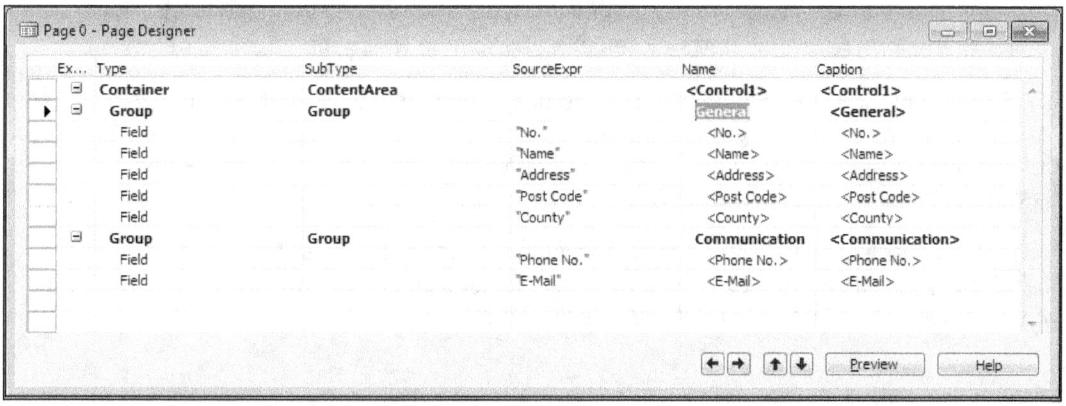

12. Compile, save, and close the page to complete our development.

13. On execution of the page from the object designer, you should see a window similar to the following screenshot:

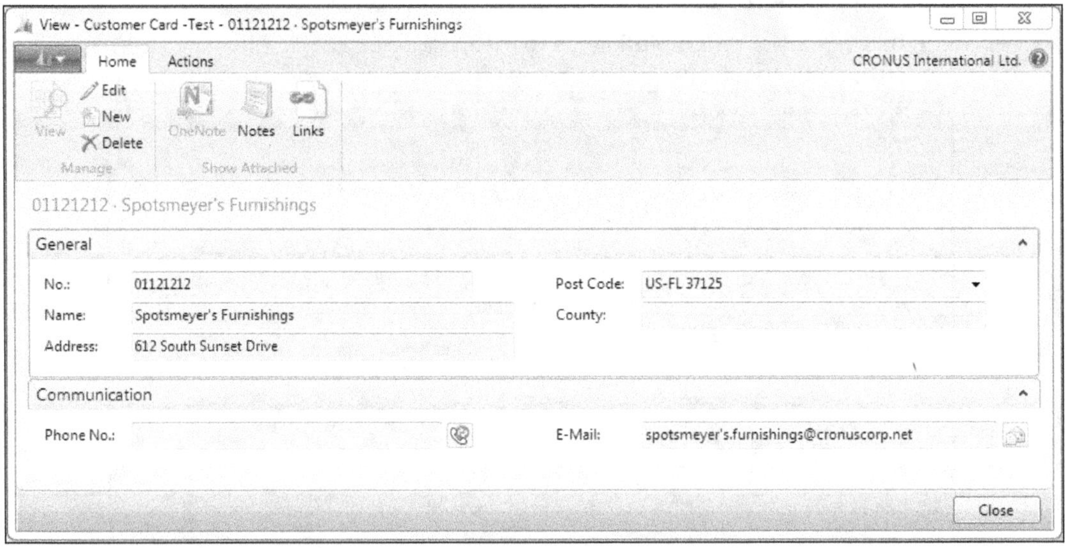

How it works...

Pages are the primary objects that capture and present data. They are similar to forms in functionality, but different in their design. There is no visual Page Designer as a Form Designer. The fastest way to design a page is by using the wizard. The page wizard is very similar to the form wizard; it starts by selecting a table on which the page will be based on.

In RTC, vertical tabs are called FastTabs. The basic functionality of the FastTab is to group the table fields as well as provide options to maximize or minimize the FastTab window. The wizard creates one default FastTab with the name `General`. In this recipe, we have added one more FastTab called `Communication`.

Now we must select fields that need to be displayed in the FastTabs. There is an option to transfer a field from a table to a selected pool. The field selection process is the same as it was available in the form wizard of the classic client.

To display additional brief information about the current record, NAV provides an option of the FactBox. These are basically divided into three types such as Page, System, and Chart. In the next dialog box, we will select a FactBox for our page. This is an optional dialog box as we can design a page without any FactBox to maintain the standard of the NAV GUI interface (I will suggest adding FactBox).

Let's look at the **Page Designer** window. `Type` and `SubType` are the two primary columns/settings to create a page. The following table will help you understand Type and SubType options.

Type	SubType	Purpose
Container		
	ContentArea	It is used as a general usage. An ordinary page (non-Role Center) has this as the topmost element.
	FactBoxArea	It is used to define FactBox controls in a page.
	RoleCenterArea	It is used for the Role Center page instead of ContentArea.
Group		
	Group	It is used to create FastTabs in the card pages and/or group several controls together.
	Repeater	It presents data in a tabular format, such as in the list page.
	CueGroup	It creates CueGroups such as in the SO Processor Activities page.
	FixedLayout	It fixes the layout of other controls, such as controls in the bottom section of journals, for example, General Journals.
	GridLayout	It is used for nesting fields in a group.
Field		It maps a data source, such as the table field or variable.
Part		It is used to add subforms or FactBox to a page.
	Page	It provides a list of pages.
	System	This is used to select a fixed page in Outlook, Notes, MyNotes, and RecordLinks
	Chart	It is used to add predefined graphical presentation of data.

Now we have an option to preview the page from Page Designer.

There's more...

In the previous recipe, we have seen that NAV does not provide any visual Page Designer. The presentation of controls depends on the type of the page; that means it's very important to select a right page type. Some of the page types and their examples are as follows:

Page	Example
Role Center	Order Processor Role Center, Page 9006
List	Customer List, Page 22
Card	Customer Card, Page 21
CardPart	Customer Details FactBox, Page 9084
ListPart	My Customers, Page 9150
Document	Sales Order, Page 42
Worksheet	General Journal, Page 39
ConfirmationDialog	Check Availability, Page 342
NavigatePage	Navigate, Page 344
ListPlus	Standard Sales Code Card, Page 170
StandardDialog	Change Exchange Rate, Page 511

See also

- *Using multiple options to run the page*
- The *Creating a table* recipe in *Chapter 3, Working with Tables, Records, and Queries*
- *Updating the subform page from a parent page*
- *Creating a FactBox page*

Using multiple options to run the page

During development or the testing phase we may need to run the page individually. This recipe has multiple subrecipes that will demonstrate the options to run the Customer Card page.

How to do it...

While using **Object Designer**, perform the following steps:

1. Open Microsoft Dynamics NAV development environment.
2. Go to the **Tools** menu, choose **Object Designer**, and then choose **Page**.
3. From the page list, select page `21` (`Customer Card`) and then click on **Run**.

While using the command prompt, perform the following steps:

1. In the command prompt window, select the `RoleTailored Client` directory by using the `CD` command.

   ```
   CD C:\Program Files (x86)\Microsoft Dynamics NAV\70\RoleTailored
   Client
   ```

2. Use the following command:

   ```
   Microsoft.Dynamics.Nav.Client.exe Dynamicsnav:////runpage?page=21
   ```

3. While using the Run window, perform the following steps:
4. On the taskbar, choose **Start** and then choose **Run**.
5. In the **Run** window, type the following command:

   ```
   Microsoft.Dynamics.Nav.Client.exe Dynamicsnav:////runpage?page=21
   ```

6. Finally, to execute our command, click on **OK**.
7. While using a browser, perform the following steps:
8. Open the Internet Explorer browser.
9. In the address bar, type the following:

   ```
   Dynamicsnav:////runpage?page=21
   ```

How it works...

It is important to have a configured NAV server and RTC to run a page using any option mentioned previously. On execution of any of the preceding options, the system will start RTC with the last used database and company.

In the preceding commands, `Microsoft.Dynamics.Nav.Client.exe` represents a RoleTailored `client`, whereas `Dynamicsnav:////runpage?page=` is a keyword to run the page object type. Number `21` represents the Customer Card Page.

There's more...

At the time of NAV installation, Windows updates the registry entry to execute NAV clients. The default value of the registry entry will always be the last NAV client installed. If you have installed NAV 2009 R2 after NAV 2013, then Windows will execute the NAV 2009 R2 RoleTailored `client` on execution of the `Microsoft.Dynamics.Nav.Client.exe` command.

A simple modification in the registry will help to execute the desired client version. In the **Run** window, type `regedit`; it will start **Registry Editor**. In **Registry Editor**, open the following folder and update `Default` and the path string value.

```
HKEY_LOCAL_MACHINE | SOFTWARE | MICROSOFT | WINDOWS | CurrentVersion | App
Paths | Microsoft.Dynamics.NAV.Client.exe
```

To execute other NAV objects, we can use the preceding method by changing the keyword. For example, to execute a report, use `Dynamicsnav:////runreport?report=`, and to execute a table, use `Dynamicsnav:////runtable?table=`.

See also

- *Creating a page using a wizard*
- The *Using multiple options to run the report* recipe in *Chapter 5, Report Design*

Applying filters on the lookup page

Execution of the page with the filtered data is the usual requirement in NAV. Read the next recipe to understand lookup options.

How to do it...

1. Create a new codeunit from **Object Designer**.
2. Then add the following global variable:

Name	Data Type	SubType
ItemRec	Record	Item

3. Write the following code in the `OnRun` trigger of the codeunit:

```
ItemRec.RESET;
ItemRec.SETRANGE("Inventory Posting Group",'FINISHED');
IF PAGE.RUNMODAL(PAGE::"Item List",ItemRec) = ACTION::LookupOK
THEN
  MESSAGE('Selected Item is %1, %2', ItemRec."No.", ItemRec.
Description);
```

4. To complete development, save and close the codeunit.

5. On execution of the codeunit, you should see a window similar to the following screenshot:

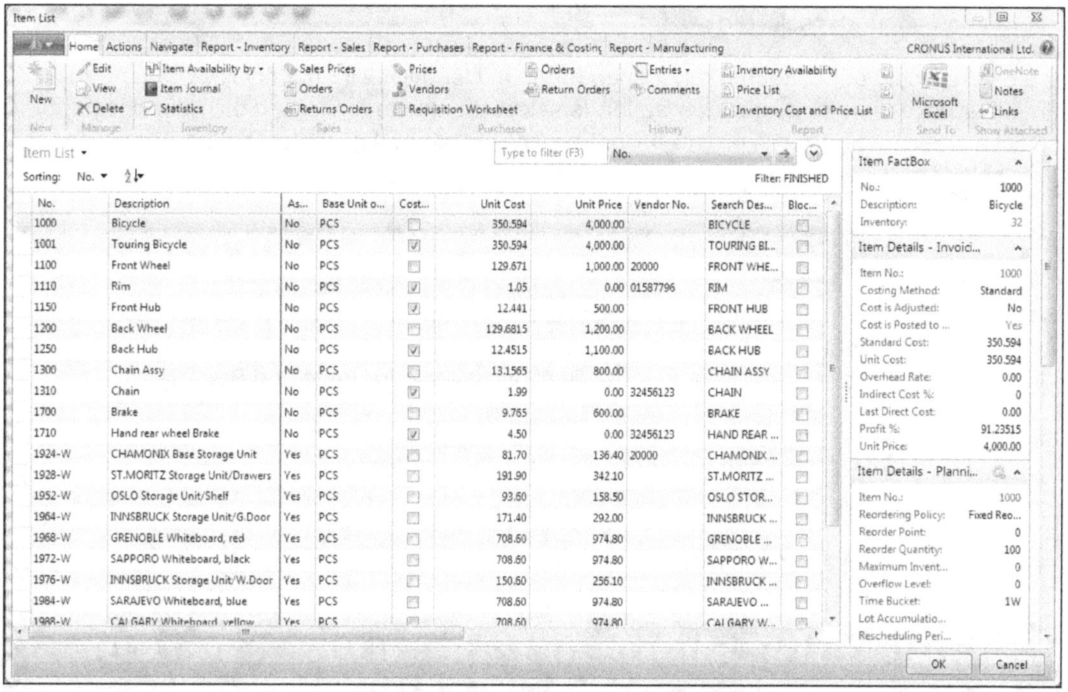

6. Select a desired record and click on **OK**, or you can even simply double-click on the record to select it.

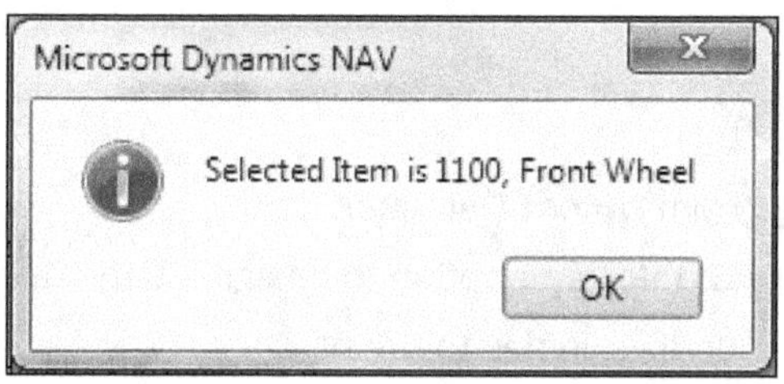

How it works...

For executing a page, NAV provides two functions `RUN` and `RUNMODAL`. If we use the `RUN` function, we need to define a page variable that we can use before we run the page. If we use the `RUNMODAL` function, we can use the variable before and after we run the page.

We added a filter on the record variable of the table on which our page is based, and passed it to our page. As we want our page to return the selected record, we are setting an action lookup on our page. Now we add the code to display a message as we want to show information about the selected record.

Once we execute our codeunit, it will open the Item List page with our filtered data. At this time, our page is waiting for a user action to select the desired record. If the user does not select any record and clicks on the **OK** button, the system will consider the first record as a user selection.

There's more...

When a page is run modally, no input, such as a keyboard or a mouse click, can occur, except for objects on the modal page. The `RUN` function is available for Page, Report, Codeunit, and XMLport, whereas the `RUNMODAL` function is only available for Page and Report.

See also

- The *Advance filters* recipe in *Chapter 3, Working with Tables, Records, and Queries*
- The *Create functions* recipe in *Chapter 2, General Development*

Updating the subform page from a parent page

The subform page only reloads data when it knows it needs to. Unfortunately, it is not very smart. This recipe will show you how to force a subform page to refresh itself.

How to do it...

1. Create a new page from **Object Designer**.
2. Choose the **Create Blank Page** option to design a page from scratch.
3. Add the following global variables to the page:

Name	Type
A	Integer
B	Integer

4. Next, add a global function called `SetValues`.

5. Add the following parameters to the function:

Name	Type
Aparam	Integer
Bparam	Integer

6. Now add the following code to the function.

```
A := Aparam;
B := Bparam;
```

7. Add another global function called `UpdateSelf`.
8. Then add the following code to the function:

```
CurrPage.UPDATE;
```

9. From the **Page Designer** window, set the following page property (*Shift* + *F4*):

Property	Value
PageType	CardPart

10. Add the following variables in the **Page Designer** window:

Type	SubType	SourceExpr	Name
`Container`	`ContentArea`		`MainContainer`
`Group`	`Group`		`MainGroup`
`Field`		`A+B`	`Sum of A & B`

11. After the previous configuration and coding, **Page Designer** will look similar to the following screenshot:

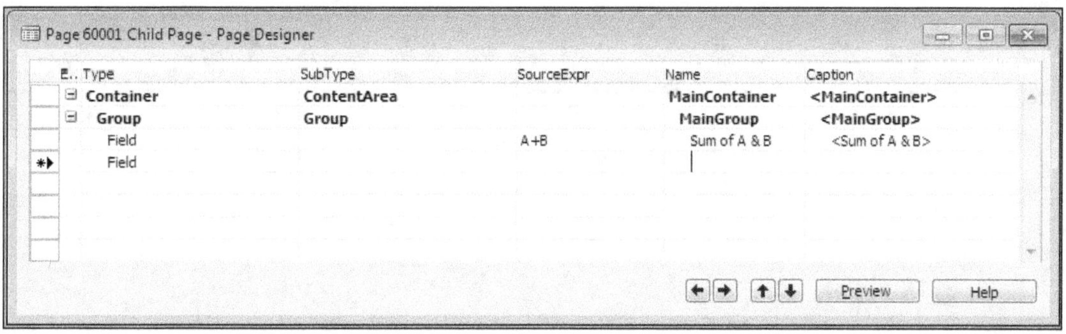

12. Save and close the page (for later use, remember the ID it is saved under).
13. Now let's create another new page using **Object Designer**.
14. Then add the following global variables:

Name	Type
A	Integer
B	Integer

15. Later, add the following variables in the **Page Designer** window:

Type	SubType	SourceExpr	Name
`Container`	`ContentArea`		`MainContainer`
`Group`	`Group`		`MainGroup`
`Field`		`A`	`Value For A`
`Field`		`B`	`Value For B`
`Part`	`Page`		`ChildPage`

16. Make sure all controls are indented under `Container` as shown in the following screenshot:

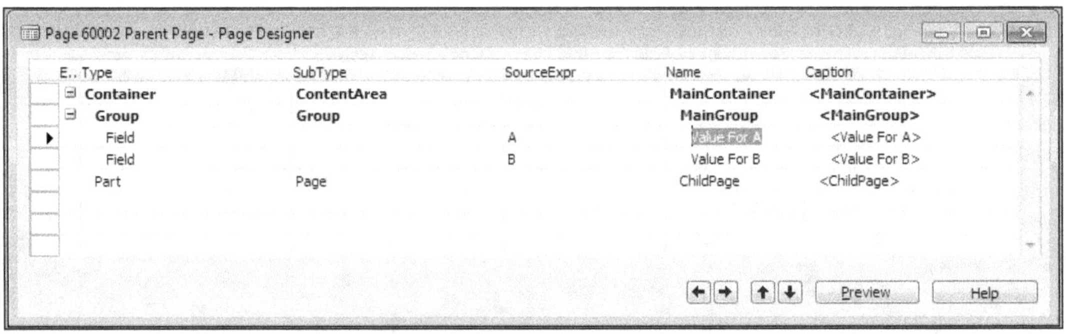

17. Next, in the `OnValidate` trigger for each field, add the following code:

```
CurrPage.ChildPage.PAGE.SetValues(A,B);
CurrPage.ChildPage.PAGE.UpdateSelf;
```

18. In the next row, add the value `Part` for the column `Type`, and for the column `SubType` add value as `Page`.
19. Set the following properties for the `Part` section (*Shift* + *F4*):

Property	Value
Name	ChildPage
PagePartID	The ID of the page you just created

20. Finally save and close the page.
21. On execution of the page, you will see a window similar to the following screenshot:

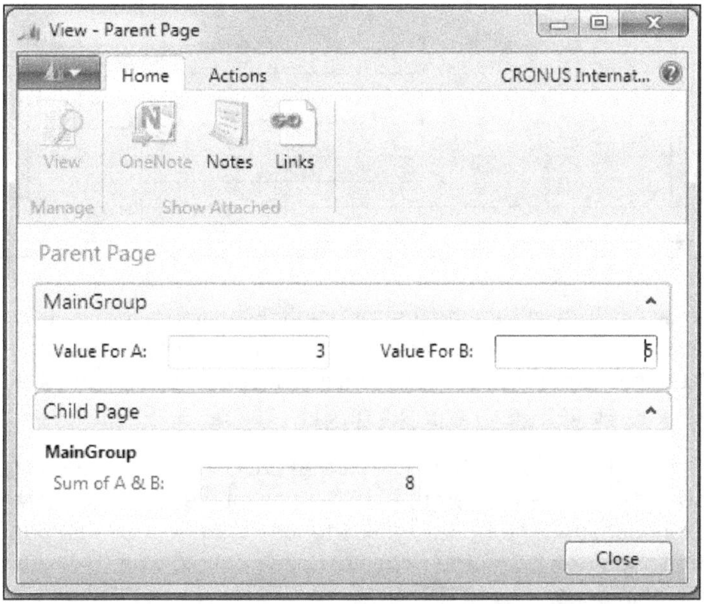

How it works...

To understand the concepts behind this recipe, we will use the following figure:

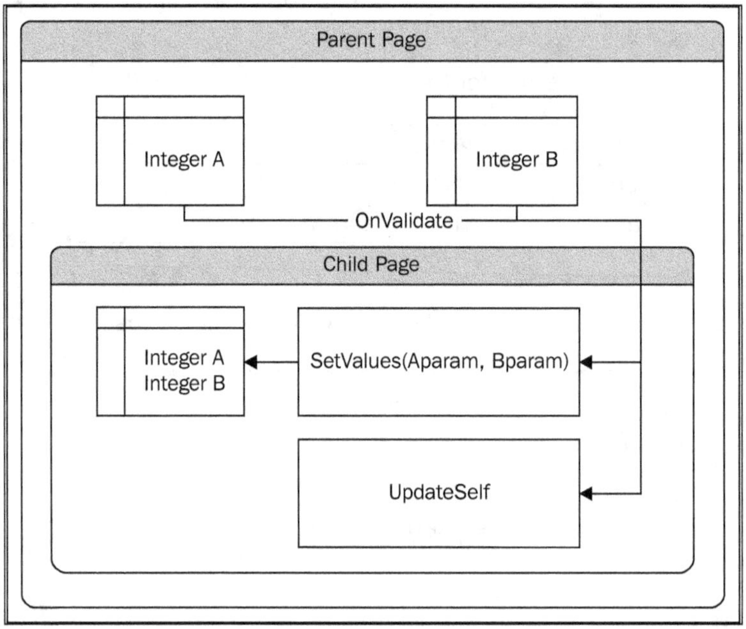

The main page knows only about things that are directly on itself, that is, two integer variables and a subform page. The main page can request the subform page to return some values and can also tell the subform page to set values if it needs to, but it cannot do it directly. The subform page can only be of type `CardPart` or `ListPart`.

Also, the subform page knows only about things that are on its own page. These include the two integer variables (completely different than the two integer variables on the main page), the `SetValues` function, and the `UpdateSelf` function. While the main page can request information from the subform page, the opposite does not hold true. The subform page knows nothing about the main page.

That explains why we add code where we do. For the subform page to display the sum of A and B, we have to tell it what the values of A and B are. Remember that just changing the values on the main page is not enough. That's why we have the `SetValues` function. We call this function every time the values are changed (`OnValidate`) in the main form.

That again is not enough, though. Just because the values have changed in the subform page, it doesn't mean the subform page is smart enough to understand that it must display the new information. Ordinarily, you would have to click on the subform page (or select it; you can do anything that makes it the active control on the page) for it to refresh. You can also do this with code, using the `CurrPage.UPDATE` command.

See also

- *Creating a page using a wizard*

Creating a FactBox page

In RTC, we can see small boxes on the right-hand side of the pages, which display brief information about the current record. To maintain the standard NAV GUI in customized pages, it is suggested to add FactBox related to the pages. In this recipe, we will create a FactBox page based on Item table and add it on the default Item List page.

How to do it...

1. Create a new page from **Object Designer**.
2. Leave the `Table Name` field blank and choose the **Create Blank Page** option to design a page from scratch.
3. From the **Page Designer** window, set the following page properties (*Shift* + *F4*):

Property	Value
PageType	CardPart
SourceTable	Item

4. Add the following variables in the **Page Designer** window:

Type	SubType	SourceExpr	Name
Container	ContentArea		MainContainer
Field		"No."	<No.>
Field		Description	<Description>
Field		Inventory	<Inventory>

5. The indented **Page Designer** window will look similar to the following screenshot:

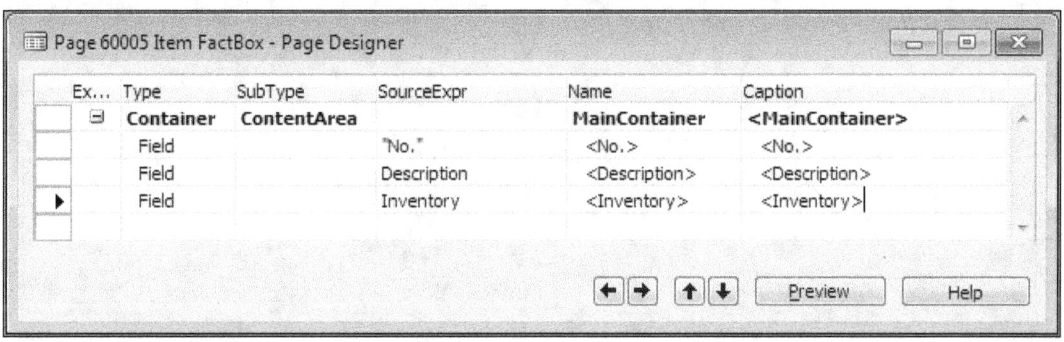

6. Save and close the page (for later use, remember the ID it is saved under).
7. Choose page 31 (`Item List`) in **Object Designer** and click on the **Design** button.
8. At the end of **Page Designer**, under `FactBoxArea`, add a new `Part` of type `Page`.
9. Now set the following properties for `Part` (*Shift* + *F4*):

Property	Value
PagePartID	The ID of the page you just created
SubPageLink	No.=FIELD(No.)

10. To adjust the sequence of FactBoxes, use the up and down arrow buttons.

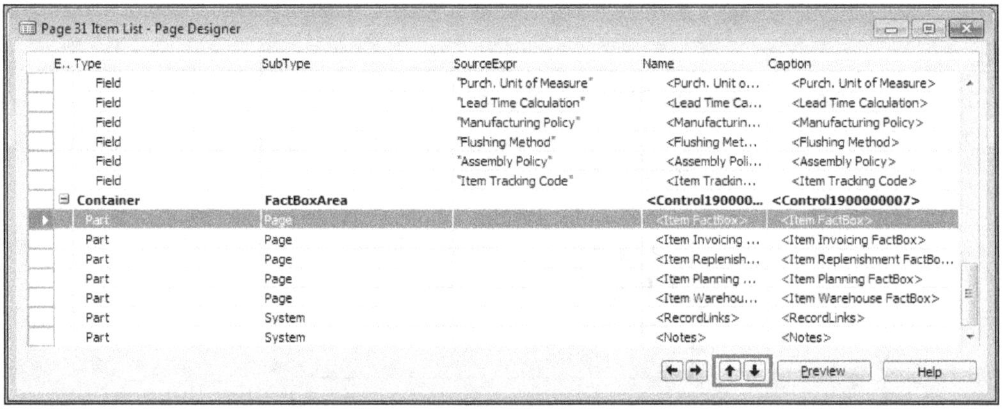

11. Save, close, and run the page. You should find your FactBox in the Item List page.

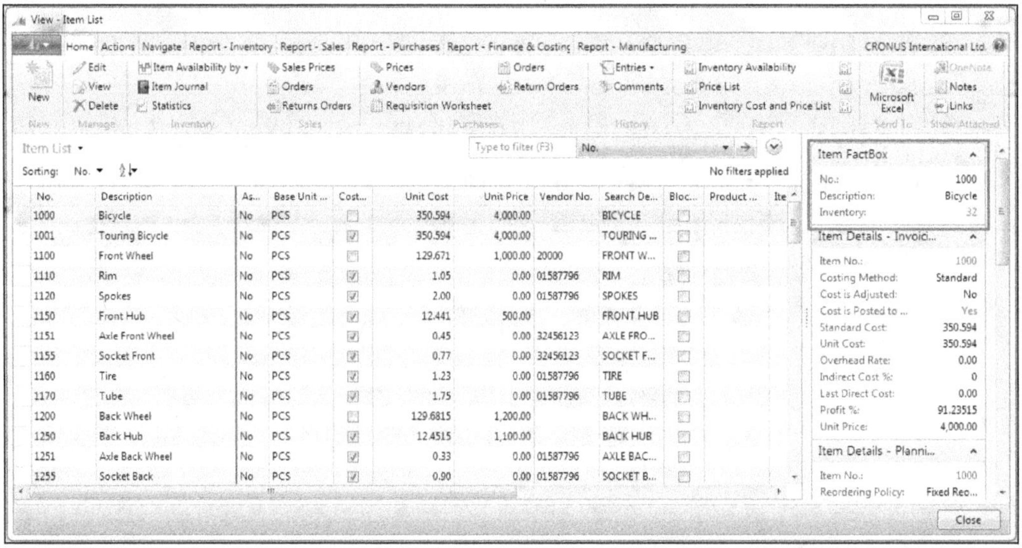

How it works...

FactBox is nothing but a subform page; that's why the page type has to be a `CardPart` or `ListPart` page. We have created our page based on the Item table with three simple fields. As we are assigning the `Inventory` field directly to a control, even though it is of type `flowfield`, we do not need to explicitly calculate it using `CALCFIELD`.

To use our new subform page as FactBox, it's important to add it under a container of type `FactBoxArea`. To set the first position (by default), we used indentation buttons. Users can use the personalization functionality of RTC and rearrange the position of FactBox as per their convenience.

To associate the FactBox data with the main page's record, we need to set up the relation between the main page and the FactBox page. To achieve this, we used the `SubPageLink` property. If we do not set this property, we will see that of all the item records, FactBox displays information of only the first record.

There's more...

Microsoft suggests using the word "FactBox" as a suffix for all the FactBox pages. It will help to identify these pages easily.

See also

- *Creating a page using a wizard*
- *Creating a Queue page*
- *Creating a Role Center page*

Creating a Queue page

The Queue page is a part of the Role Center page. This recipe will help us to create a Queue page, which we will be utilizing in our next recipe, *Creating a Role Center page*.

How to do it...

1. Create a new blank page from **Object Designer**.
2. Set the properties of the page as follows:

Property	Value
Caption	Activities
PageType	CardPart
SourceTable	Sales Cue

3. Add the following variables in the **Page Designer** window:

Type	SubType	SourceExpr	Name	Caption
`Container`	`ContentArea`		`MainContainer`	`<MainContainer>`
`Group`	`CueGroup`		`ForReleaseGroup`	`For Release`
`Field`		`"Sales Quotes - Open"`	`OpenQuotes`	`Open Sales Quotes`
`Field`		`"Sales Orders - Open"`	`OpenOrders`	`Open Sales Orders`

4. Set the following property in the `OpenQuotes` line:

Property	Value
DrillDownPageID	Sales Quotes

5. Set the following property in the `OpenOrders` line:

Property	Value
DrillDownPageID	Sales Orders

6. After the previous configuration and coding, our page should look similar to the following screenshot:

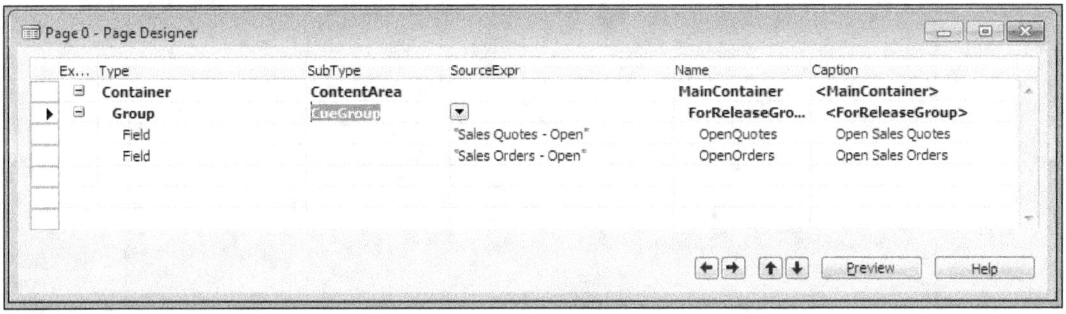

7. Keep the cursor on the `ForReleaseGroup` line and navigate to **View | Control Actions**.
8. Then add the following variables:

Type	Name	Caption
Action	Action1	`New Sales Quote`
Action	Action2	`New Sales Order`

9. Set the following property in the `New Sales Quote` line:

Property	Value
RunObject	`Page Sales Quotes`

10. Set the following property in the `New Sales Order` line:

Property	Value
RunObject	`Page Sales Order`

11. Compile, save, and close the page.

12. When you run the page, you will see a window similar to the following screenshot:

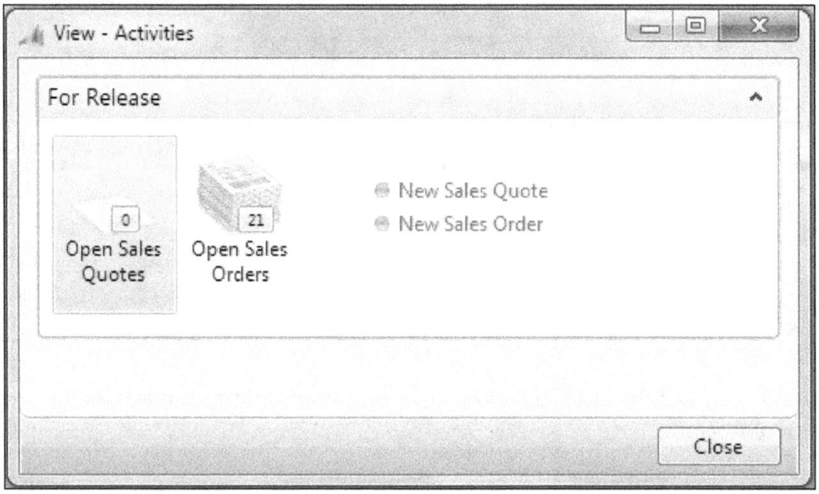

How it works...

The first part of the Role Center is known as activities. This is where the users look to know what actions they need to perform. The activities are built on top of special tables known as cues. These cue tables are made mostly of `FlowFields` and `FlowFilters`. We are going to build our activities part on the `Sales Cue` table. It should display any Open Sales documents we are working on.

By adding the `Group` line to our page and specifying `SubType` as `CueGroup`, we tell the RTC to display the fields indented beneath it in a specific way. Activities are displayed as stacks of paper that grow and shrink based on the numbers returned by the `FlowFields` in the cue table. Additionally, in order to provide the same type of data access that you would gain on a form, we specify `DrillDownFormID` for each of the fields or activities. We can also define actions on our group lines. In this example we have created simple links to create new sales quotes and sales orders.

See also

- *Creating a page using a wizard*
- *Creating a FactBox page*
- *Creating a Role Center page*
- *Adding a chart to the page*

Creating a Role Center page

The Role Center is like a dashboard that displays data and functionality related to a specific user role. This recipe will show you how to create a Role Center page for the new RTC.

How to do it...

1. Create a new page from **Object Designer**.
2. Set the properties of the page as follows:

Property	Value
PageType	RoleCenter

3. Add the following variables in the **Page Designer** window:

Type	SubType	SourceExpr	Name
Container	RoleCenterArea		Content
Group	Group		LeftSide
Part	Page		Activities
Part	System		Outlook
Group	Group		RightSide
Part	Page		MyCustomers
Part	Page		MyItems
Part	System		MyNotes

4. All of the previous lines should be indented as shown in the following screenshot:

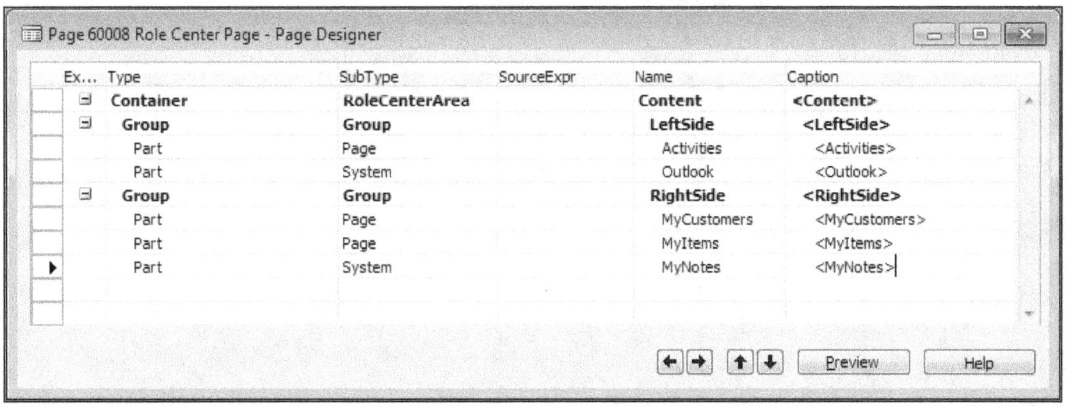

5. Now set the following properties in the `Activities` line:

Property	Value
PartType	Page
PagePartID	The Queue ID of the Activities page that we created in the previous recipe

6. Then set the following properties in the `Outlook` line:

Property	Value
PartType	System
SystemPartID	Outlook

7. Set the following properties in the `MyCustomers` line:

Property	Value
PartType	Page
PagePartID	My Customers

8. Set the following properties in the `MyItems` line:

Property	Value
PartType	Page
PagePartID	My Items

9. Set the following properties in the `MyNotes` line:

Property	Value
PartType	System
SystemPartID	Notes

10. Compile, save, and close the page. The resulting Role Center should look similar to the one shown in the following screenshot:

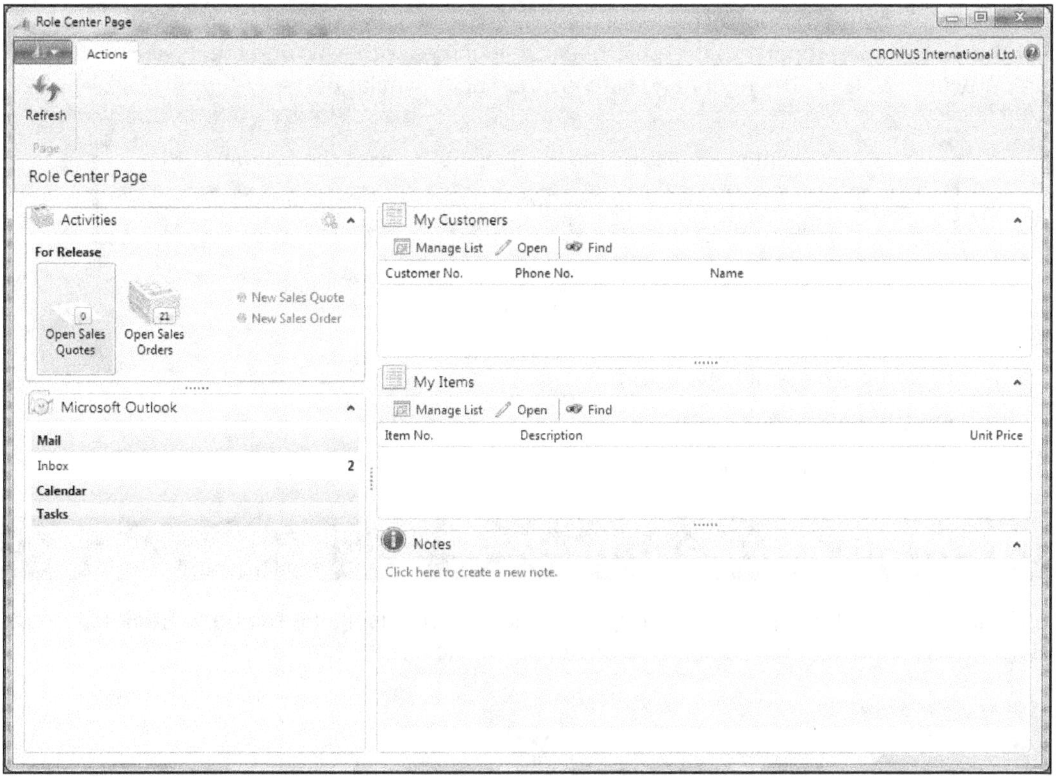

How it works...

We begin with a container, but this time we set the `SubType` field to `RoleCenterArea`. This essentially divides the page vertically into a left and right section. We add groups for each of these sections and then choose what to display.

Deciding what to display is fairly straightforward. Instead of adding fields to our group, we add parts. First we choose what type of part will be shown. For our activities, this will be a `Page` object, so we set the `PartType` property to `Page` and `PagePartID` to the object ID of the page. Directly beneath that part, we are displaying the built-in `Outlook` part. For this, we set the `PartType` property to `System`, because it comes with NAV, and the `SystemPartID` property to `Outlook`. The right-hand side is made up of similar parts.

> For more details on the PartType option, visit the following URL:
> `http://msdn.microsoft.com/en-us/library/dd355029(v=nav.70).aspx`

See also

- *Creating a page using a wizard*
- *Creating a FactBox page*
- *Creating a Queue page*

Creating a wizard page

A wizard is a page that takes you through specific sections using the **Next** and **Back** buttons. Here we will show you how to design a page that will do exactly that.

How to do it...

1. Create a new blank page from **Object Designer**.
2. Set the properties of the page as follows:

Property	Value
PageType	NavigatePage

3. Create the following global variables:

Name	Type	Length
FullName	Text	200
Address	Text	200
DateofBirth	Date	
ContactNo	Text	30
BackEnable	Boolean	
NextEnable	Boolean	
FinishEnable	Boolean	

Name	Type	Length
Step1Visible	Boolean	
Step2Visible	Boolean	
Step3Visible	Boolean	
Step4Visible	Boolean	

4. Add the following variables in **Page Designer**:

Type	SubType	SourceExpr	Name
`Container`	`ContentArea`		`Content`
`Group`	`Group`		`Step1`
`Field`		`FullName`	`Enter Your Full Name`
`Group`	`Group`		`Step2`
`Field`		`Address`	`Enter Your Present Address`
`Group`	`Group`		`Step3`
`Field`		`DateofBirth`	`Enter Your Date of Birth`
`Group`	`Group`		`Step4`
`Field`		`ContactNo`	`Enter Your Contact no.`

5. They should be indented as shown in the following screenshot:

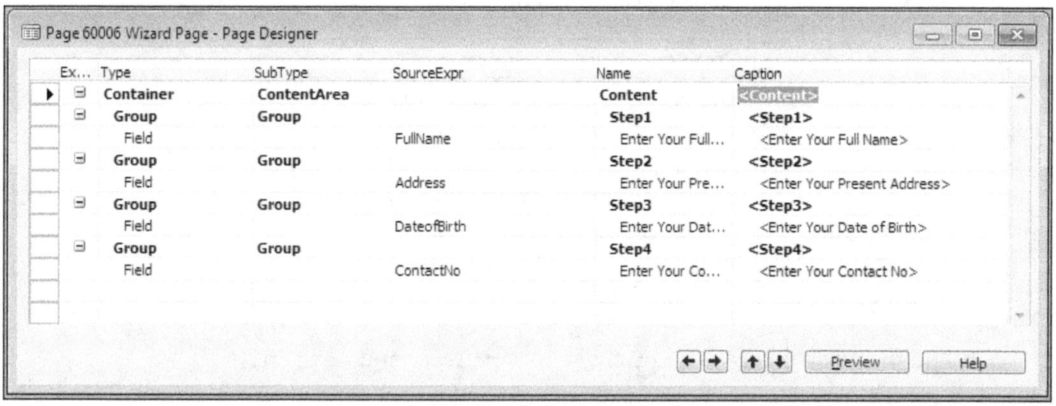

6. Select `Group` and `Step1` and set the `Enable` property with a value `Step1Visible`.
7. Select `Group` and `Step2` and set the `Enable` property with a value `Step2Visible`.
8. Select `Group` and `Step3` and set the `Enable` property with a value `Step3Visible`.
9. Select `Group` and `Step4` and set the `Enable` property with a value `Step4Visible`.
10. Then navigate to **View** | **Page Actions** (*Ctrl* + *Alt* + *F4*) to add actions on the page.

11. In `Action Designer`, add the following variables:

Type	Name	Caption
Action	Action1	&Back
Action	Action2	&Next
Action	Action3	&Finish

12. Set the following properties for `Action1`:

Property	Value
Enabled	BackEnable
Image	PreviousRecord
InFooterBar	Yes

13. Set the following properties for `Action2`:

Property	Value
Enabled	NextEnable
Image	NextRecord
InFooterBar	Yes

14. Set the following properties for `Action3`:

Property	Value
Enabled	FinishEnable
Image	Approve
InFooterBar	Yes

15. Add this code on the `action` trigger of `Action1`:

```
DoStep(CurrentStep-1);
CurrPage.UPDATE;
```

16. Add this code on the `action` trigger of `Action2` and `Action3`:

```
DoStep(CurrentStep+1);
CurrPage.UPDATE;
```

17. Next, create a new function `DoStep`.
18. Add the following parameters to the function:

Name	Type
Step	Integer

19. Add the following code to the function:

```
CurrentStep:=Step;
CASE Step OF
  1:
    BEGIN
      Step1Visible:=TRUE;
      Step2Visible:=FALSE;
      BackEnable := FALSE;
      NextEnable := TRUE;
      FinishEnable := FALSE;
    END;
  2:
    BEGIN
      Step2Visible:=TRUE;
      Step1Visible:=FALSE;
      Step3Visible:=FALSE;
      BackEnable := TRUE;
      NextEnable := TRUE;
      FinishEnable := FALSE;
    END;
  3:
    BEGIN
      Step3Visible:=TRUE;
      Step2Visible:=FALSE;
      Step4Visible:=FALSE;
      BackEnable := TRUE;
      NextEnable := TRUE;
      FinishEnable := FALSE;
    END;
  4:
    BEGIN
      Step4Visible:=TRUE;
      Step3Visible:=FALSE;
      BackEnable := TRUE;
      NextEnable := FALSE;
      FinishEnable := TRUE;
    END;
  5:
    BEGIN
    MESSAGE('%1\%2\%3\%4',FullName,Address,
      DateofBirth,ContactNo);
    CurrPage.CLOSE;
    END
  END;
CurrPage.UPDATE;
```

20. To start with step 1, add the following code to the `OnOpenPage` trigger:

    ```
    DoStep(1);
    ```

21. Compile, save, and close the page.
22. When you run the page, you will see a window similar to the following screenshot:

How it works...

The page contains four steps, only one of which is visible at any given time. To control this, we assigned a Boolean variable to all the `StepxVisible` properties. To control the movement of steps, we need to control our actions. To achieve this, we added other Boolean variables to the `Enable` property of our actions.

Our custom function `DoStep` decides what should be visible and what should not. It is just a large `CASE` statement based on the `Step` variable. In the first frame, for example, we can't move backwards to disable the **Back** button. We can't finish until we get to the last frame, so the **Finish** button is disabled until that point.

In the **Back** and **Next** buttons, we decrement and increment the `Step` variable, so that the `DoStep` function knows what to do. To keep track of the current step, we assign a value to the global `CurrentStep` variable; on the back action, we subtract 1 whereas on the next action we add 1 into `CurrentStep`.

See also

- *Creating a page using a wizard*

Displaying a .NET add-in on a page

The Microsoft Dynamics NAV Page Designer is limited in what it can do and what data it can display. By creating a visual .NET add-in and adding it to a page, you can display your data in the same formats that are available in .NET Windows Forms.

Getting ready

Microsoft Visual Studio must be installed on your system to use this recipe. I have used Visual Studio 2010; however, this recipe is compatible with Visual Studio 2008 as well.

How to do it...

1. Create a new class library project in Visual Studio.
2. Add the following references to the project:

   ```
   System.Windows.Forms
   Microsoft.Dynamics.Framework.UI.Extensibility
   ```

3. The latter can be found in the NAV's installation folder under `RoleTailored Client`.
4. Add the following code to the program:

   ```
   using System.Xml;
   using System.Data;
   using System.Windows.Forms;
   using Microsoft.Dynamics.Framework.UI.Extensibility;
   using Microsoft.Dynamics.Framework.UI.Extensibility.WinForms;
   namespace RSSReader
   {
     [ControlAddInExport("NAV_RSS")]
     public class RSSReaderAddIn : WinFormsControlAddInBase
     {
       private DataGridView grid;
       public void LoadRSS(string URL)
       {
         System.Net.WebRequest myRequest =
           System.Net.WebRequest.Create(URL);
         System.Net.WebResponse myResponse =
           myRequest.GetResponse();
         System.IO.Stream rssStream =
           myResponse.GetResponseStream();
         System.Xml.XmlDocument rssDoc = new
           System.Xml.XmlDocument();
         rssDoc.Load(rssStream);
   ```

```
        System.Xml.XmlNodeList rssItems =
          rssDoc.SelectNodes("rss/channel/item");
        XmlNode attribute;
        int i = 0;
        foreach (XmlNode node in rssItems)
        {
          attribute = node.SelectSingleNode("title");
          string[] rowArray = new string[] {
            attribute.InnerText };
          grid.Rows.Add(rowArray);
          i++;
        }
      }
      public override bool AllowCaptionControl
      {
        get
        {
          return false;
        }
      }
      protected override Control CreateControl()
      {
        grid = new DataGridView();
        grid.Columns.Add("Title", "Title");
        grid.Columns["Title"].Width = 600;
        grid.Height = 500;
        LoadRSS(
"http://mibuso.com/forum/smartfeed.php?u=7776&e=dGmFiU150Nty0r
hD8WG9KPwqlx38DiyvBH0tybeha8xNIA6Pr4x6EA..&lastvisit=1&filter_
foes=1&forum=32&limit=NO_LIMIT&count_limit=10&sort_by=postdate_
desc&feed_type=RSS2.0&feed_style=HTML");
        return grid;
      }
    }
}
```

5. Go to the project's properties and click on the **Signing** tab. Check the **Sign the assembly** checkbox.

6. Under choose a strong name key file, select an existing key or create a new one.
7. Build, save, and close the project.
8. Copy the `NAV_RSS.dll` file from your default project folder, usually under `C:\Users\Your Username\Documents\Visual Studio 2008\Projects\RSSReader\RSSReader\bin\Debug` folder for the `RoleTailored client`, usually under `C:\Program Files (x86)\Microsoft Dynamics NAV\70\RoleTailored Client\Add-ins`.
9. Run the command prompt as the administrator.
10. Locate the `sn.exe` file. The default folder for the Microsoft .NET Framework SDK is `C:\Program Files (X86)\Microsoft SDKs\Windows\v7.0\Bin`.
11. In the command prompt, change to the directory that contains the `sn.exe` utility.
12. Type the following command:

    ```
    sn.exe -T "C:\Program Files (x86)\Microsoft Dynamics NAV\70\RoleTailored Client\Add-ins\NAV_RSS.dll"
    ```

13. Record the `Public Key Token` number.
14. From **Object Designer**, run the 2000000069 table in **Client Add-in**.
15. Create a new record for `NAV_RSS` as shown in the following screenshot:

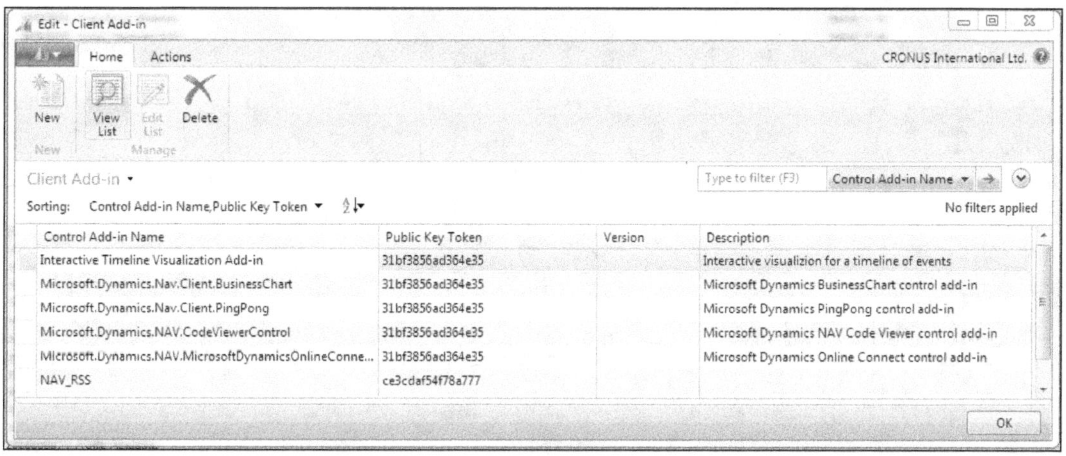

16. Then click on **OK**.
17. The add-in should be registered.
18. Create a new page from **Object Designer**.
19. Add the following variables:

Caption	Type	SubType	Name
`<MainContainer>`	`Container`	`ContentArea`	`MainContainer`
`<NAV_RSS>`	`Field`		`NAV_RSS`

20. Set the following property in the `NAV_RSS` line and use the `Public key token` value, which we searched for earlier in this recipe:

Property	Value
`ControlAddIn`	NAV_RSS;PublicKeyToken=Your Public Key Token

21. Use the lookup arrow to select the add-in. Your page should look similar to the following screenshot:

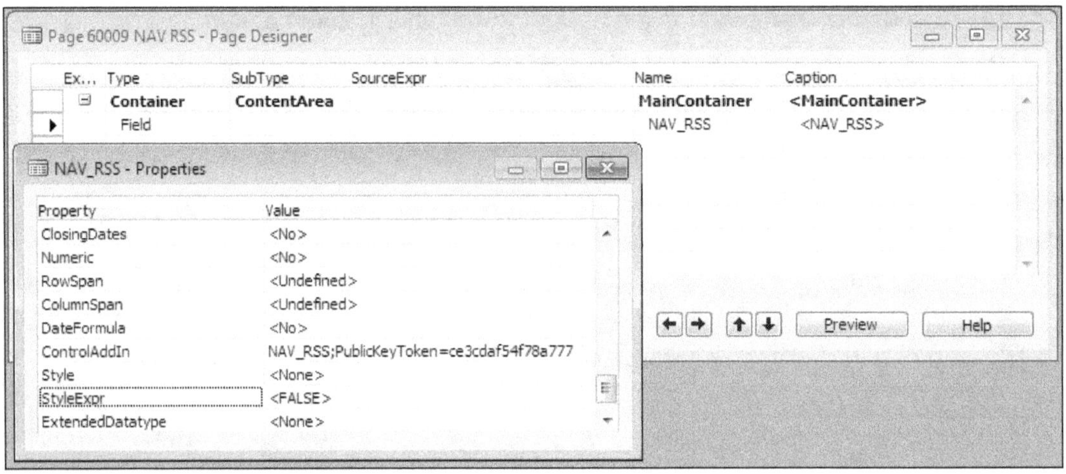

22. When you run the page, it should look similar to the following screenshot:

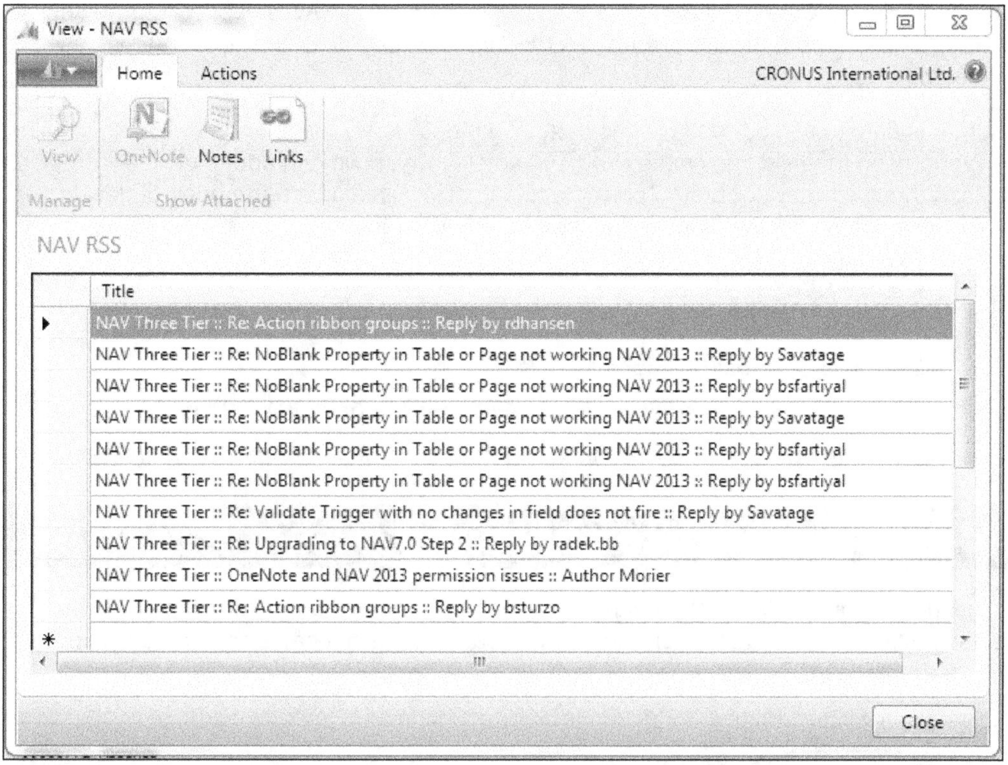

How it works...

In NAV 2013, you can use your own .NET objects to display in RTC pages. This is done using the functionalities in `Microsoft.Dynamics.Framework.UI.Extensibility dll`.

The `LoadRSS` function is the bulk of our class, but it is not important to the recipe, so we will only discuss it in brief. Many sites publish data in a format called **Really Simple Syndication** (**RSS**). This RSS format is just a form of XML, which can be parsed and used for our own use, in this case to fill in our `GridView`.

We have two functions that allow us to control the way we interact with pages in NAV 2009. The first is `AllowCaptionControl`. By overriding this function in `extensibility.dll`, we can force our control to not display a label. The second function, which is `CreateControl`, is the most important one. It returns a control object that tells the RTC what to display. Our function sets up a simple grid with one column called `Title`. We then call our `LoadRSS` function to fill in the actual data.

In order to use this new DLL in NAV 2013, we have to also make sure it is a signed assembly.

With the `Client Add-in` tool, registering the new control in NAV is easy. When we select the file to register, it automatically determines the `Public Key Token` number that is used to identify the DLL.

Finally, it is time to use our control in a page. We create a new page and add a field line. There is a property on the field line called `ControlAddIn`, which we can add to our newly registered add-in. Although it may not be the prettiest add-in, it will give us a better idea of developing add-ins. Our control is now ready to be used anywhere in the RTC.

See also

- *Creating a page using a wizard*
- The *Zipping folders and files within NAV* recipe in *Chapter 9, OS Interaction*
- The *Using SHELL to run external applications* recipe in *Chapter 9, OS Interaction*

Adding a chart to the page

Microsoft Dynamics NAV 2013 provides functionality to design unlimited charts. These charts can be based on a table or query. Users can add these charts on FactBoxes and Role Center pages.

How to do it...

1. Start Microsoft Dynamics NAV 2013 RoleTailored client.
2. Go to **Departments** | **Administration** | **Application Setup** | **RoleTailored Client** | **Generic Charts**.
3. Select the **New** action to create a chart.
4. In `General FastTab`, provide an `ID` and `Name` field to the chart (for later use, remember the ID it is saved under).
5. Select the `Source Type` table and set the `Source ID` value `112`.
6. Set `Measures` as follows:

Data Column	Aggregation
Amount	Sum

7. Then set `Salesperson Code` as `X-Axis` and `Currency Code` as `Z-Axis`.
8. Update the description text as `Salesperson sales by currency`.
9. Close the window.

10. Go to **Home** | **Role Center**.
11. Go to the **Application** menu and navigate to **Customize** | **Customize This Page...**.

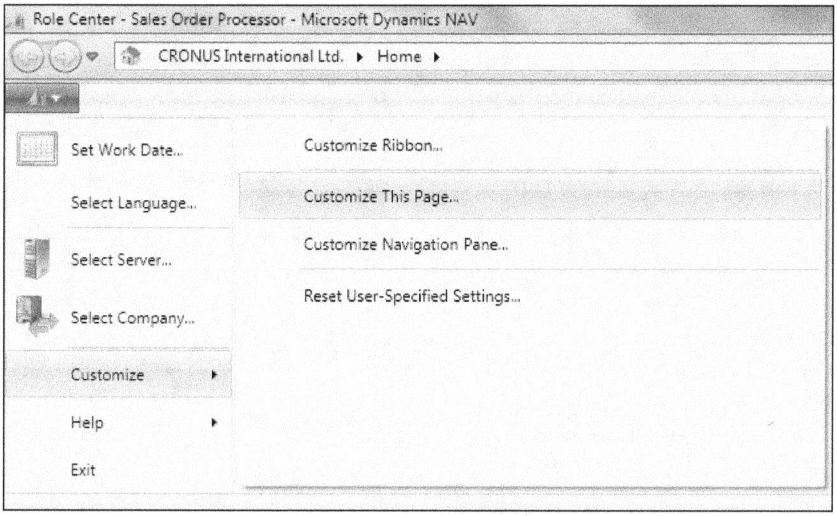

12. In the **Customize the Role Center** window, in the **Available parts:** field, choose **Chart Part**, and then click on **Add>>**.
13. To select our chart, click on the **Customize Part...** button at the right-hand side of the window.

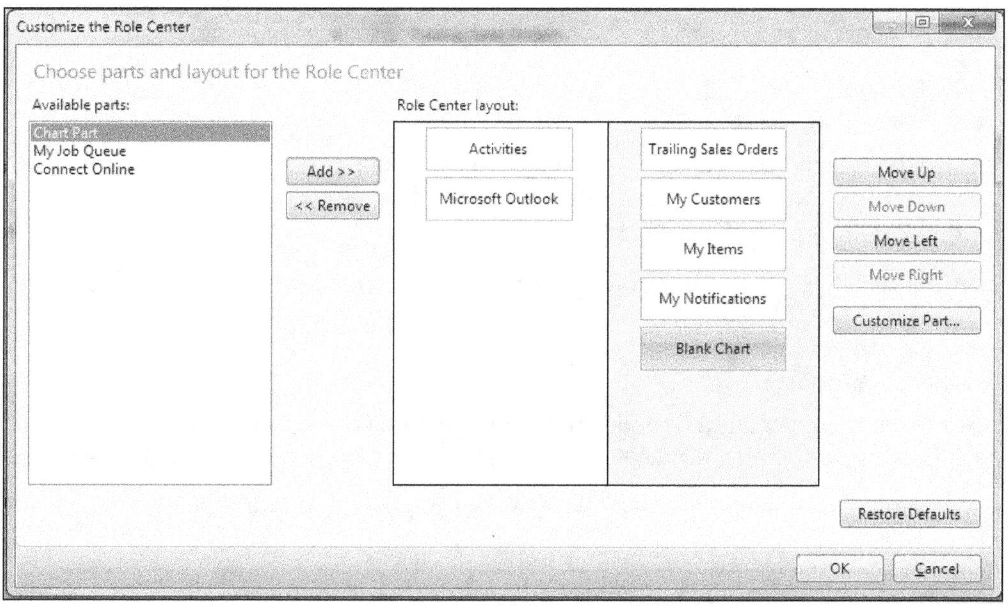

14. In the **Customize Chart** window, choose the last generic chart we created. Then click on the **OK** button.
15. Now on the Role Center page, in the FactBox area, we can see our newly added chart.

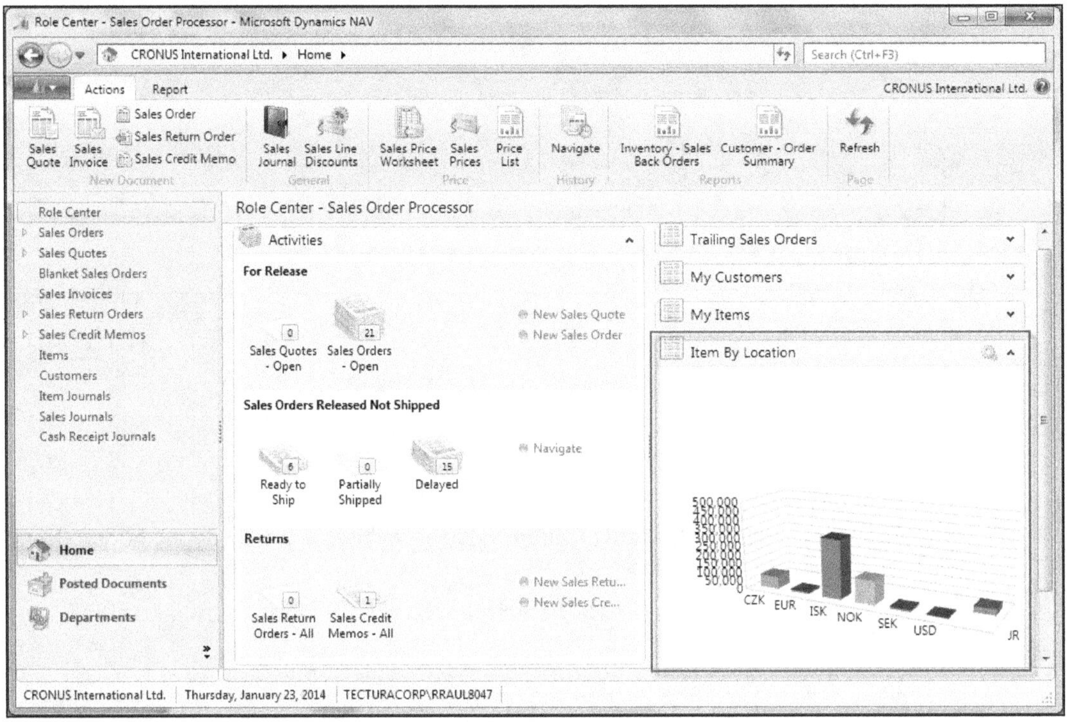

How it works...

To display the salesperson's sales by currency, we based our chart on the `Posted sales Invoice` table. The `Amount` field is a measure, whereas `Salesperson Code` and `Currency Code` are dimensions.

By personalizing RTC, we add our own customized charts and FactBoxes on the Role Center.

There's more...

Microsoft Dynamics NAV 2013 Generic Charts provide 14 different graph types to choose from. In addition to generic charts, Microsoft provides specific charts such as Finance Performance.

For more information on Finance Performance, visit the Microsoft MSDN site.

`http://msdn.microsoft.com/en-us/library/hh895991(v=nav.70).aspx`

See also

- *Creating a Role Center page*
- The *Creating an RDLC report* recipe in *Chapter 5, Report Design*
- The *Creating a Matrix report* recipe in *Chapter 5, Report Design*

5
Report Design

In this chapter, we will cover:

- Creating an RDLC report
- Using multiple options to run a report
- Adding custom filters to the Request Page
- Setting filters when report is loaded
- Creating reports to process data
- Creating a link from report to page
- Creating a link from report to report
- Adding totals on decimal field
- Adding interactive sorting on reports
- Creating a matrix report

Introduction

Although reports are similar to pages, they serve a different purpose in NAV. Pages exist primarily for data entry while reports show a higher-level view of what is going on in the database. Reports can be customer-facing documents, such as order confirmations and invoices or used for internal analysis, such as aged accounts receivables and aged accounts payable. They can also be used to process large amounts of data.

As developers, it is our job to design the dataset and visual layout of these reports. First, we use the **Report Dataset Designer** in **Microsoft Dynamics NAV Development Environment** to define the dataset of the report by choosing `table` as `dataItem` and `field`, `variable`, `expression`, or a text constant as `column`. Next, we design **Client Report Definition Layout** (**RDLC**) for reports that are used to print or display data. We use the Visual Studio report designer to design an RDLC layout. The following table will help to understand the different types of reports:

Report type	Details	Example
List report	A list report contains a single data item based on either a master or supplemental table to print the list. A report name contains the table name and the word `List`.	`Customer - List` `Inventory - List`
Test report	A test report is generally based on journal tables. The purpose is to test each journal line before posting and presenting the missing information to the user. The name of this report contains the type of journal and the word `Test`.	`General Journal -Test` `Resource Journal - Test`
Posting report	Posting reports are printed from the **Post and Print** options of the journals. They contain a list of transactions posted to register. The report name is the name of the register.	`G/L Register` `Customer Register`
Transaction report	A transaction report is based on two tables, the master table and the related ledger table. It presents all the ledger entries for each transaction record with a subtotal for each transaction record and the grand total at the end. There is no standard name for these reports.	`Trial Balance` `Customer - Trial Balance`
Document report	This type of report is generally divided into three sections—header, body, and footer. The header and footer information is generally repeated on each page, whereas the body mostly contains the column layout presenting transaction details.	`Sales - Invoice` `Purchase - Invoice`
Processing-only report	This type of report does not have a print layout; the report itself does the processing. To make any report a processing-only report, we need to set the `ProcessingOnly` property to the report.	`Import Budget from Excel` `Update Analysis Views`
Other reports	These reports are designed as per client requirements. There is a fixed format for these reports.	

Creating an RDLC report

This recipe will guide you to develop a simple RDLC report of the type list.

How to do it...

1. Create a new report from **Object Designer**.
2. Then add the following lines in the **Report Designer**:

Data type	Data source	Name
DataItem	Customer	<Customer>
Column	"No."	No_Customer
Column	Name	Name_Customer
Column	Address	Address_Customer
Column	City	City_Customer
Column	Balance	Balance_Customer

3. After the previous step, the **Report Dataset Designer** should look like the following screenshot:

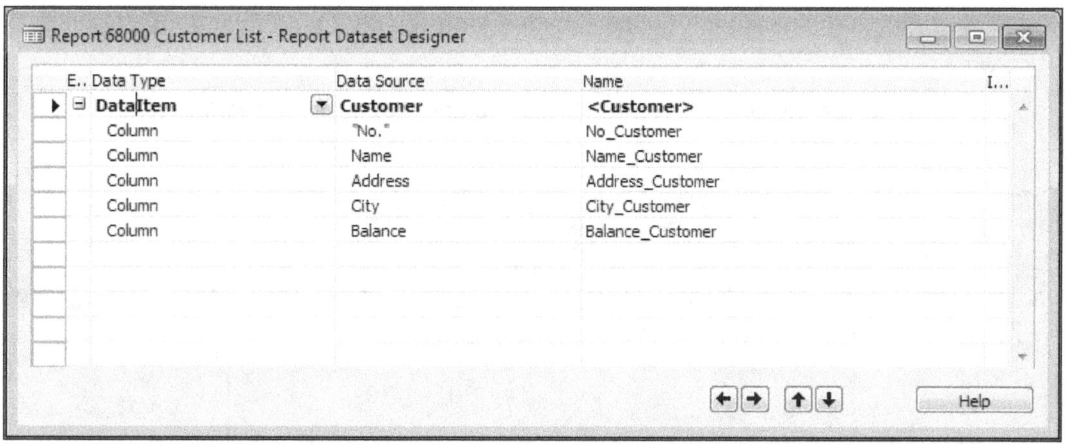

4. From the **View** menu, choose **Layout**. You should see a window similar to the following screenshot:

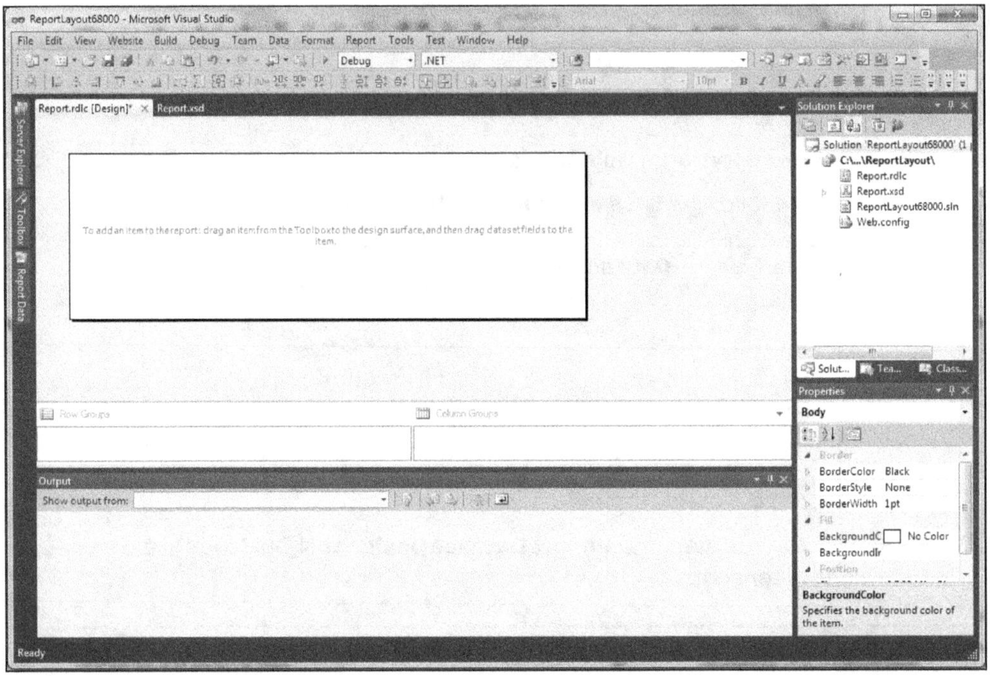

5. From the **Toolbox** explorer, select **Table** and add it to design as shown in the following screenshot:

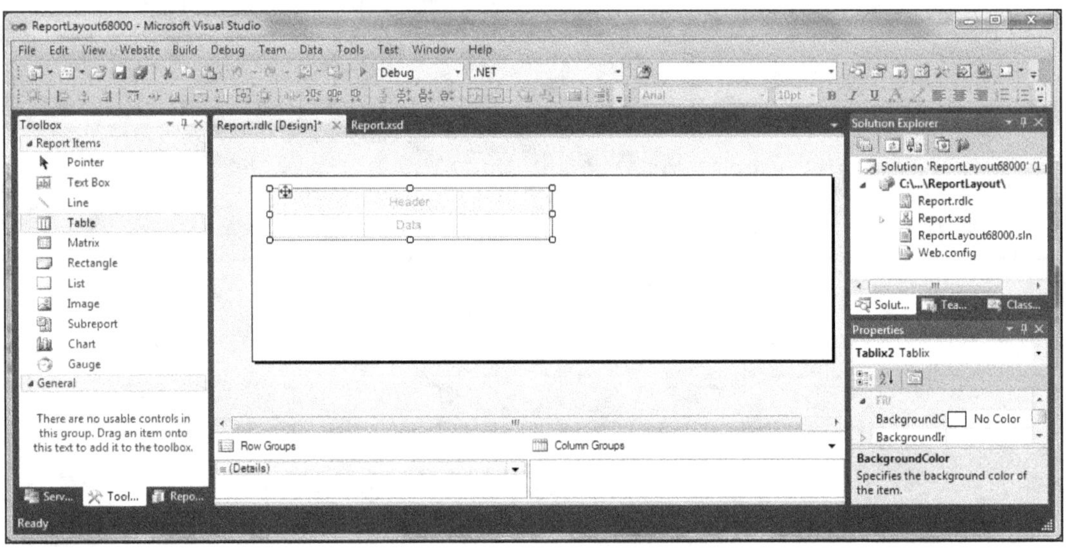

6. Display the **Report Data Explorer** window from the **View** menu in Visual Studio or press *Ctrl + Alt + D*. From the **Report Data Explorer**, select all the dataset items, and add them to the table in the designer. After adding the dataset items to the Visual Studio report designer, it should look like the following screenshot:

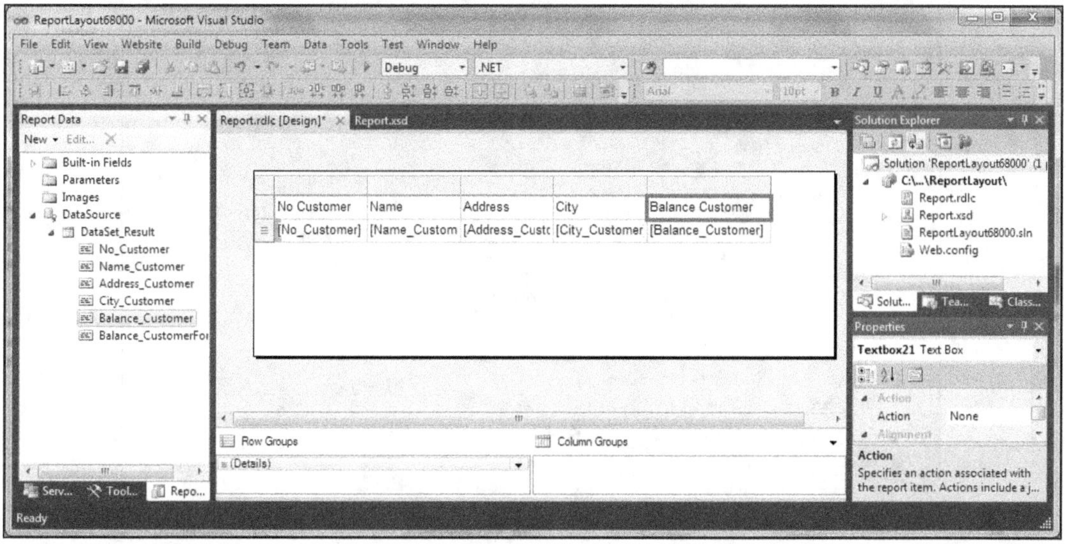

7. Save and close the Visual Studio report designer.

8. On clicking on the report designer in NAV, you will see the following confirmation dialog. Click on **Yes**.

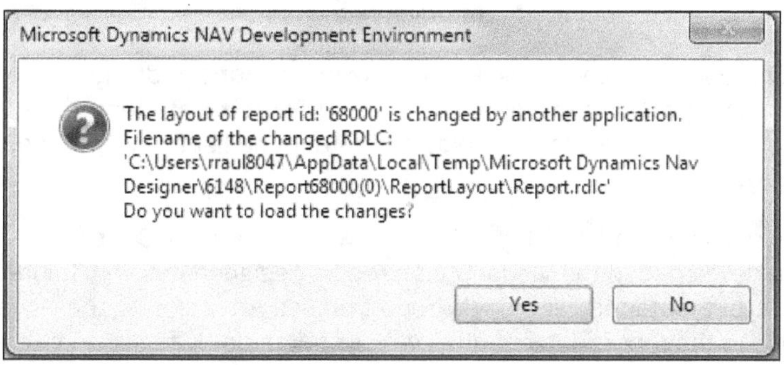

9. **Save** and **close** the report.

10. On execution of the report from the NAV **Object Designer** page, you should see a window similar to the following screenshot:

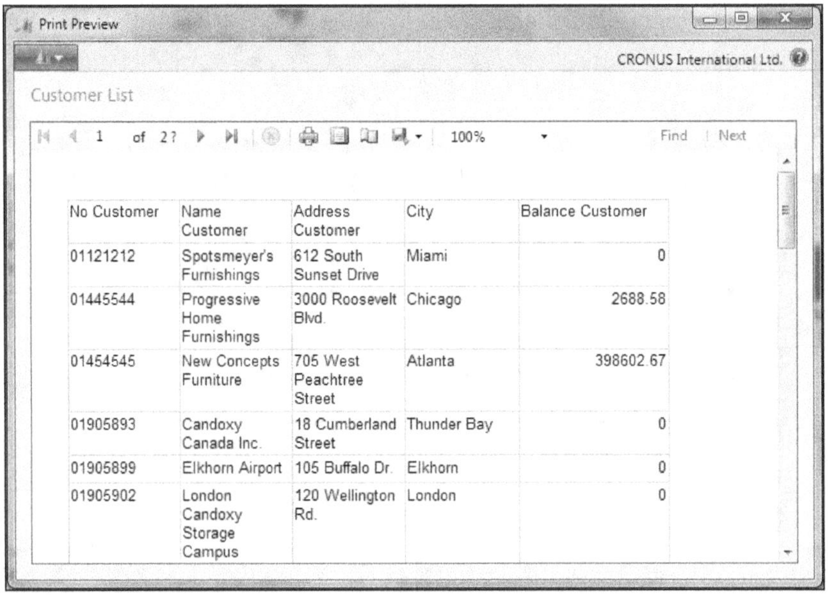

How it works...

The **Report Dataset Designer** provides options to select the tables and fields on which we want to base our report. After selecting the desired table as `DataItem`, we can simply type the field details or select it from the **Field** menu.

The Visual Studio report designer provides very flexible options to design a visual layout of reports. To view the report data explorer, go to **View** | **Report Data** (or press *Ctrl* + *Alt* + *D*). We selected the **Table** data region to display our data in the list format. We added fields from the report data explorer.

NAV objects are designed and developed in C/AL, whereas an RDLC report visual layout is designed and developed in the Visual Studio report designer. It is very important to save/integrate layout metadata with a NAV report object. After closing the visual designer and coming back to the report dataset designer, we get a dialog to save/integrate the visual layout information with the report.

There's more...

Microsoft Dynamics NAV 2013 provides an option to upgrade NAV 2009 reports. The following table will help to understand how the upgrade process will develop the NAV 2013 report. To upgrade the report from the **Microsoft Dynamics NAV Development Environment**, go to **Object Designer,** select the report which needs to be upgraded, and then go to **Tools | Upgrade Report**.

NAV 2009 Report	After upgrade
Reports with both classic report layouts and RDLC layouts	The report dataset is upgraded to NAV 2013 dataset definition and the RDLC 2005 layout is upgraded to RDLC 2008
Classic report	The report dataset is upgraded to NAV 2013 dataset definition, the request page is deleted, and an RDLC 2008 layout is created
Processing-only reports	The report dataset is upgraded to NAV 2013 dataset definition

See also

- *Using multiple options to run a report*
- *Adding custom filters to the Request Page*
- *Creating a link from report to page*
- *Creating a link from report to report*

Using multiple options to run a report

During the development or testing phase, we may need to run a report individually. This recipe has multiple subrecipes that will demonstrate options to run the `Customer - List` report.

How to do it...

1. Open **Microsoft Dynamics NAV Development Environment**.
2. From the **Tools** menu, choose **Object Designer** and then choose **Report**.
3. Select the report `101, Customer - List` and then choose **Run**.
4. Firstly using command prompt, in the command prompt window, select `RoleTailored client` directory by using the `CD` command:

   ```
   CD C:\Program Files (x86)\Microsoft Dynamics NAV\70\RoleTailored
   Client
   ```

Secondly, use the following command:

```
Microsoft.Dynamics.Nav.Client.exe Dynamicsnav:////runreport?report
= 101
```

5. Firstly, using the **Run** window, on the taskbar, choose **Start**, and then choose **Run**. In the **Run** window, type the following command:

   ```
   Microsoft.Dynamics.Nav.Client.exe Dynamicsnav:////runreport?Report
   =101
   ```

   secondly, choose **OK**.

6. Using browser - Open the browser. In the address bar, type the following command:

   ```
   Dynamicsnav:////runreport?report=101
   ```

How it works...

It is important to have a configured NAV server and the `RoleTailored client` to run a report using any of the options mentioned in the previous section. On execution of any of the previous options, the system will start the `RoleTailored client` with the last used database and company.

In the previous commands, `Microsoft.Dynamics.Nav.Client.exe` represents the `RoleTailored client`, whereas `Dynamicsnav:////runreport?report=` is a keyword to run the object type `report`. The number `101` represents the `Customer - List` report.

See also

- *Creating an RDLC report*
- *Using multiple options to run the page*

Adding custom filters to the Request Page

When running a report, sometimes we want the user to be able to filter on something that is not a field in a table. This recipe will show you how to add a filter to the request page for this purpose.

How to do it...

1. Create a report by following the *Creating an RDLC report* recipe.
2. Reopen the report in the designer mode and add the following global variables:

Name	Type	Length
`CustomerNoFilter`	`Code`	`250`

3. Navigate to **View** | **Request Page** (*Alt* + *V*, *A*).
4. Add the following lines in the page designer:

Type	SubType	SourceExpr	Name
`Container`	`ContentArea`		`MainContainer`
`Group`	`Group`		`MainGroup`
`Field`		`CustomerNoFilter`	`Customer No. Filter`

5. The request page should look like the following screenshot:

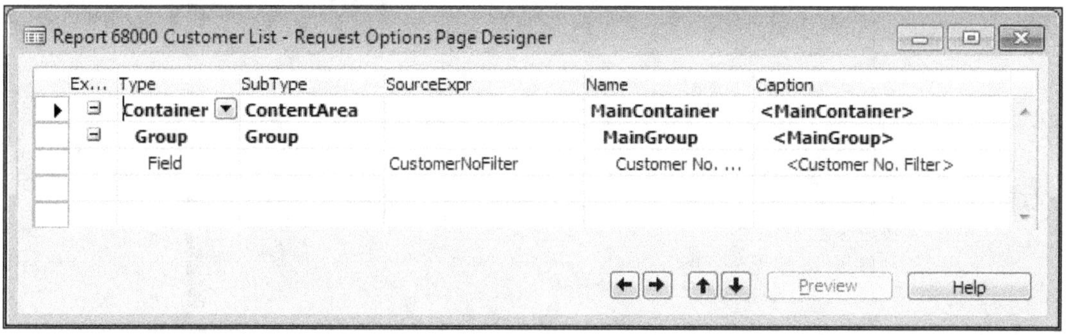

6. Add the following code to the `OnPreDataItem` trigger for the `customer` data item:

```
IF CustomerNoFilter <> '' THEN
  SETFILTER("No.", '%1', CustomerNoFilter);
```

7. Save and close the report.

How it works...

The request page is just a normal page. We design it in the same way we would design any other page.

Our example is basic. We could easily add the `No.` field to the filters on the data item. Instead, we store the filter in a global text variable and then use that text variable to set the filter properly before loading the data by adding the code to the `OnPreDataItem` trigger. The trick is to set the filter only if the user has entered any value. If the filter was left blank, and this blank was filtered, we would get an empty recordset.

Ordinarily when you run a report, assuming you have added fields to the `ReqFilterFields` property and nothing has been added to the request page, you would see a window similar to the following screenshot:

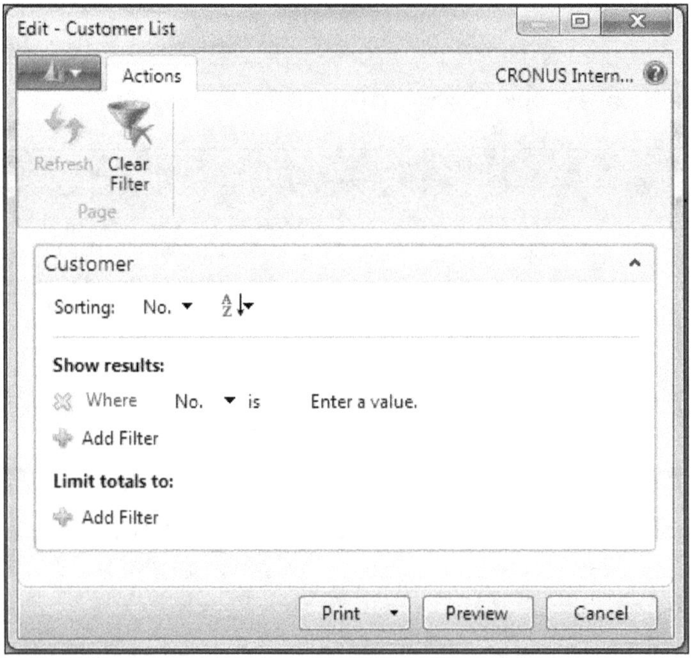

When you run this report, you'll notice that a new FastTab is created. This is the tab that holds the request page, but it only appears when you have added something to it:

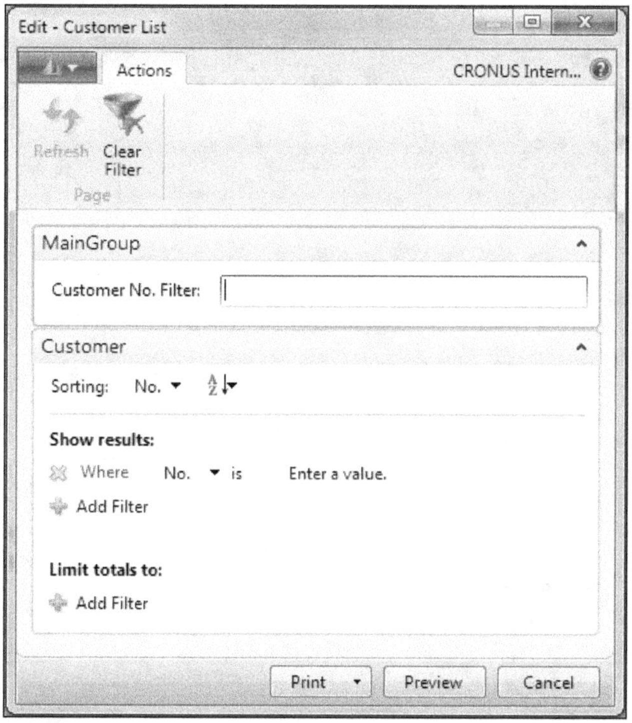

There's more...

The fields on the request page have the same triggers and properties as textboxes on a normal page. This means that you don't have to rely on the user to remember the customer number. We can add the lookup functionality as shown:

Add the following local variables to the `OnLookup` trigger for the field:

Name	Type	Subtype
Customer	Record	Customer

Add the following code to the `OnLookup` trigger:

```
IF PAGE.RUNMODAL(22,Customer) = ACTION::LookupOK THEN
  CustomerNoFilter:=Customer."No.";
```

This code enables the lookup arrow on the field. It runs the **Customer List** page in lookup mode and retrieves the selected record. That value is assigned to the `CustomerNoFilter` variable, which is what the field displays as shown in the following screenshot:

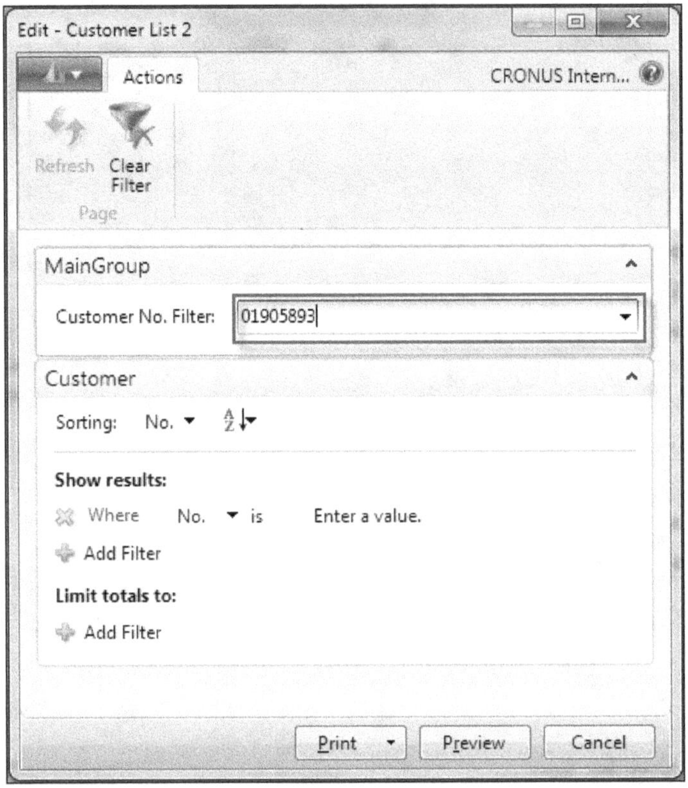

See also

- *Creating an RDLC report*
- *Setting filters when report is loaded*
- *Adding totals on decimal field*

Setting filters when report is loaded

You will often want to run a report on a specific record. This recipe will show you how to set the record that the report will use to execute.

How to do it...

1. Create a new codeunit from **Object Designer**.
2. Then add the following global variables:

Name	Type	Subtype
Customer	Record	Customer

3. Write the following code in the `OnRun` trigger of the codeunit:

```
Customer.FINDFIRST;
Customer.SETRANGE("No.", Customer."No.");
REPORT.RUN(REPORT::"Customer List", TRUE, FALSE, Customer);
```

4. Save and close the codeunit.

How it works...

The `FINDFIRST` value in this example is used here so that we have some data to work with. It is not necessary to implement this example. We use this data to apply a filter for the first customer number in the table.

Next comes the important part. NAV has a built-in variable named `REPORT` that has several methods associated with it. One of these is the `RUN()` method that takes four parameters. The first parameter is the ID of the report to run. It is best to reference the report using the same syntax as an `Option` variable, `REPORT::"Name of Report"`.

The second and third parameters are Booleans. The second tells the system whether or not to display the request page. We definitely want to display it because we want to see how it looks when we run it on a specific record. The third parameter tells it whether or not to use the system printer.

Our final parameter is a record variable that matches the first data item of the report. This parameter holds all of the filters that have been previously applied. When you run the codeunit, the report request page will be shown and the `No.` filter will be filled in.

There's more...

The most common place in NAV to see the final parameters being used is when printing reports-page-specific documents, such as an invoice. You can take a look at the flow of data between the actual pages and the document-print codeunit to get a better understanding.

See also

- *Using multiple options to run a report*
- *Adding custom filters to the Request Page*

Creating reports to process data

If we want to carry out some process without an output, we can use a report with the **Process-only** option. It allow us to use the built-in processing loop along with sorting and filtering capabilities to create a variety of data updating routines with minimum programming. In addition to this, it gives access to the **Request Page** to allow user inputs and guidance for the run. We can create the same functionality using codeunit, but for user inputs, we need to develop an additional page. Here we will see how to build a processing-only report.

How to do it...

1. Create a new blank report from **Object Designer**.
2. Set the following property on the report:

Property	Value
`ProcessingOnly`	`Yes`

3. Now, the previous property system will open a dialog box to confirm the auto changes done after setting this property. Click on **Yes**:

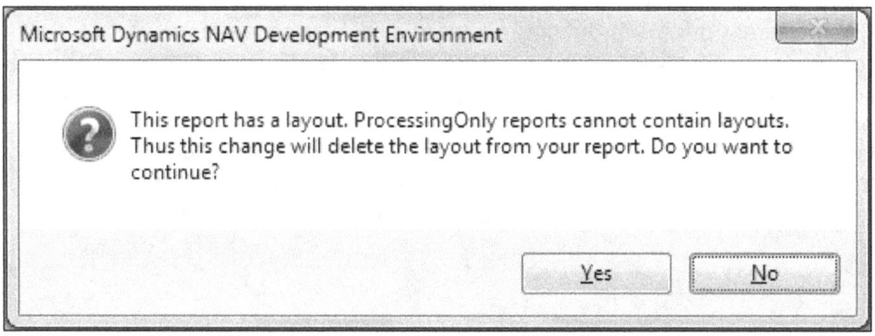

4. Add a data item with `Customer` as the table data source.

5. In the `OnAfterGetRecord` trigger for the `customer` data item, add the following code:

```
"Last Date Modified" := TODAY;
MODIFY;
```

6. Save and close the report.

How it works...

A data item is a record variable. However, instead of us writing our own code to loop through each record, this functionality is built inside a report. That makes a report a great place to perform mass processing of records. For this type of report, we don't want any pages to be displayed. This slows down the processing speed dramatically. To do this, we set the `ProcessingOnly` property of the report to `Yes`.

The `OnAfterGetRecord` trigger is fired after each record is retrieved from the database. This is where we need to place our code. Here we are just changing the `Last Modified Date` field, but you could do any sort of change that you want. When you run the report, you will see different buttons on the **Request Page**. Instead of the normal print and preview button, there is an **OK** button in its place:

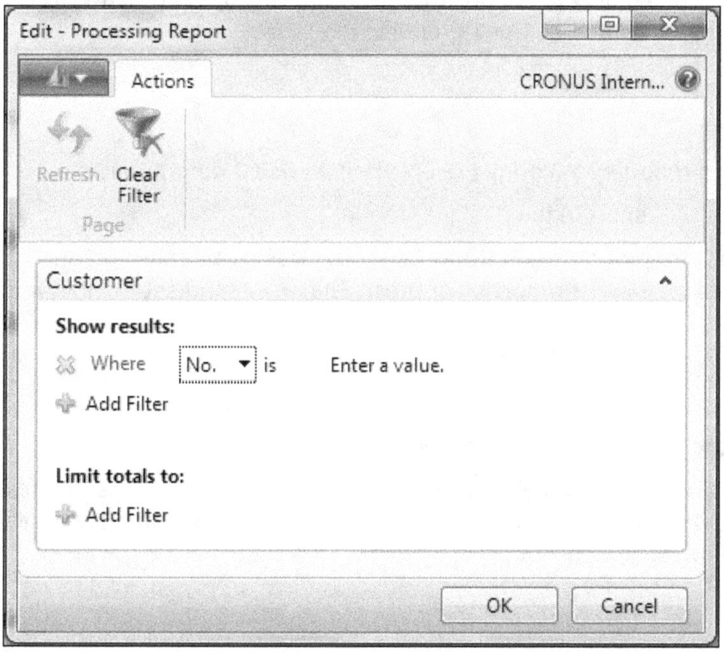

There's more...

When a normal report is running, the system displays a dialog box, which contains the count of processed records. This lets the user know that the system is still doing something and has not stopped. The processing-only reports don't tell the user what is going on. This means that it is your responsibility to keep the user informed. The best way to do this is by displaying a progress bar. You can assign the variables and open the dialog in the `OnPreDataItem` trigger. The `OnAfterGetRecord` trigger is used to update the progress bar while the `OnPostDataItem` trigger can be used to close the dialog.

See also

- *Creating an RDLC report*
- *Using multiple options to run a report*
- *Creating a matrix report*

Creating a link from report to page

RDLC reporting offers plenty of options to make reports more interactive. This recipe will demonstrate how to call a page from a report.

How to do it...

1. Create a report by following the *Creating an RDLC report* recipe.
2. Reopen the report in the designer mode.
3. Go to report properties. In **Report Dataset Designer**, select an empty line, and then navigate to **View** | **Properties** or press *Shift* + *F4*, and set the following property:

Property	Value
`EnableHyperlinks`	`Yes`

4. From the **View** menu, choose **Layout**.
5. In the **Visual Layout Designer**, right-click on the `No_Customer` table box field and select **Table Box Properties**. You should see a window similar to the following screenshot:

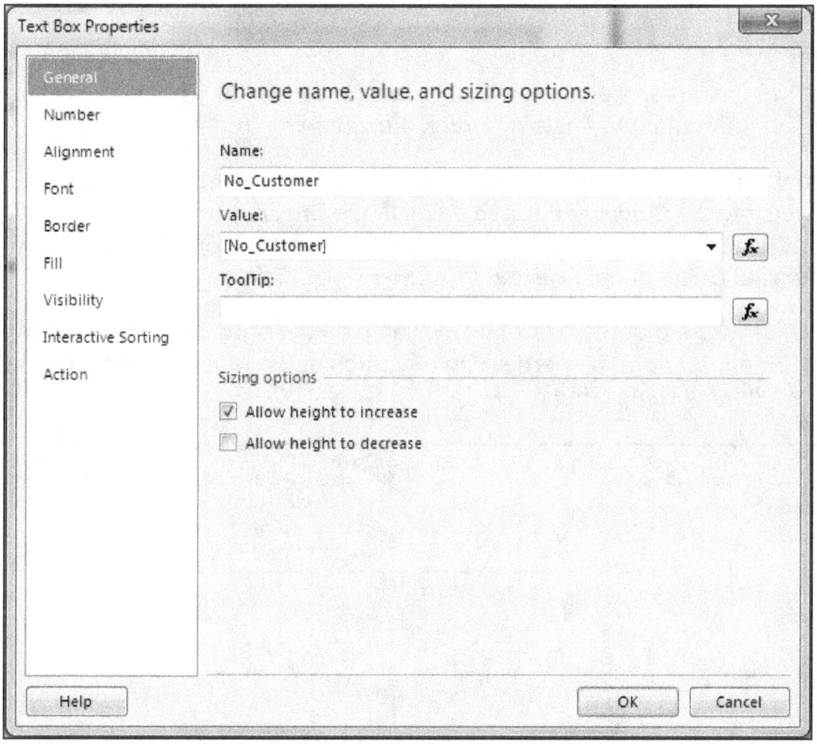

6. In the **Properties** window, choose the **Action** tab.
7. Select the **Go to URL** option.
8. Click on the **Fx** button to enter the following URL in the **Select URL** field and click on the **OK** button:

```
="dynamicsnav://///runpage?page=21&$filter=Customer.'No.'%20IS%20
'''%40" + Fields!No_Customer.Value + "*''''"
```

9. In the **Properties** window, choose the **Font** tab and set the following properties:

Property	**Value**
`Color`	`Blue`
`Effects`	`Underline`

10. Save and close the visual layout designer.
11. Save and close the report.

How it works...

By updating two properties we can link a page to a report. Firstly, update the report properties to let the report know that there is a hyperlink present in the report.

Secondly, configure the URL action for the `report` field. We selected the `Customer No.` field and linked it to the `Customer Card` page. In the URL, `dynamicsnav://///runpage?page=` is the keyword to run page and `21` is the `Customer Card` page ID. Finally, we applied a filter of our selected `Customer No.` field.

Now, to make us aware that there is a link available on the `Customer No.` field, we have the updated `Color` and `Effect` properties. On execution of the report you should see a screen similar to the following screenshot:

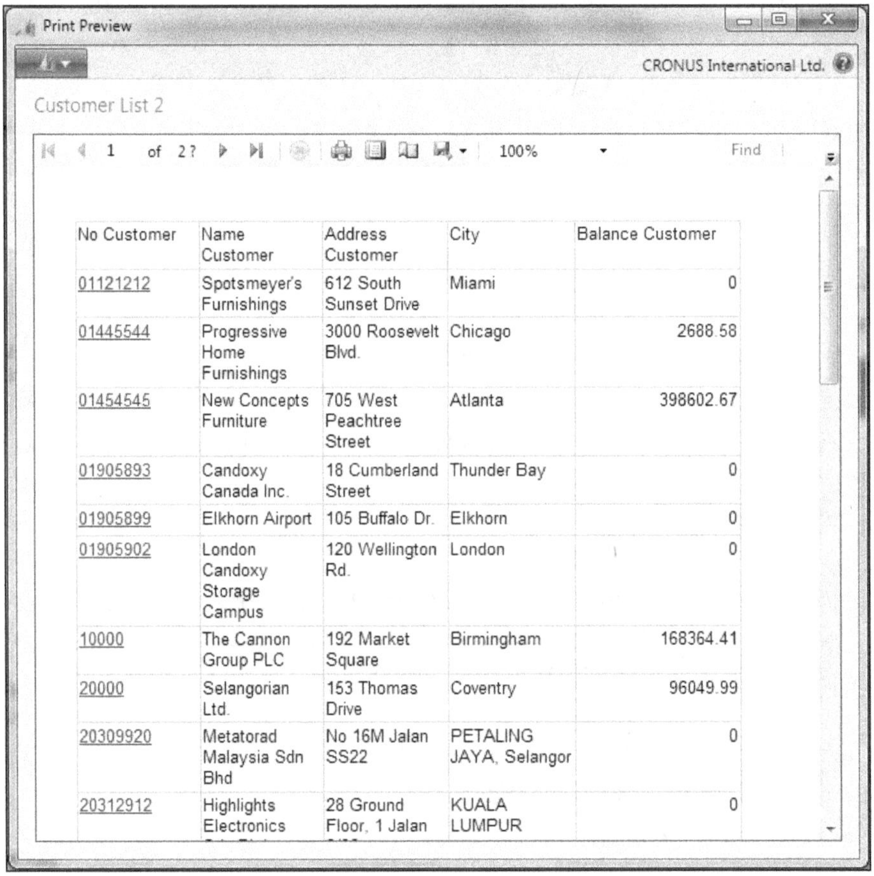

There's more...

We have seen how to link a report with a page using URL. Now the question is—how do we get the right URL? The following steps will help you to get the proper URL to open a page:

1. Apply the required filter on the page using the `RoleTailored client`.
2. Go to the application menu and navigate to **Page** | **Copy Link**.
3. To view the copied link, paste it on a Notepad.

See also

- *Creating an RDLC report*
- *Creating a link from report to report*
- *Creating a matrix report*

Creating a link from report to report

Linking one report to another report is very similar to the previous recipe *Creating a link from report to page*. Let's see how it works.

How to do it...

1. Create a report by following the *Creating an RDLC report* recipe and open the report in the designer mode.
2. Go to report properties. In **Report Dataset Designer**, select an empty line and then navigate to **View** | **Properties** or press *Shift* + *F4*, and set the following property:

Property	Value
`EnableHyperlinks`	`Yes`

3. On the **View** menu, choose **Layout**.
4. In the visual layout designer, right-click on the `No_Customer` table box and select **Table Box Properties**.
5. In the **Properties** window, choose the **Action** tab.
6. Select the **Go to URL** option.
7. Click on the **Fx** button to enter the following URL in the **Select URL** field:

```
="dynamicsnav:////runreport?report=104&filter=Customer.%22No.%22:"
+Fields!No_Customer.Value
```

8. In the **Properties** window, choose the **Font** tab and set the following properties:

Property	Value
Color	Blue
Effects	Underline

9. Save and close the visual layout designer.
10. Save and close the report.

How it works...

The principle of linking pages is applied here; the only difference is that we have changed the keyword:

```
="dynamicsnav://///runpage?page=21&$filter=Customer.'No.'%20IS%20
'''%40" + Fields!No_Customer.Value + "*''''"
```

Reports can be linked to pie charts as well by configuring the series properties.

See also

- *Creating an RDLC report*
- *Creating a link from report to page*
- *Creating a matrix report*

Adding totals on decimal field

As the reporting solution is changed, most of the old functions are either removed or replaced. The next small recipe will show you a very basic but widely used function to get a total.

How to do it...

1. First, create a report by following the *Creating an RDLC report* recipe.
2. Open the report in the designer mode and navigate to **View** | **Layout** (*Alt* + *V*, *Y*) to alter the report visual layout.
3. Select the last row of the table control, right-click and navigate to **Insert Row** | **Outside Group - Below**.
4. In the newly added row, right-click on the cell of column `Balance_Customer` and select **Expression**.

5. Set the following value for the expression as you reach a form similar to the following screenshot:

   ```
   =SUM(Fields!Balance_Customer.Value)
   ```

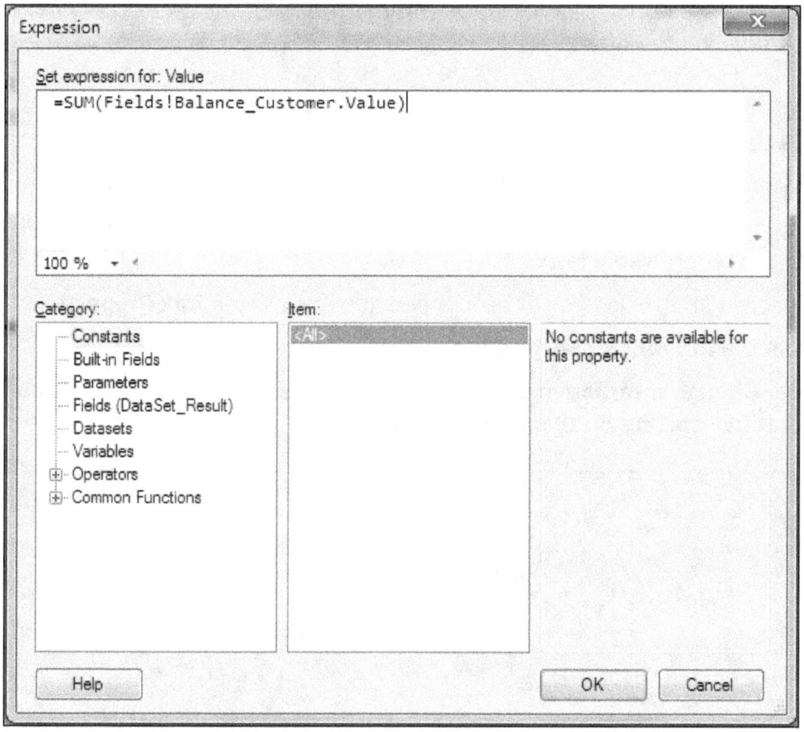

6. Save and close the report.

How it works...

In NAV classic reporting, we used to set the data item property `TotalFields` or function `CREATETOTALS`. As both these options are not available for the NAV 2013 report, we need to base our report totals on Visual Studio functions.

`Expression` and `Scope` are the two parameters for the Visual Studio report designer `SUM` function. `Expression` is required field on which aggregation need to be done whereas a `video scope` is the name of a grouping, dataset, or data region.

See also

- *Creating an RDLC report*
- *Creating a matrix report*

Adding interactive sorting on reports

After a classic report is generated, no change can be made on the sorting of data, whereas an RDLC report offers the option of interactive sorting. The following recipe will guide you to add interactive sorting on a report.

How to do it...

1. First, create a report by following the *Creating an RDLC report* recipe.
2. Open the report in the designer mode and navigate to **View** | **Layout** (*Alt* + *V*, *Y*) to alter the report visual layout.
3. Right-click on the `No. Customer` cell and select **Table Box Properties**.
4. Select the **Interactive Sorting** tab.
5. Under **Change interactive sort options for the text box**, select the **Enable interactive sorting on this text box** checkbox:

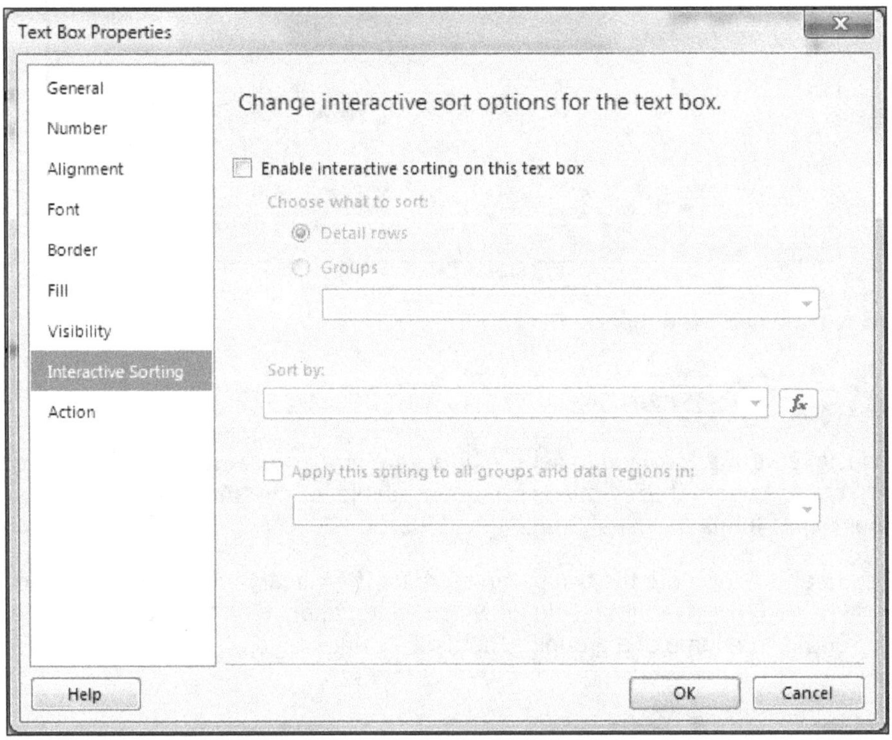

6. In the **Sort by** drop-down list, select the `No_Customer` field. Click on **OK** to close the properties window:

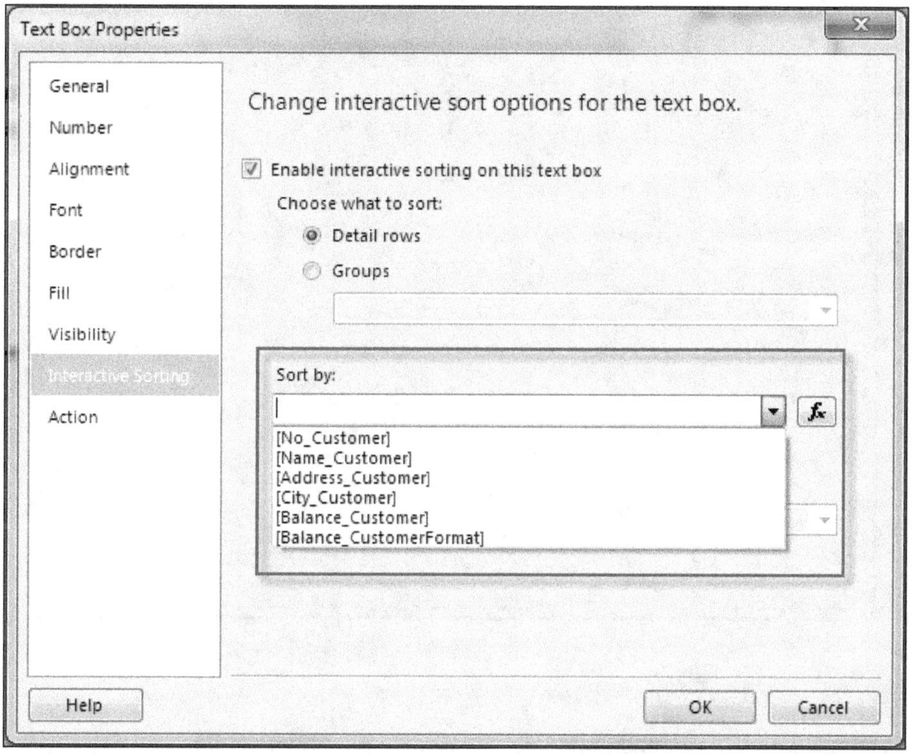

7. Right-click on the **Name** cell and select **Table Box Properties**.
8. Select the **Interactive Sorting** tab.
9. Under **Change interactive sort options for the text box**, select the **Enable interactive sorting on this text box** checkbox.
10. In the **Sort by** drop-down list, select the `Name_Customer` field. Click on **OK** to close the properties window.
11. Save and close the report.

12. On execution of the report, you should see a window similar to the following screenshot:

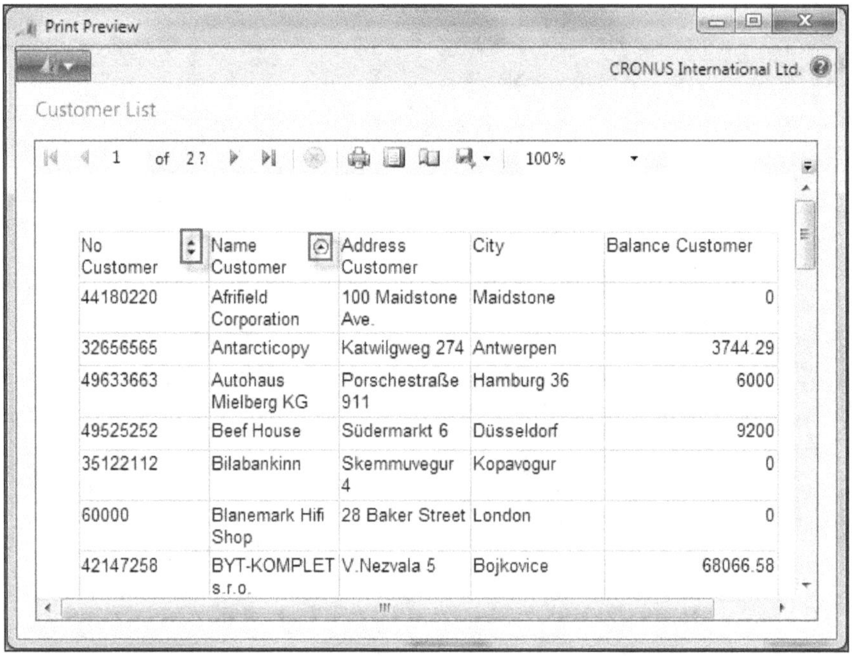

How it works...

Interactive sorting will enable users to interactively change the sort order for the data columns. To change the sort order between ascending and descending order, select the sort control button in the column header.

See also

- *Adding custom filters to the Request Page*
- *Setting filters when report is loaded*

Creating a matrix report

Matrix report!!! This word suggests complexity. In reality, it's not that tough. In this recipe, I tried to keep it as simple as possible.

How to do it...

1. Create a new report from **Object Designer**.
2. Create global text constant with the following details:

Name	ConstValue
ReportNameLbl	Item by Location

3. Add the following lines in the **Report Designer**:

Data type	Data source	Name
DataItem	Location	<Location>
Column	Code	Location_Code
Column	Name	Location_Name
Column	ReportNameLbl	ReportName
DataItem	Item	<Item>
Column	"No."	Item_No
Column	Description	Item_Description
Column	Inventory	Item_Inventory

4. After making the previous changes, **Report Dataset Designer** should look like the following screenshot:

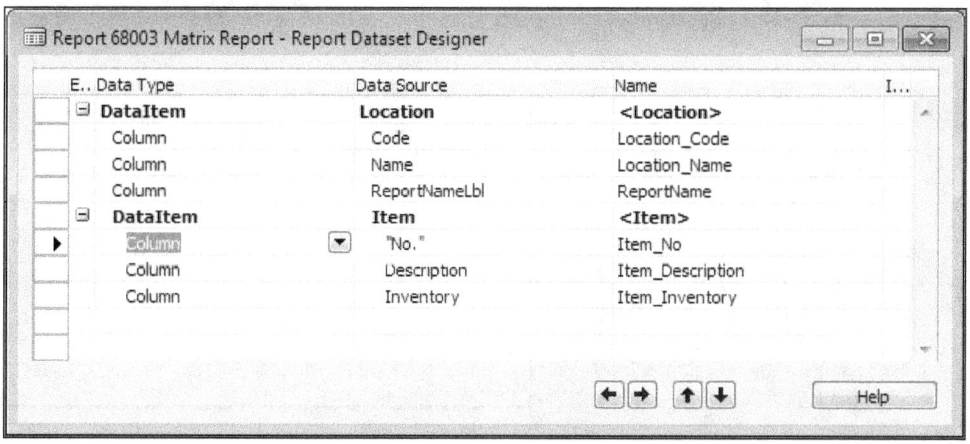

5. Set the following property for the `Location` data item:

Property	Value
`DataItemTableView`	`SORTING(Code)` `ORDER(Ascending)`

6. Set the following property for the `Item` data item:

Property	Value

`DataItemTableView`	`SORTING(No.)`
	`ORDER(Ascending)`
	`WHERE(Inventory=FILTER(<>0))`

`DataItemLink`	`Location Filter=FIELD(Code)`

7. To design the visual layout, go to **View** | **Layout** (*Alt* + *V*, *Y*).
8. From the **Toolbox** explorer, select **Matrix** and add it to design.
9. Right-click on the first cell of the matrix control and go to **Insert Column** | **Inside Group Left**.
10. To merge two cells of the first row, select both the cells, right-click, and select **Merge Cells**.
11. From the **Report Data** explorer, drag `ReportName` to the top-left cell in the matrix control:

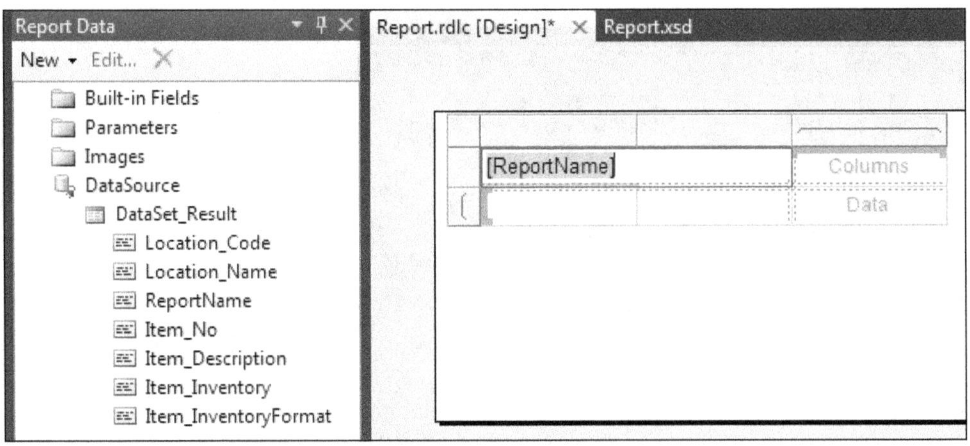

12. In the next row, drag `Item_No` and `Item_Description` to the first two columns:

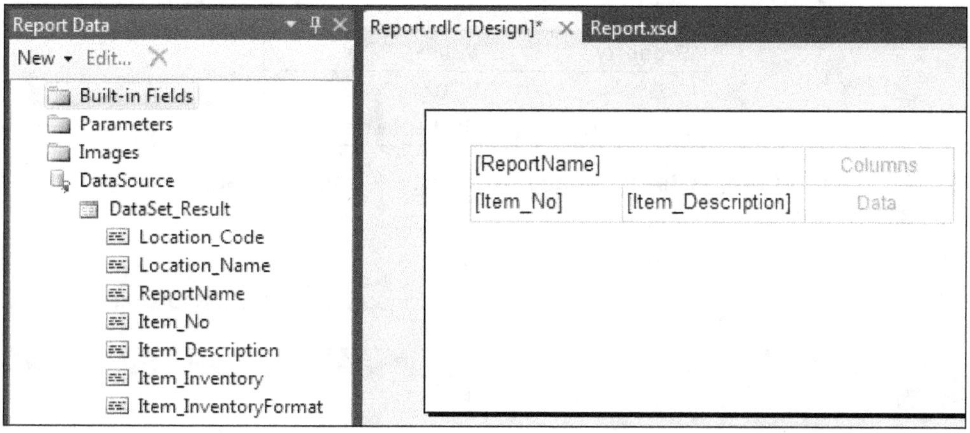

13. In the last column of the first row, drag the `Location_Name` field.
14. In the data cell, add the `Item_Inventory` field.
15. The **Visual Designer** should look like the following screenshot:

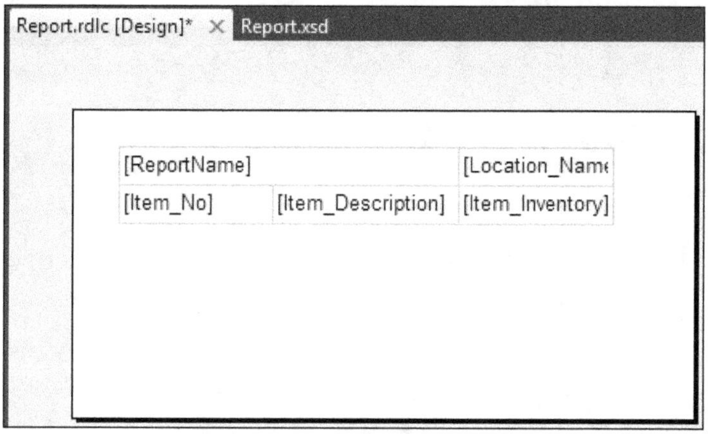

16. Select the `Item_Inventory` data cell, **Table Box Properties**, and go to the **Action** tab.
17. Select the **Go to URL** option and add the following value as the URL expression:

```
="DynamicsNAV:////runreport?Report=705&Filter=Item.%22Location
Filter%22:"+Fields!Location_Code.Value+"&Filter=Item.%22No.%22:
"+Fields!Item_No.Value
```

18. In the data cell `Table Box Properties`, go to the **Font** tab and set the following properties:

Property	Value
`Color`	`Blue`
`Effects`	`Underline`

19. Go to **Report Properties** from the NAV report designer and set the `EnableHyperlinks` property to `Yes`.
20. Save and close the report.
21. On execution of the report, you should see a window similar to the following screenshot:

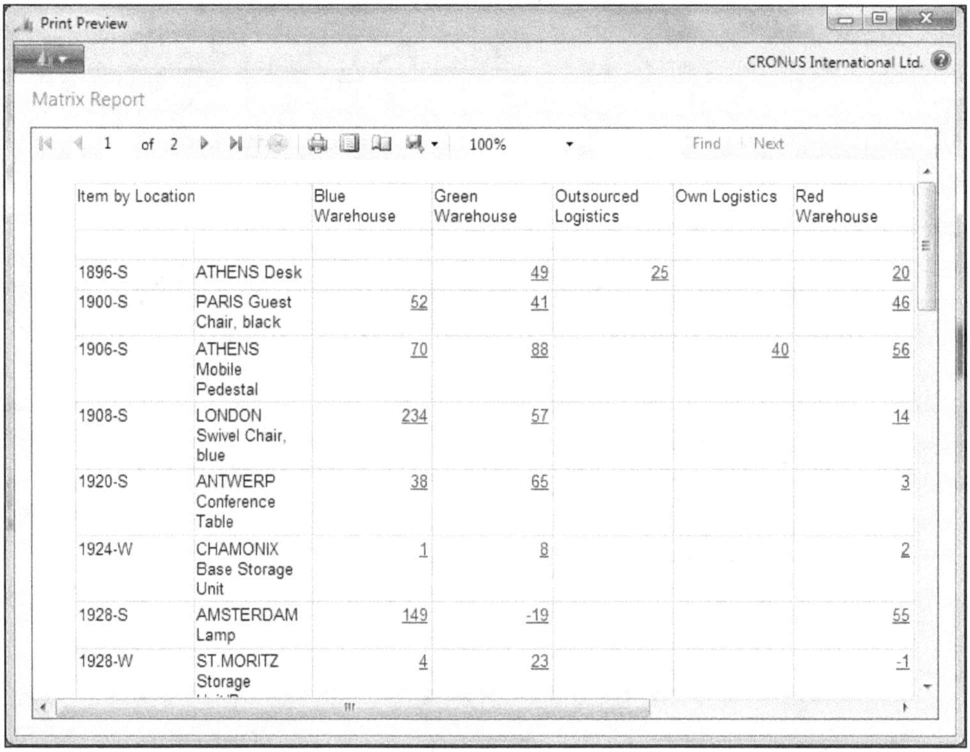

How it works...

Our matrix report is based on the `Item` and `Location` table. We are expecting an inventory count per item by location. In the `Location` data item, we have added one column which is taking the value from text constants. This field will be used as the matrix name. To pass any information to the Visual Studio designer, we need to add that information as a column.

After creating the required data items and columns, we need to set up a relation between the two data items. Otherwise, we will receive the same value per item for all locations. To avoid this, we have applied the location filter by using the `DataItemLink` property. To avoid data with zero inventory value, we have added a filter on the inventory field of the `Item` table.

The matrix control simplifies our process of designing by allowing the dragging-and-dropping of the required fields inside control, and we are now ready to run the report. Here, we have added a hyperlink on our values to link the matrix report with the report `705 (Inventory Availability)` to offer more visibility on an inventory value.

There's more...

We can export an RDLC report in different ways.

Exporting an RDLC report from viewer

After the report is generated, it can be exported to Excel, Word, and PDF. The following screenshot will show you the export options:

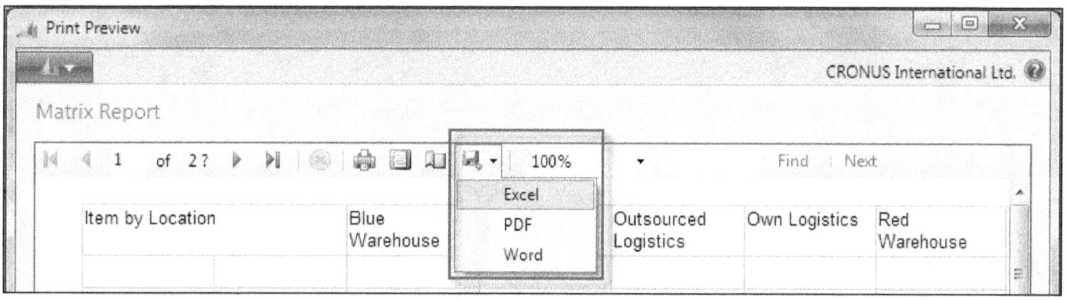

Exporting an RDLC report from C/AL code

Using the following C/AL code, a report can be exported to Excel, Word, PDF, XML, and HTML:

1. Excel:
   ```
   REPORT.SAVEASEXCEL(Number, FileName[, Record])
   ```
2. Word:
   ```
   REPORT.SAVEASWORD(Number, FileName[, Record])
   ```
3. PDF:
   ```
   REPORT.SAVEASPDF(Number, FileName[, Record])
   ```
4. XML:
   ```
   REPORT.SAVEASXML(Number, FileName [, SystemPrinter] [, Record])
   ```

5. HTML:

```
REPORT.SAVEASHTML(Number, FileName [, SystemPrinter] [, Record])
```

6. NAV 2013 executes C/AL code on the NAV server, so the NAV server will search for the file path on the server machine and not on the client machine. To avoid confusion about the file location, create a folder on the server machine and share that folder with all the users and use it as the `EXPORT` and `IMPORT` location for NAV.

See also

- *Using multiple options to run a report*
- *Adding custom filters to the Request Page*
- *Creating a link from report to page*
- *Creating a link from report to report*
- *Adding totals on decimal fields*
- *Adding interactive sorting on reports*

6
Diagnosing Code Problems

In this chapter, we will cover:

- Using the debugger
- Setting breakpoints
- Handling runtime errors
- Using About This Page and About This Report
- Finding errors while using NAS

Introduction

No one writes perfect code on their first attempt. When running hundreds or even thousands of lines of code at a time, it can be extremely difficult to determine where exactly an error occurred and what caused it. That's why we have tools such as the debugger in Microsoft Dynamics NAV.

For the most part of the recipes in this chapter, we will not deal with writing your own code or writing better code. Instead, we will focus more on how you can determine what is happening with the code you have already written.

Using the debugger

This recipe will show you how to use the debugger to examine the code that is currently executing. We will demonstrate how to go through the code line-by-line and watch how values and objects change.

How to do it...

1. First create a new codeunit from **Object Designer**.
2. Then add the following global variable:

Name	Type	Subtype
Customer	Record	Customer

3. We need to add the following global text constant as well:

Name	ConstValue
Text001	Rakesh Raul

4. Add a global function called `ChangeCustomerName`.
5. The previous function should take the following parameter:

Name	Type	Length
NewName	Text	50

6. Add the following code to the function:

```
Customer.Name := NewName;
```

7. Add the following code to the `OnRun` trigger:

```
Customer.FINDFIRST;
ChangeCustomerName(Text001);
Customer.VALIDATE("Post Code");
```

8. Save and close the codeunit.
9. Now from the **Tools** menu in the NAV client, go to **Debugger** | **Debug Session** (*Shift* + *Ctrl* + *F11*).
10. You should see the currently running session list:

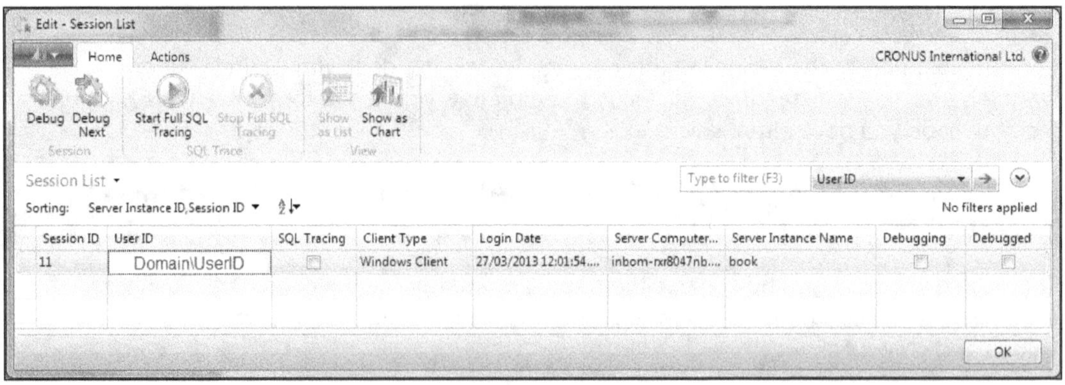

11. To debug the session, select the session that has the login permissions used to run the client.
12. From the ribbon, select the **Debug** action.
13. You should see a window similar to the following screenshot:

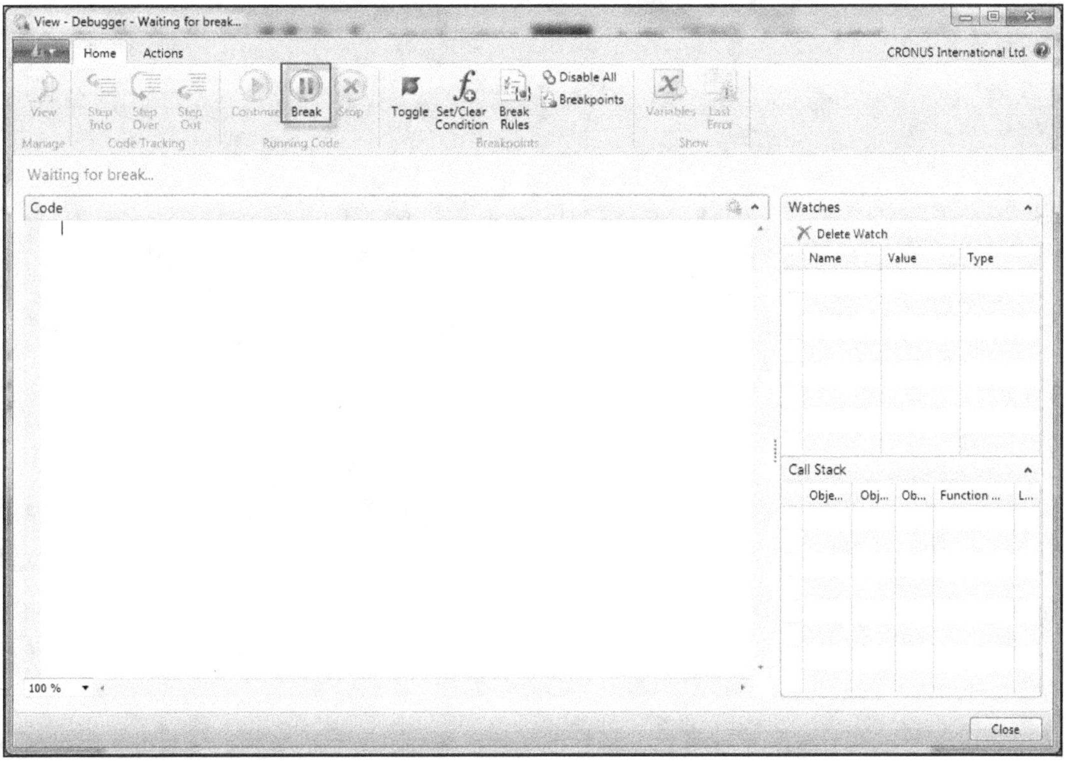

14. From the ribbon, select the **Break** action.
15. Run the codeunit.

How it works...

When you run the codeunit, the Microsoft Dynamics NAV debugger window will appear, just like the one shown in the following screenshot:

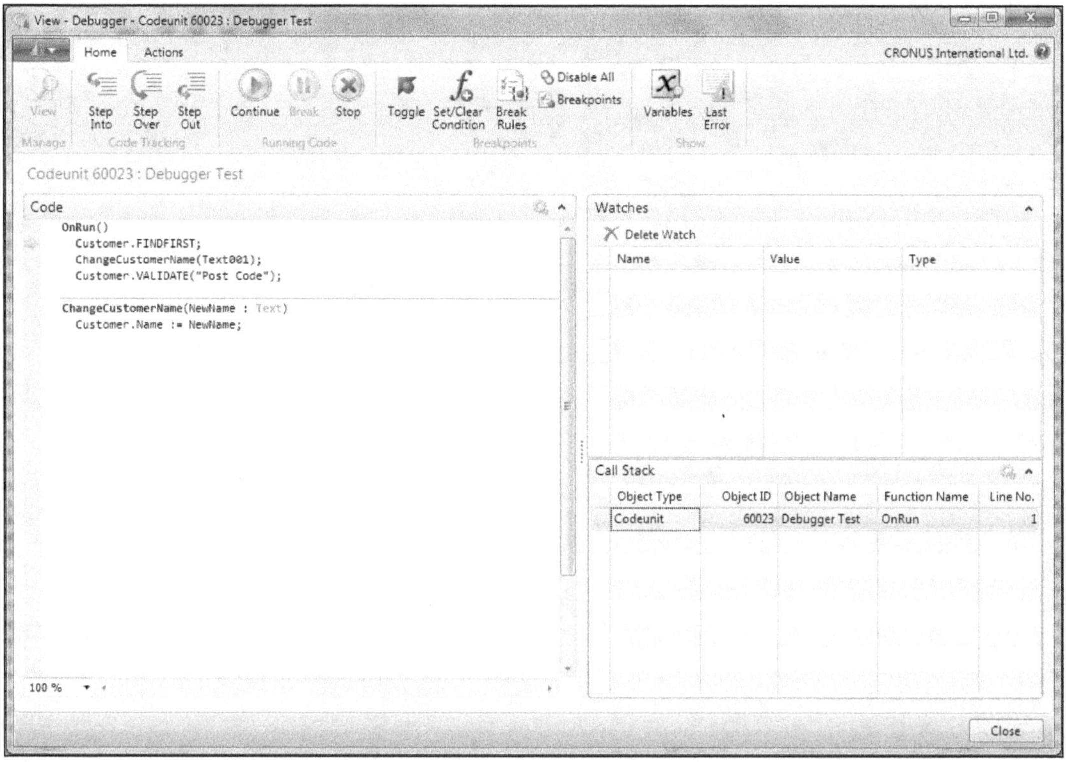

Before we get into the details of this window, we need to understand what caused it to appear. Setting the debugger for a particular session means that the debugger window will open every time the system encounters an error; in this case, though, we know our code doesn't produce any errors. We want to look at it anyway, so we turn on the **Break** option as well.

There are five components to the debugger window. The first is the **Actions** option on the ribbon at the very top. We can hover over each button to get a tool tip of what it does.

The second component sits right below and contains the actual code from the current object. Here you can see a small yellow arrow pointing to the first line of our codeunit in the `OnRun` trigger. This is the line that is about to execute. Note that it has *not* yet executed. We'll explore each of the other three components as we move through our code.

Use the *F11* key or click on the **Step Into** action on the ribbon. The window will now look like the one shown in the following screenshot:

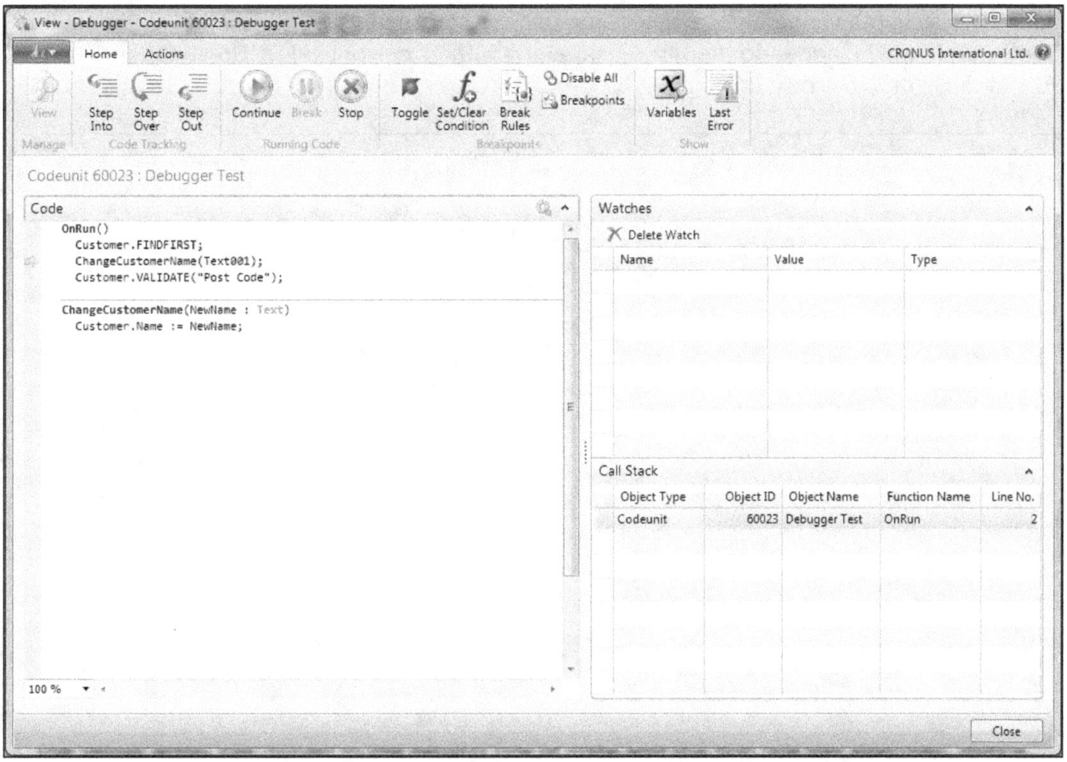

The yellow arrow has moved to the second line of the code and the first line has executed. Click on the **Variables** action on the ribbon. It lists all the variables and their values in the current object. At first, our `Customer` variable was uninitialized because we had not executed the `Customer.FINDFIRST` line. That line retrieved a record from the database causing the value of the variable to change.

The following is the next line of code that will be executed:

```
ChangeCustomerName(Text001);
```

What is this `Text001` variable? If you're unsure of the value of a text constant, or you don't want to open a new page of variables and scroll through a possibly long list of variables to view a variable's value repeatedly, you can add a shortcut to the `Watch` list (the **Watches** FactBox). Open the variable page, select the text constant, and select the **Add Watch** action. The variable will be added to the `Watch` list along with its current value. Go ahead and hit *F11* to move onto the next line.

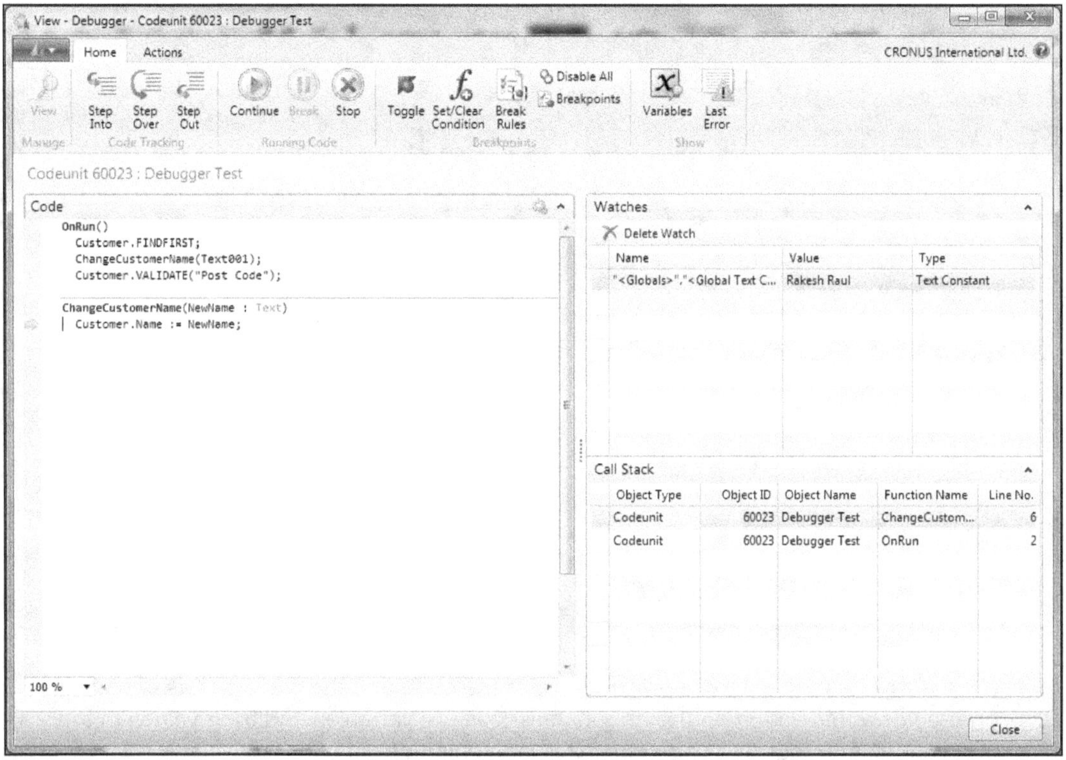

The yellow arrow jumps to the function that we just called. That brings us to our last window, the **Call Stack** window (the second FactBox). It is important to know how we got to the code that we are currently viewing. By looking at the **Call Stack** window, we can see that we were in the `OnRun` trigger of the codeunit and then jumped to the `ChangeCustomerName` function. We can click on each level of the stack to see the code for that object:

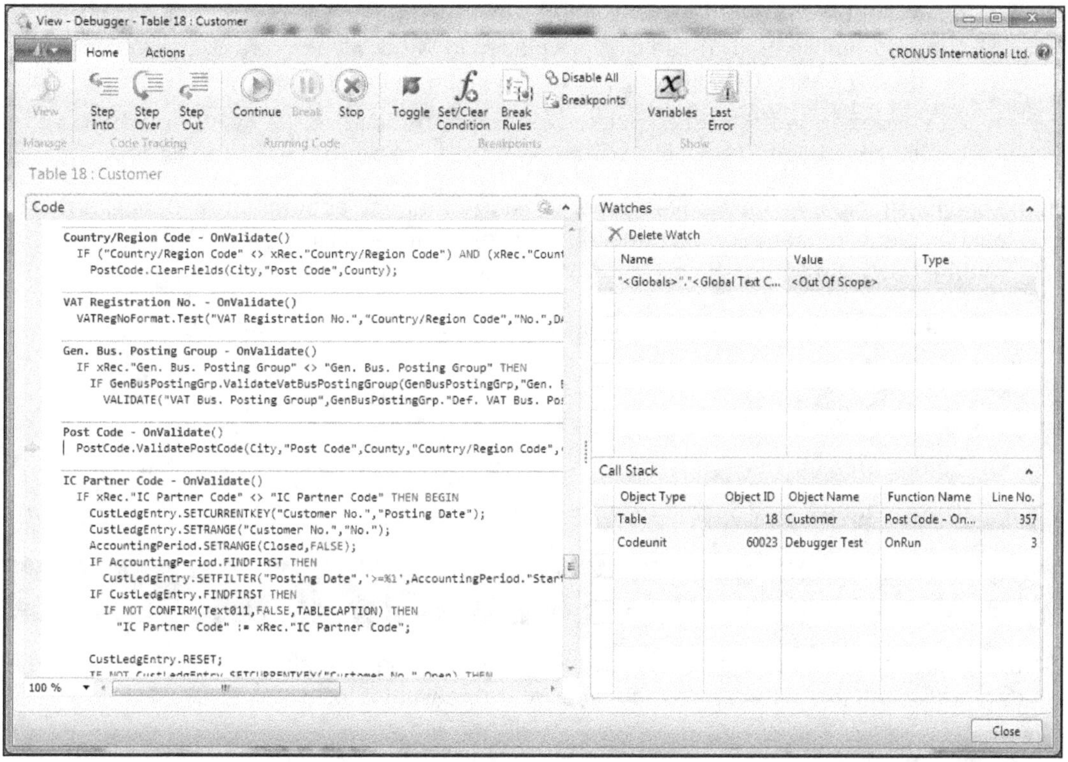

You may not always want to go through your code line-by-line, though. Try hitting the *F5* key or the **Go** command from the **Debug** menu. This will cause you to jump to the next function that is called instead of the next line. You will find yourself in a completely new object, the `Customer` table. Notice how the **Context** menu completely changes because the old variables are no longer in scope. They do not belong to the current object being examined.

There's more...

There are few facts we should be aware of before debugging:

- Only one debugging session can be activated on a single NAV instance; this means that if we need multiple debugging sessions at the same time, we need to have those many NAV Server instances.
- There is a setting available on the NAV Server instance to activate or deactivate debugging, and that is **Debugging Allowed**.

- As we enable the debugger for the first time, the system will create C# files for the complete application. These files are placed in Windows' `ProgramData` folder. For Windows 7 users, the following path will help them to find these files:

  `C:\ProgramData\Microsoft\Microsoft Dynamics NAV\70\Server\MicrosoftDynamicsNavServer$YourNAVServerInstance\source\Codeunit`

In the previous recipe, we only looked at very basic information about the NAV debugger; but this tool has plenty of features and benefits. I suggest that you visit the following URL to learn more on the debugging process and the NAV debugger:

`http://msdn.microsoft.com/en-us/library/dd338786(v=nav.70).aspx`

See also

- *Setting breakpoints*
- The *Creating a NAV Server instance* recipe in *Chapter 12, NAV Server Administration*

Setting breakpoints

Stepping through the code line-by-line or function-by-function can take forever. Luckily, there is an easy way to tell the debugger to stop right where we want it to.

How to do it...

1. Create and save the same codeunit discussed in the *Using the debugger* recipe in this chapter.
2. Design the codeunit.
3. Go to the following line of code in the `OnRun` trigger:

   ```
   ChangeCustomerName(Text001);
   ```

4. Press *F9* twice.
5. Then go to the following line of code in the `OnRun` trigger:

   ```
   VALIDATE("Post Code");
   ```

6. Press *F9* once.

7. Your window should look like the following screenshot:

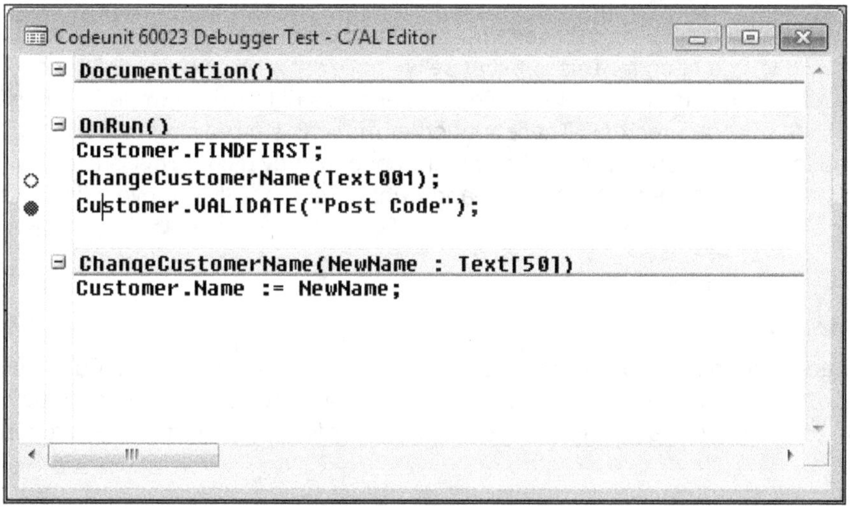

8. Save and close the codeunit.
9. From the **Tools** menu of the **Microsoft Dynamics NAV Development Environment** page, navigate to **Debugger** | **Debug Session** (*Shift* + *Ctrl* + *F11*).
10. From the debugger window, select the user session and click on **Debug** (*Ctrl* + *Shift* + *S*) to activate the debugger.
11. On execution of the codeunit, the system will take you to the debugging window; the debugging screen should be identical to the following screenshot:

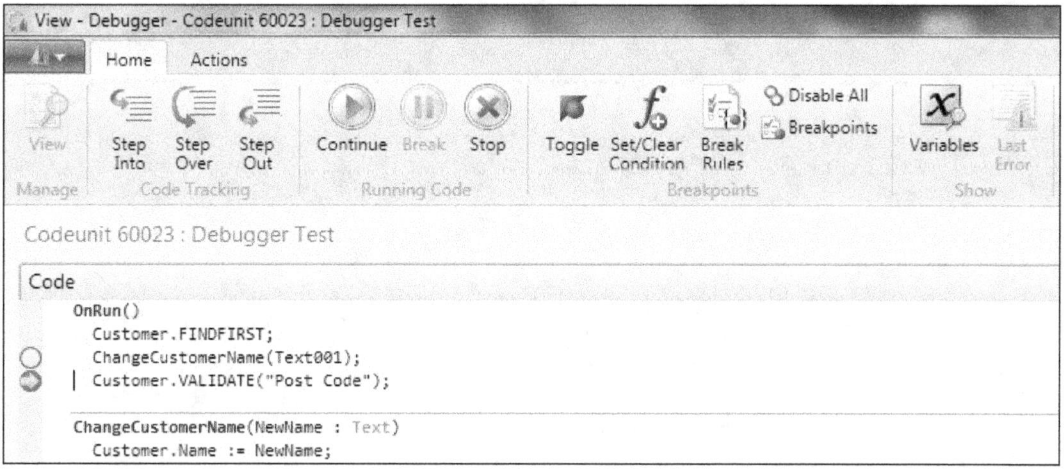

How it works...

While running the debugger on this codeunit, it should stop on the `Customer.VALIDATE ("Post Code")` line of code. This is because we have set a breakpoint here, which was the filled red circle at the left of that line. The debugger stops right where we tell it to, that is, right before that line of code executes. There is another mark; it is a red circle that is not filled. This is used to mark old breakpoints that we are not currently using. This is useful when we are trying to debug large amounts of code and want to temporarily remove a breakpoint or remember where we had one.

There's more...

The debugger is not perfect by any means. Some might even say it has a mind of its own sometimes. It doesn't always stop exactly where you want it to. It is a common practice to set a breakpoint on a few successive lines of code in order to ensure that you stop in the general area.

Breakpoint options in the debugger

The NAV 2013 debugger is pretty advanced as compared to the old versions. It provides some nice options related to breakpoints.

By selecting the **Toggle** action, we can add or remove breakpoints while debugging:

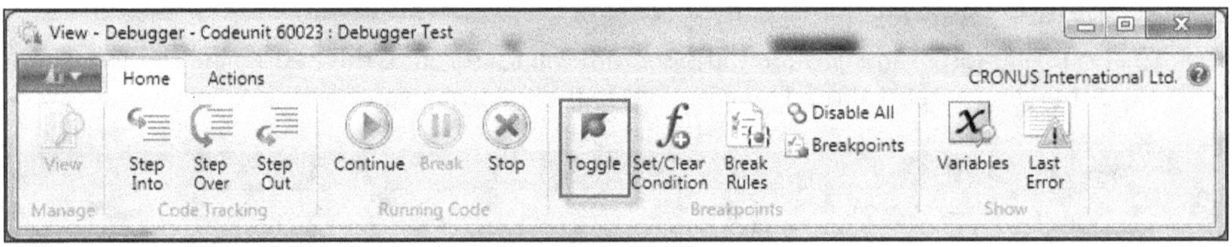

The **Breakpoints** action will provide the list of all breakpoints and options to enable or disable them:

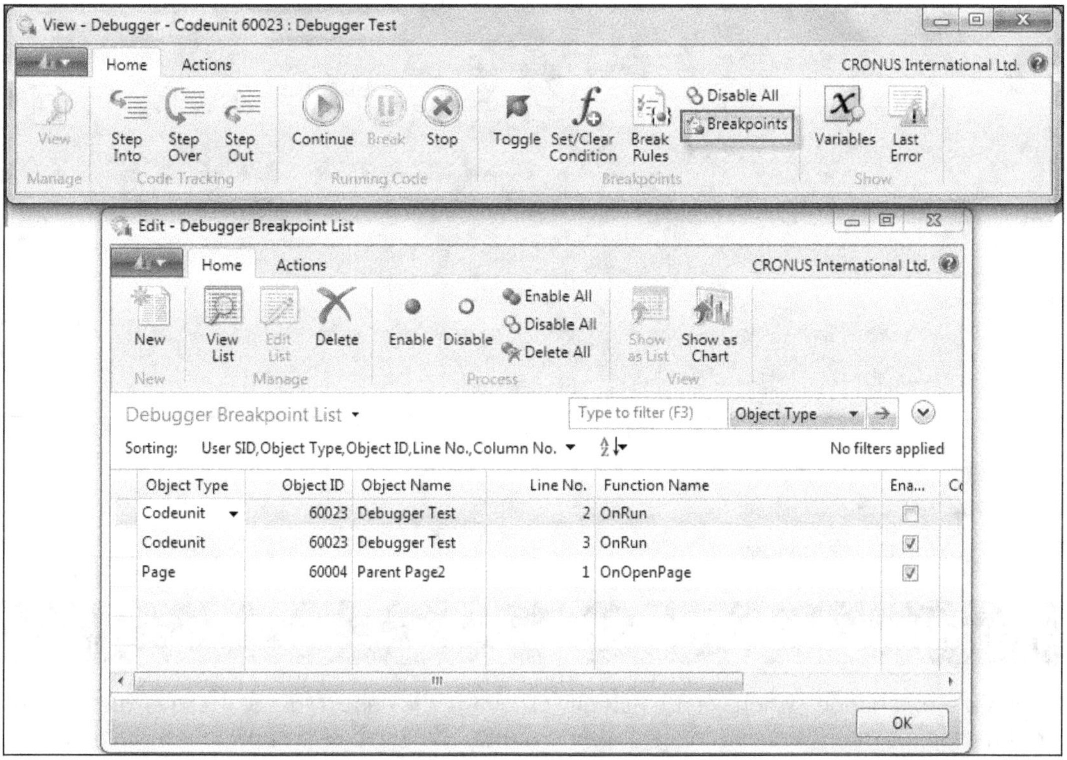

The following three options are provided under the **Break Rules** action:

- **Break on Error**: Debuggers break the execution when an error occurs.
- **Break on Record Changes**: If a record is going to be changed by using `INSERT`, `MODIFY`, `MODIFYALL`, `DELETE`, and `DELETEALL`, this option will break the execution before the change happens.
- **Skip Codeunit 1**: The codeunit `1` is the base set of functions for NAV, which is used in almost all actions/executions. This option will skip the codeunit `1` from the debugger.

The following screenshot shows the options in the **Break Rules** action:

See also

- *Using the debugger*

Handling runtime errors

Runtime errors happen when we are actually executing the code. Most of these errors present error messages that users cannot easily understand. This recipe will show how to handle these errors as well as some of the most common errors.

How to do it...

1. Let's create a new codeunit from **Object Designer**.
2. Then add the following global variables:

Name	DataType	SubType
`Customer`	`Record`	`Customer`
`Selection`	`Integer`	

3. Write the following code in the `OnRun` trigger of the codeunit:

```
Selection := STRMENU('Show Error,Handle Error', 1);
IF Selection = 1 THEN
  Customer.GET
ELSE
  IF NOT Customer.GET THEN
    ERROR('Unable to find a customer with a blank number.'+
          '\Are you sure you have selected a customer?');
```

4. Save and close the codeunit.
5. On execution of the codeunit, we will see a window with two options, as shown in the following screenshot:

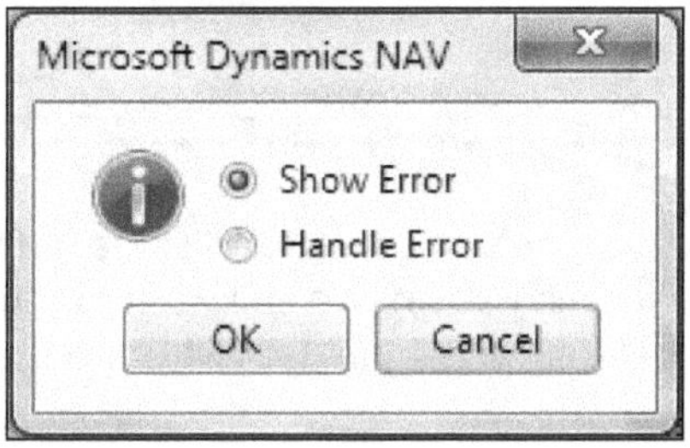

How it works...

This codeunit allows you to select between having NAV handle an error for you or handling it with custom code. If you choose to let NAV handle the error for you, you will be presented with the following error message:

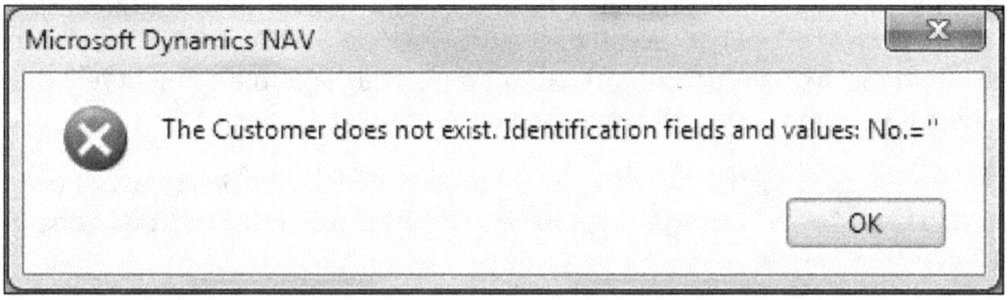

This message can be confusing for new users. Its interpretation can be different depending on the user.

For those who have been using NAV for a while, this message is obvious. Those users know that two single quotes represent something blank, and that this message is saying that a customer's record with a blank number does not exist.

Now look at the message that is displayed when we handle the error:

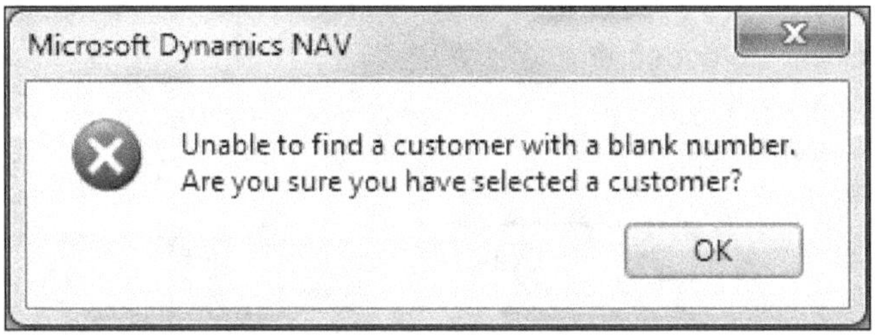

The `GET` function, and many others, returns a Boolean value. If this value is not used by the developer and it is `false`, an error is thrown. We still want to throw an error, but we want one that makes sense to everyone. Here, we tell the user what went wrong and a possible solution.

There's more...

With an older version of NAV, we used to have a very important and useful tool, that is, **code coverage**; unfortunately, from NAV 2013, Microsoft has removed this tool. The code coverage tool logs every line of code that is executed during a process; in addition to this, it also provides a percentage of code (coverage ration) that was executed in the object.

NAV blogs are a great help for developers, thanks to all the contributors who share their research. The following URL will take you to the MSDN blog on NAV 2013 code coverage; it includes the solutions' explanation (in the German language) and an object text file. Online translation tools can help you to translate the German text to English.

`http://blogs.msdn.com/b/german_nav_developer/archive/2012/08/26/pimp-your-nav-2013-code-coverage-in-30-minuten-nachr-252-sten.aspx`

See also

- *Using the debugger*
- *Using About This Page and About This Report*

Using About This Page and About This Report

When a user reports that there is a bug, our first question is, in which object? We often find errors on pages or reports, as these are the two main GUI objects used to present the data. This recipe will help you to get more information about the page and report objects.

How to do it...

This recipe has two parts that will provide steps to use the about this feature on the object type's page and report.

About This Page

The following are the steps to use **About This Page**:

1. Start the `RoleTailored client`.
2. Go to the **Department** menu.
3. Navigate to **Sales & Marketing** | **Order Processing** | **Sales Order**.
4. Select the first sales order and click on the **View** action.
5. On the **Sales Order** page, go to the **Application** menu and navigate to **Help** | **About This Page**.
6. You should see a window similar to the following screenshot:

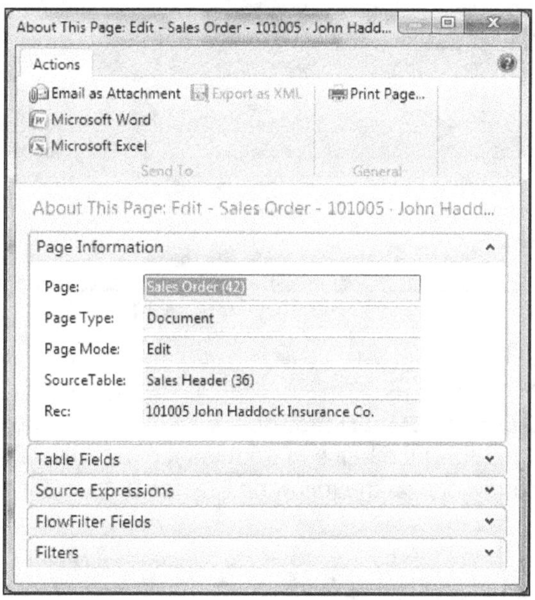

About This Report

The following are the steps to use **About This Report**:

1. Start the `RoleTailored client`.
2. Go to the **Department** menu.
3. Select **Sales & Marketing** and choose the **Report and Analysis** category.
4. Select the **Customer List** report and click on **Preview**.
5. In the **Customer List** report, go to the **Application** menu and navigate to **Help** | **About This Report**.

> The first time you run this option, the program will open **About This Report** for the first time and ask the user to run the report again and select **About This Report** to see the details!

6. The system will open a window displaying the row data on which the report is based:

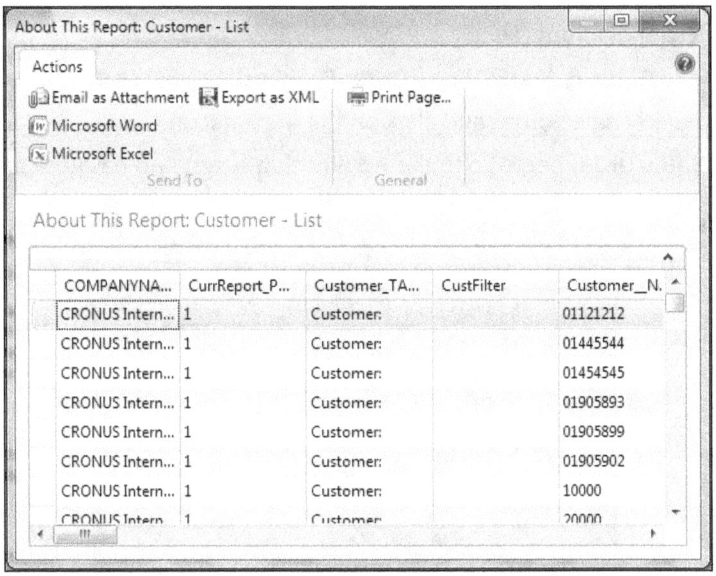

How it works...

About This Page and **About This Report** provide the inside view of objects from the `RoleTailored client`, which helps in troubleshooting and debugging issues. The **About This Page** window shows the following FastTabs:

- **Page Information**
- **Table Fields** (sorted first by key fields, then alphabetically)

- **Source Expressions**
- **FlowFilter Fields**
- **Filters**

All the information displayed in the about this section can be exported in Word and Excel, and can be set as an e-mail attachment or can be printed.

There's more...

If you try to run **About This Page** for a subform page, by selecting the **Application** menu and then **About This Page**, you will see all the information about the main page.

How to get the subform information

The trick is to use the shortcut keys. *Ctrl* + *Alt* + *F1* are the shortcut keys for the about this feature. Select a record for the subform page and press *Ctrl* + *Alt* + *F1*, and you will see the desired information, as shown in the following screenshot:

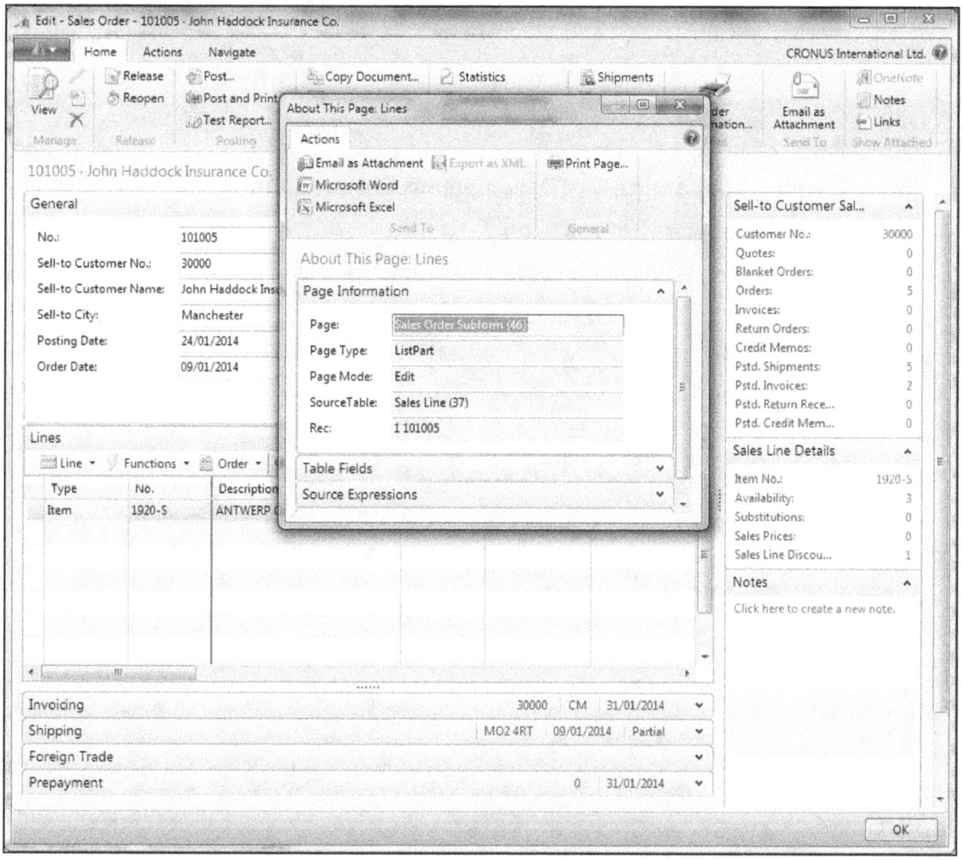

> On a few computers, we need to add a Windows key in the about this shortcut (*Ctrl* + *Alt* + the Windows key + *F1*).

See also

- *Using the debugger*

Finding errors while using NAS

Navision Application Server (**NAS**) is just a NAV client without GUI. This can present challenges in figuring out what has gone wrong while running your code using NAS. This recipe will show how to debug NAS.

Getting ready

You must already have the NAV Application Server service installed on the machine on which you are working.

How to do it...

1. Start **Microsoft Dynamics NAV Development Environment**.
2. Go to **File** | **Database** | **Information**.
3. The following screenshot will provide an idea about the expected window:

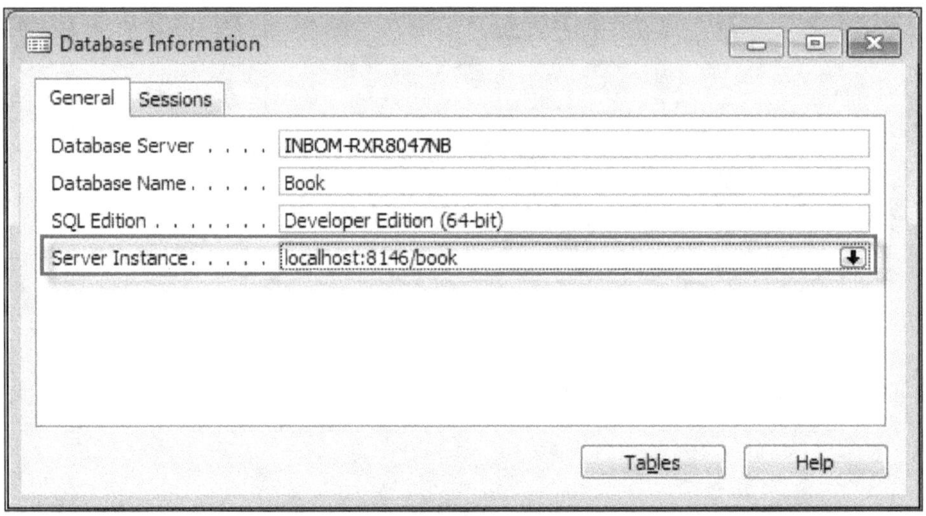

4. In the **Server Instance** drill-down list, select the service instance that is running NAS.
5. From the **Tools** menu in the NAV client, navigate to **Debugger** | **Debug Session** (*Shift* + *Ctrl* + *F11*).
6. You should see the currently running session list.
7. Select the NAS session.
8. From the ribbon select the **Debug** action.
9. From the ribbon select the **Break** action.

How it works...

In NAV 2013, debugging NAS is pretty much the same as debugging an RTC client; the only difference is in selecting a right session. If you activate the debugger from an RTC client service, you won't even see the NAS session.

To connect our development environment with the NAV Server, we need to select the NAS service instance. A service instance field is non-editable, but you can select the required service from the drill-down list.

Now, after this, if we activate the debugger we get a session list that contains our NAS session entry. After this point, everything is the same regarding debugging.

> The NAV Server instance has a dedicated tab to configure NAS; it includes setting **Enable Debugging**, which provides a lead time of 60 seconds before executing the first C/AL statement to allow time for activating the debugger.

There's more...

From the `RoleTailored client`, go to **Departments** | **Administration** | **IT Administration** | **General** | **Sessions** to get the list of active sessions.

The following screenshot of the session table showing **Client Type** is considered in the session list for debugging:

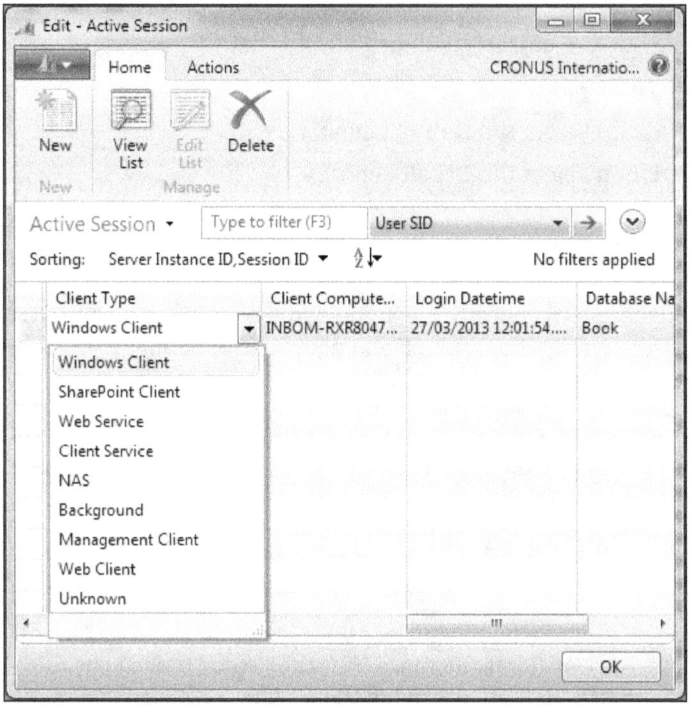

The **Session List** page not only shows all clients but also allows us to debug the sessions of other users. Even if you want to debug the immediate next session-accessing breakpoint code, it is possible only by selecting the **Debug Next** action from the **Session List** page:

See also

- *Using the debugger*
- *Using About This Page and About This Report*
- The *Configuring NAS to run Job Queue* recipe in *Chapter 12, NAV Server Administration*

7

Roles and Security

In this chapter, we will cover:

- Assigning a role to a user
- Creating a new role
- Using the FILTERGROUP function
- Using security filters
- Applying security filter modes
- Field-level security
- Assigning permission to use the About This Page function
- Killing a user session

Introduction

Enterprise resource planning (**ERP**) systems such as Dynamics NAV need a built-in security model to make sure that the appropriate people have access to the appropriate information. NAV supports four forms of user authentication: **Windows**, **Username**, **NavUserPassword**, and **ACS**. Each login has assigned roles, which in turn have permissions, which the system checks every time data is accessed or an object is run.

NAV security is somewhat limited and difficult to maintain. However, as system-security data is stored in tables of the NAV database, we can write a custom code to handle permissions in any way we like. We can even make calls to the Active Directory to examine user groups and other Windows properties. As you will see in this chapter, the boundaries of NAV security are limitless, but there will be a large amount of work involved for certain tasks.

Assigning a role to a user

To provide access to certain areas of NAV, we need to assign permission of that area to the user. In order to limit the complexity of assigning individual object permission to every user, the NAV group-related permission under one head calls the role (`Permission Set`). This recipe will show you how to assign the role (`Permission Set`) to a NAV user.

How to do it...

1. From the `RoleTailored client`, navigate to **Department** | **Administration** | **IT Administration** | **General** | **Users**.
2. Now open **User Card** in the edit mode and add the role (`Permission Set`).
3. Then go to **User Permission Set** fast tab.
4. In the `Permission` column, click on the dropdown. You should see a window similar to the following screenshot:

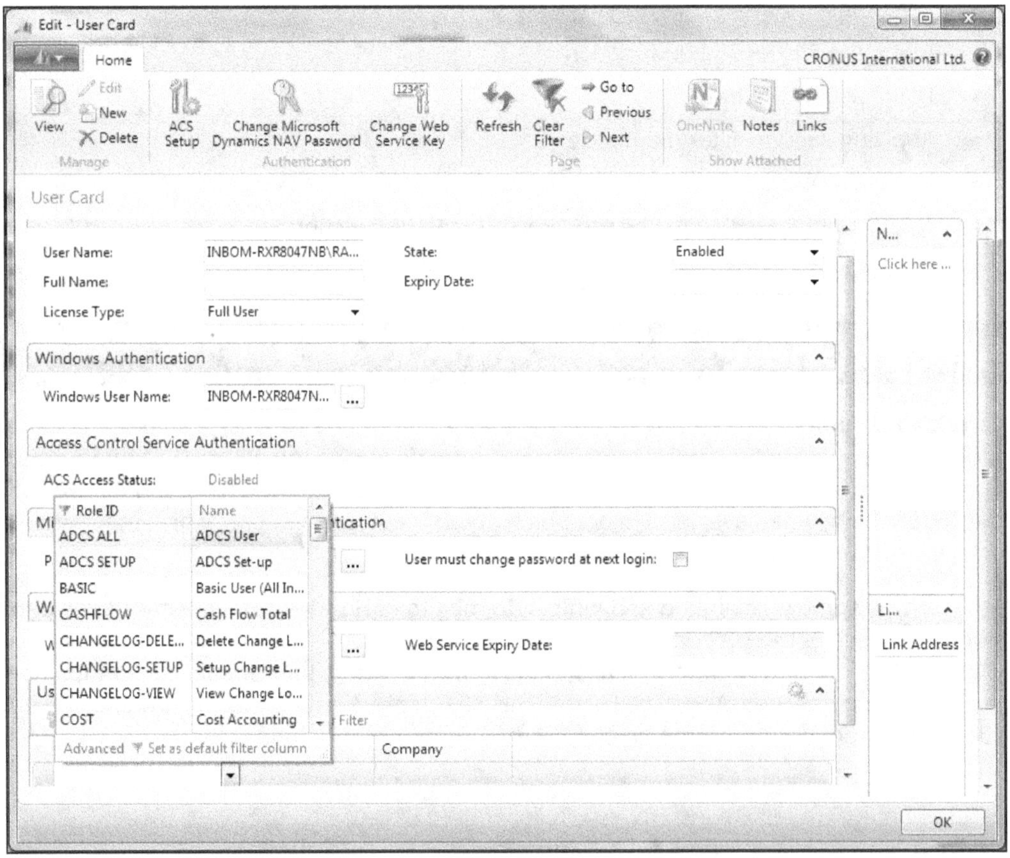

5. From the role list, select `Role ID` and then `Basic`.
6. Click on **OK**.

How it works...

The security system in NAV is maintained using roles (`Permission Sets`) and permissions. A role (`Permission Set`) is made up of permissions to access specific objects, such as tables, pages, and reports in the database. These roles are then assigned to the users.

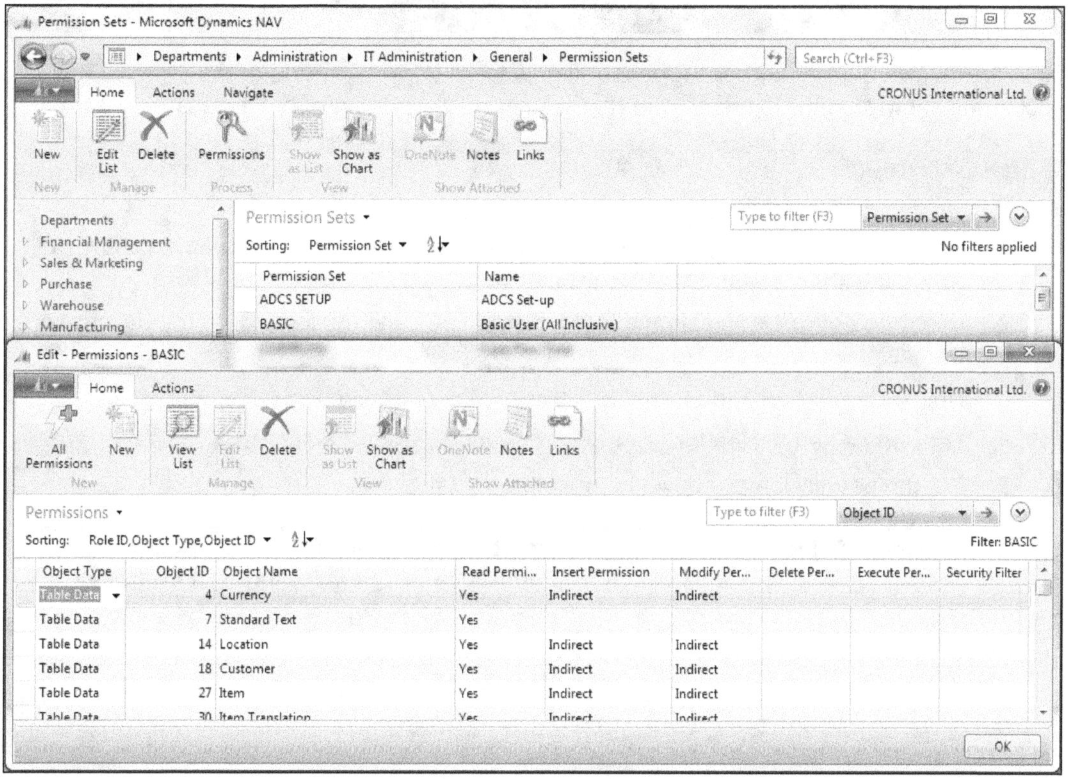

Everything related to security in NAV can be found under the **Department** | **Administration** | **IT Administration** | **General** menu in the `RoleTailored client`. The NAV system has built-in roles categorized by user activity. The role `Basic` contains permission to access the NAV system; all NAV users need to have this role in their permission set.

There's more...

Access permission can be restricted for a particular company by applying a filter on the role.

See also

- *Creating a new role*
- *Using security filters*
- *Field-level security*
- *Assigning permission to use the About This Page function*

Creating a new role

NAV has its own built-in methods for controlling access to certain parts of the system. This recipe will show you how to create role (`Permission Set`) to limit that access.

How to do it...

1. From the `RoleTailored client`, navigate to **Department** | **Administration** | **IT Administration** | **General** | **Permission Set**.
2. Use the `New` (*Ctrl* + *N*) action to enter a new role called `SAMPLE` with the description `PACKT - Sample Role`.
3. Now with your cursor on the `SAMPLE` line, click on the action `Permissions`.
4. Let's add a permission for `Object Type` as `TableData` and `Object ID` as `18`.
5. Set the permission as shown in the following table:

Object Type	Object ID	Read Permission	Insert Permission	Modify Permission	Delete Permission
`Table Data`	`18`	`Yes`	`Yes`	`Yes`	`Yes`

6. After setting the permission, the NAV window will look like the following screenshot:

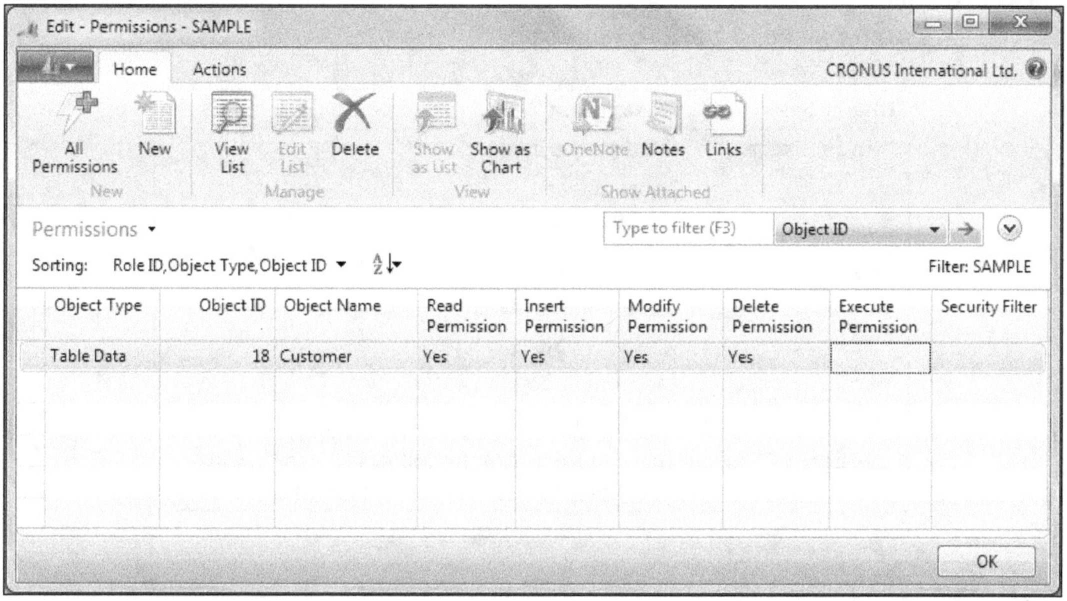

7. Click on **OK**.

How it works...

Roles are inserted into the system using the same shortcuts as in every other record, by using the *Ctrl* + *N* key. These roles have a short name called the `Role ID` and a longer description field.

Our role contains a permission that will allow the user full access to customer records. For `Table Data` object types, there are four permission levels that can be combined in any order. They include the ability to read, insert, modify, and delete records from this table. The fifth permission level is run or executed and is used for the other object types. The options for each of these permission levels are `No`, `Yes`, and `Indirect`.

In order to test this, we will need to assign the role to a user who does not already have permission to the Customer table. Once that role is assigned, the user will need to close the NAV client and reopen it in order to gain new permissions.

There's more...

Permission can be defined for the following objects:

Object type	Description
`Table Data`	Data stored in table
`Table`	Table object
`Page`	Page objects
`Report`	Report objects
`Codeunit`	Codeunit objects
`XMLPort`	XMLport object
`MenuSuite`	MenuSuite object
`Query`	Query object
`System`	The system tables that allow the user to make backups, change license files, and so on.

See also

- *Assigning a role to a user*
- *Using security filters*
- *Field-level security*

Using the FILTERGROUP function

The `FILTERGROUP` function is used to apply filters that cannot be removed by the user. This recipe will show you how to write a code to utilize them and what to watch out for.

How to do it...

1. Create a new codeunit from **Object Designer**.
2. Now add the following global variables:

Name	Type	Subtype
`CurrFilterGroup`	`Integer`	
`Customer`	`Record`	`Customer`

3. Write the following code in the `OnRun` trigger of the codeunit:

```
CurrFilterGroup := Customer.FILTERGROUP;

Customer.FILTERGROUP(255);
Customer.SETRANGE("No.", '50000');
Customer.FILTERGROUP(CurrFilterGroup);
Customer.FINDFIRST;

MESSAGE('Filters: %1\First Customer: %2', Customer.GETFILTERS,
Customer.Name);
```

4. Save and close the codeunit.

How it works...

The `FILTERGROUP` function is used to set filters on a `Record` variable that cannot be removed by the user. This function does not have any direct relation to roles, but it is part of the complete security solution for NAV. It takes in a single integer as a parameter between the numbers `0` and `255`. Although you can use numbers one to six, they are reserved by the system and manually assigning filters to those groups can override default functionality; for example, NAV uses `FILTERGROUP` number four to apply the link between the header and line values on pages such as **Sales Order** and **Purchase Order**.

In our short code segment, we first need to determine the `FILTERGROUP` function that is currently assigned to the user, so that we can set it back when we are finished. Like other functions in NAV, when the optional parameter is not used, the function returns the current value. Next we set the `FILTERGROUP` to `255`, assign a filter, and then reset the `FILTERGROUP`. Finally, we find the first record in the table and then display a message with the filters applied and the record that was found.

As you can see from the expected output, we cannot view filters that we have applied to the record. However, if we look at the **Customer List** from the standard page, we can see that **Guildford Water Department** is not the first customer on the list.

See also

- The *Advanced filtering* recipe in *Chapter 3, Working with Tables, Records, and Query*

Using security filters

Microsoft Dynamics NAV allows you to specify record-level security using the `Security Filters` field on `Permissions`. Here we will discuss how to set up these filters and some pitfalls to watch out for when using them.

How to do it...

1. From the `RoleTailored client`, navigate to **Department** | **Administration** | **IT Administration** | **General** | **Permission Set**.
2. View permission for the role **HR-EMPLOYEE**.
3. Using the assist button, set the `Security Filter` field of `Object ID 5200` to a filter based on `City` equal to 'Cambridge'.
4. Close the **Security** window.
5. Create a new codeunit from **Object Designer**.
6. Add the following global variables:

Name	Type	Subtype
Employee	Record	Employee

7. Write the following code in the `OnRun` trigger of the codeunit:

```
Employee.SETPERMISSIONFILTER;
PAGE.RUNMODAL(0, Employee);
```

8. Save and close the codeunit.

9. The resulting form will contain the details of a single `Employee` variable:

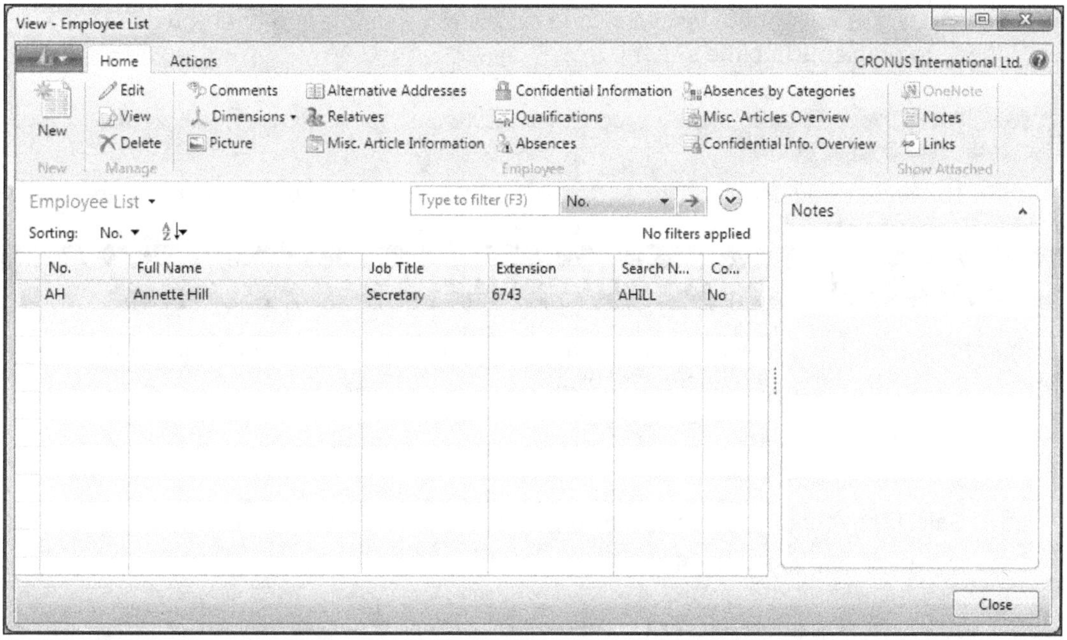

How it works...

We can limit the records, which the user can see in a table, using the **Security Filter** option. This attribute is assigned in a way similar to the `read/insert/modify/delete` attributes in the `Permissions` window for a `Role`.

If the user opens a page, these filters will automatically be applied. This is not the case, though, when the page is opened through the code. In these cases you must call the `SETPERMISSIONFILTER` function on the `Record` variable that is passed to the page.

There's more...

When used correctly, security filters can be of great use when setting up permissions. On the other hand, they can also cause a lot of headaches.

For example, let's imagine a manager who needs to view the `General Ledger` entries to make sure his department is not going over budget. He should be able to view the entries only in the accounts that relate directly to his department. This seems like a great use for security filters. But what about all the other `General Ledger` entries that are created when he posts the documents? Tax and VAT are great examples. That security filter will not allow him to post those accounts and he will receive errors during posting.

Be careful when and how you use this type of security. If you apply a security filter to a `Customer` permission, don't just open the **Custom List** page to test it out. As with all the security pages, you will want to test your code extensively to make sure that you do not introduce any problems into the system.

See also

- The *Advanced filtering* recipe in *Chapter 3, Working with Tables, Records, and Query*

Applying security filter modes

In this recipe we will see how to apply security filter modes on record variables, records on page, reports, XMLports, and query variables.

How to do it...

1. Select the record variable on which you want to add a security filter mode.
2. Use the following syntax to apply a filter:

```
RecordVar.SecurityFiltering := SecurityFilter:: <Disallowed|Filter
ed|Ignored|Validated>
```

How it works...

To change the security filtering property on the record variable, we have to simply apply the desired filter value to a property. The filter values are as follows:

- **Disallowed**: No security filters are allowed on variables; if there is any filter applied, the system will fire error.
- **Filtered**: All security filters are applied on the record variable.
- **Ignored**: All security filters are ignored on the record variable.
- **Validated**: All security filters are applied; on violation of a filter, an error will be generated.

There's more...

For more details, search security filter modes in the **Help** | **Developer and IT Pro Help** menu of Microsoft NAV Development Environment.

See also

- *Using security filters*
- *Field-level security*

Field-level security

Field-level security does not exist out of the box in NAV and is not easy to implement. In fact, a real field-level security is impossible to implement. This recipe will show you an example of how to quickly create a work around this type of security model in your system.

How to do it...

1. Create a new table from **Object Designer** of the name `Field Level Security`.
2. Then add the following fields:

Name	Type	Length
Table No.	Integer	
Field No.	Integer	
Applied To	Code	50
Editable	Boolean	
Visible	Boolean	

3. Set the following properties for these fields:

Field name	Property	Value
Table No.	TableRelation	Object.ID WHERE (Type=CONST(Table))
Field No.	TableRelation	Field.No. WHERE (TableNo=FIELD(Table No.))
Applied To	TableRelation	User."User Name"
Applied To	NotBlank	Yes
Applied To	ValidateTableRelation	No
Applied To	TestTableRelation	No

4. Set the primary key for the table to `Table No.,Field No.,Applied To`.
5. Create the following global variable:

Name	Type	Subtype
UserMgt	Codeunit	User Management

6. Write the following code in the `OnValidate` trigger of the `Applied To` field:

```
UserMgt.ValidateUserID("Applied To")
```

7. Write the following code in the `OnLookup` trigger of the `Applied To` field:

```
UserMgt.LookupUserID("Applied To")
```

8. Save and close the table.
9. Using page generation wizard, create a **List** page that displays all the fields from this table.
10. Save and close the page.
11. A sample page with data might look like this:

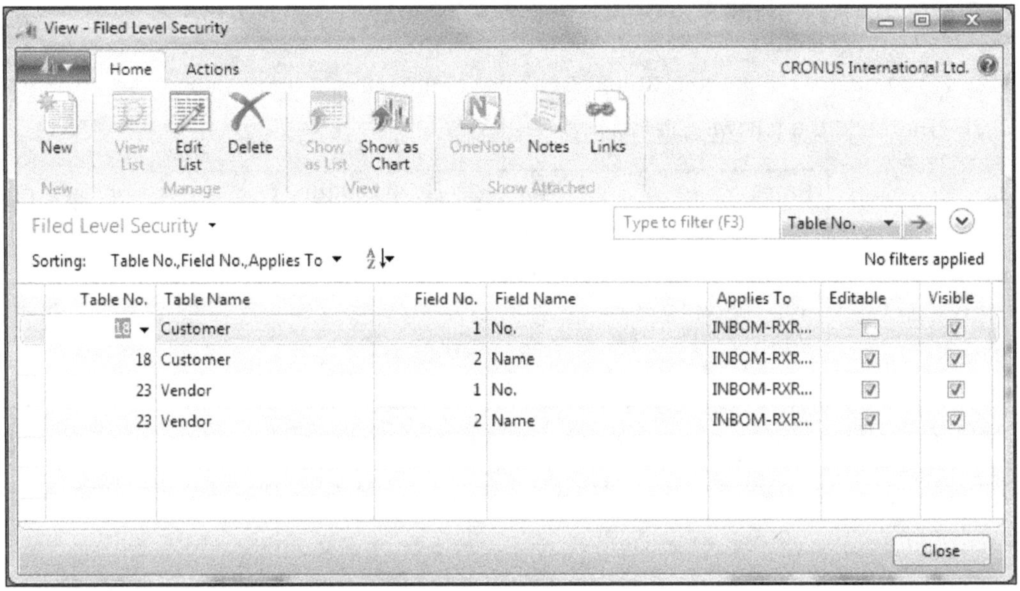

12. Create a new codeunit from **Object Designer**.
13. Create a global function named `CheckSecurity`.
14. This function should take in the following parameters:

Name	Type	Length
`UserIDIn`	`Code`	`119`
`TableID`	`Integer`	
`FieldID`	`Integer`	
`CurrentStatus`	`Boolean`	
`PropertyToCheck`	`Boolean`	

15. Set the following property for these fields:

Field name	Property	Value
PropertyToCheck	OptionString	Editable,Visible

16. The function should return a Boolean value.
17. Define the following local variables in the function:

Name	Type	Subtype
FieldLevelSecurity	Record	Field Level Security
SessionRec	Record	Session

18. Add the following code to the `CheckSecurity` function:

```
FieldLevelSecurity.SETRANGE("Table No.", TableID);
FieldLevelSecurity.SETRANGE("Field No.", FieldID);
FieldLevelSecurity.SETRANGE("Applies To", UserIDIn);
IF FieldLevelSecurity.FINDFIRST THEN
  CASE PropertyToCheck OF
    PropertyToCheck::Editable:
      EXIT(FieldLevelSecurity.Editable AND CurrentStatus);
    PropertyToCheck::Visible:
      EXIT(FieldLevelSecurity.Visible AND CurrentStatus);
  END;
EXIT(CurrentStatus);
```

19. Save and close the codeunit.
20. Create a page of type list for table `18`, `Customer`. Add field `No.` and `Name` on the page.
21. Add the following global variable to the page:

Name	Type	Subtype
FieldLevelSecurity	Codeunit	Field Level Security
NoEditable	Boolean	
NoVisible	Boolean	

22. Set the following properties for these variables:

Variable	Property	Value
NoEditable	IncludeInDataset	Yes
NoVisible	IncludeInDataset	Yes

23. Add the following code to the `OnInit` trigger:

```
NoVisible := TRUE;
NoEditable := TRUE;
```

24. Set the following properties for these fields:

Field	Property	Value
No.	Visible	NoVisible
No.	Editable	NoEditable

25. Add the following code to the `OnOpenPage` trigger:

```
NoVisible := FieldLevelSecurity.CheckSecurity(USERID,
DATABASE::Customer, Rec.FIELDNO("No."),NoVisible, 1);

NoEditable := FieldLevelSecurity.CheckSecurity(USERID,
DATABASE::Customer, Rec.FIELDNO("No."),NoEditable, 0);
```

26. Save and close the page.
27. The resulting page might look something like the one shown in the following screenshot, depending on the security assigned:

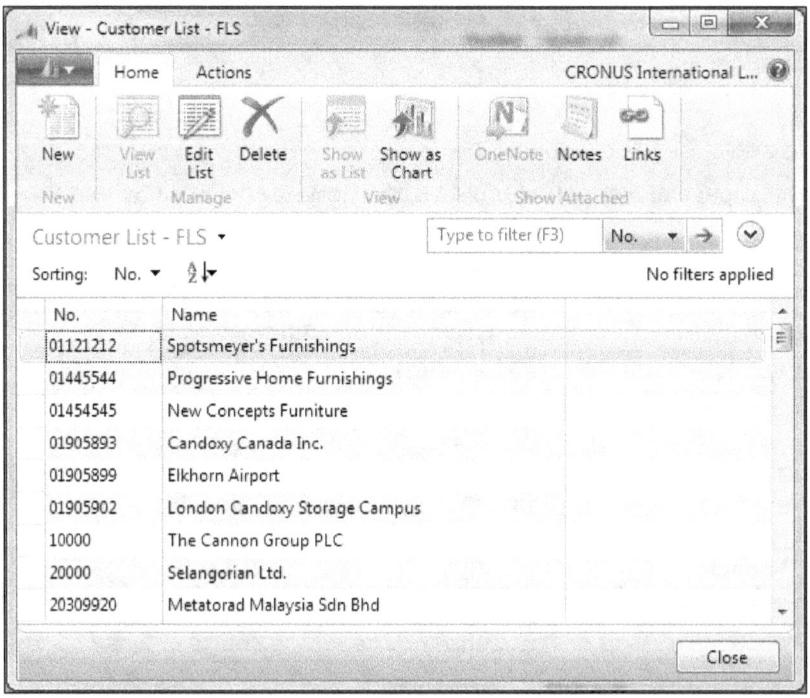

How it works...

NAV does not have a place to store the security settings on a field-level, so we need to create our own table and page to hold this information. This table will hold the user, table, and field number that security needs to be tracked for. Similar to the `read/insert/modify/delete` permissions, we will track the `Editable` and `Visible` properties.

We also need a codeunit to check the permissions when the fields are accessed. This function will take in the table and field to check, the ID of the user, the current status of the property, and the property to check. We set appropriate filters on the **Field Level Security** table based on our parameters. If a record is found, we return the value and current status in the table. This is so that we do not change the default value of the page to allow more access. For example, if a field is not editable on a page, we do not want to allow our code to make the field editable. It would be fine if it was the other way round. If no value is found, we return the current value of the property.

Finally, we need a test page. When the page opens, we need to set the properties of the fields based on the `Field Level Security` table. We will set an initial value to our variables, which is assigned to the `field` property. We will be setting security for the `No.` field in the customer table so that we can add the appropriate code to the `OnOpenPage` trigger.

There's more...

The concept of field-level security is neither difficult to understand nor something you will need to write a code for. The problem is that in order to do it properly we have to add a code to every page in the database. For this to work on a large scale, you would need to build your own parser to analyze NAV objects in their text form. The code would then be added to the correct areas and the objects imported into the system.

Adding too much code to the pages before they open can also cause some slowness. `Customer Card`, for example, has 68 fields on it. That is, 136 checks (68 for `Editable`, 68 for `Visible`) that need to be made before the page can appear on the screen. Of course many of these fields will never have security set up for them, but you would need to determine that before making any modifications. You would also need to keep a documentation of the fields whose security you won't be checking, as those fields could still be added to the permissions table, but never utilized.

See also

- The *Checking for conditions using an IF statement* recipe in *Chapter 2, General Development*
- The *Creating a table* recipe in *Chapter 3, Working with Tables, Records, and Query*
- The *Creating a page using a wizard* recipe in *Chapter 4, Designing Pages*

Assigning permission to use the About This Page function

In this recipe we will see how to add permission to use the `About This Page` function.

How to do it...

1. From the `RoleTailored client`, navigate to **Department** | **Administration** | **IT Administration** | **General** | **Permission Set**.
2. Use the `New` (*Ctrl* + *N*) action to enter a new role called `SAMPLE-ATP` with a description of `About This Page - Sample Role`.
3. Now, with your cursor on the `SMPLE-ATP` line, click on action `Permissions`.
4. Add permission for `Object Type` as `System`, and for `Object ID` as `5330`.
5. Set `Execute Permission` as `Yes`.
6. Close the `Permissions` window and the `Permission Sets` window.

How it works...

The standard role (permission set) does not include permission to run or view all the information for `About This Page`. To provide this permission, we can just add permission in any existing role or create a new role which can be added to any user permission set.

Here we have created a new role and added permission to execute object ID 5330. The object name field will be filled in automatically with **Tools**, **Zoom**. As object type is the system's only permission type, `Execute` needs to be configured for providing permission.

There's more...

In the previous versions of NAV, we have a function call `Zoom` that allows us to see the complete record information from object type form. In NAV 2013, this functionality has been expanded with some new features. Let's take a quick look at these features.

About This Page for subform page

Typically, a subform is a tabular form, that is, a form with a table box. If you need to get information on subform page and you execute the `About This Page` function from the menu, you will be disappointed. This is because you will not get the subform details of the parent. The solution for this is to keep the cursor on the subform page and use a shortcut for `About This Page`, that is (*Ctrl* + *Alt* + *F1*). It will give you details of the subform page. Follow these steps to validate it:

1. From the `RoleTailored client`, navigate to **Department** | **Sales & Marketing** | **Order Processing** | **Sales Order**.
2. Select any sales order record and click on the action **View**.
3. Select the first line record and use the shortcut *Ctrl* + *Alt* + *F1*.

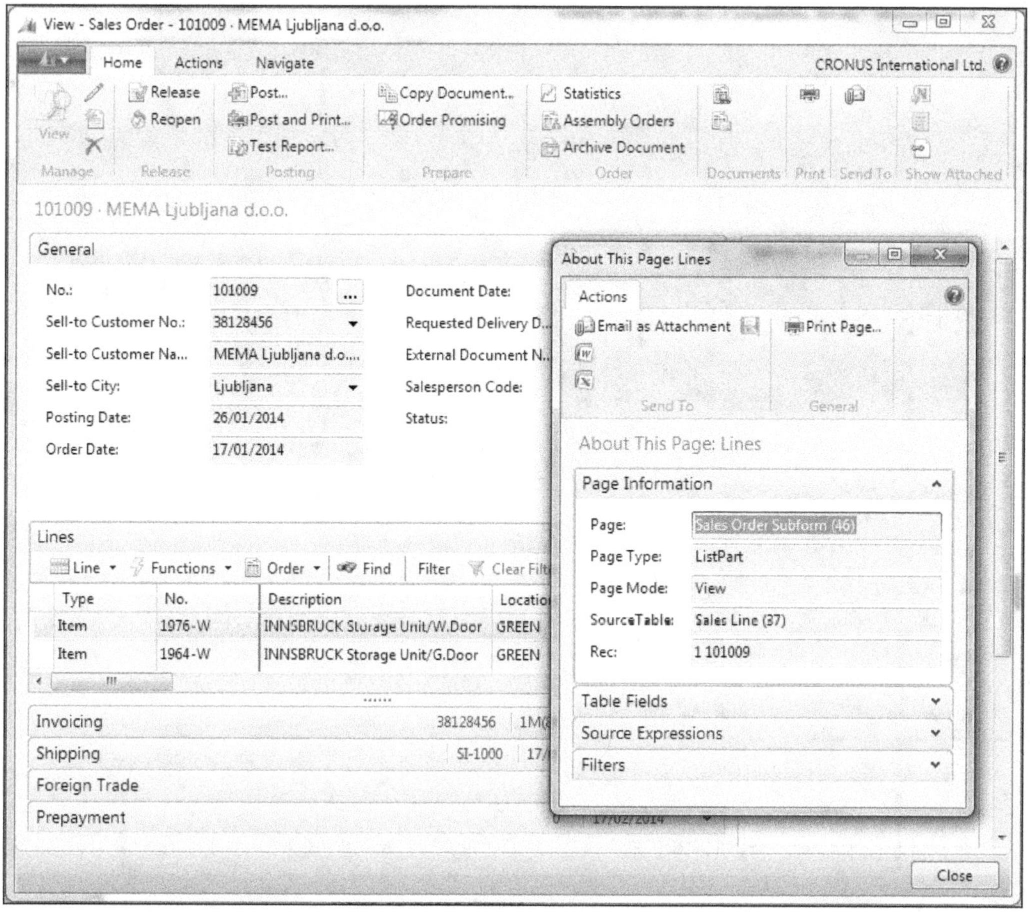

About This Page for report

When we run the `About This Page` function on the request page of any report, the details displayed in `About This Page` is related to report, and not to the subform page. Just neglect the caption **Page**.

1. From the `RoleTailored client`, navigate to **Sales Order Processor** role center and run the `Customer - Order Summary` report.
2. From the request page, navigate to the application menu **Help** | **About This Page** or use the shortcut *Ctrl* + *Alt* + *F1*.

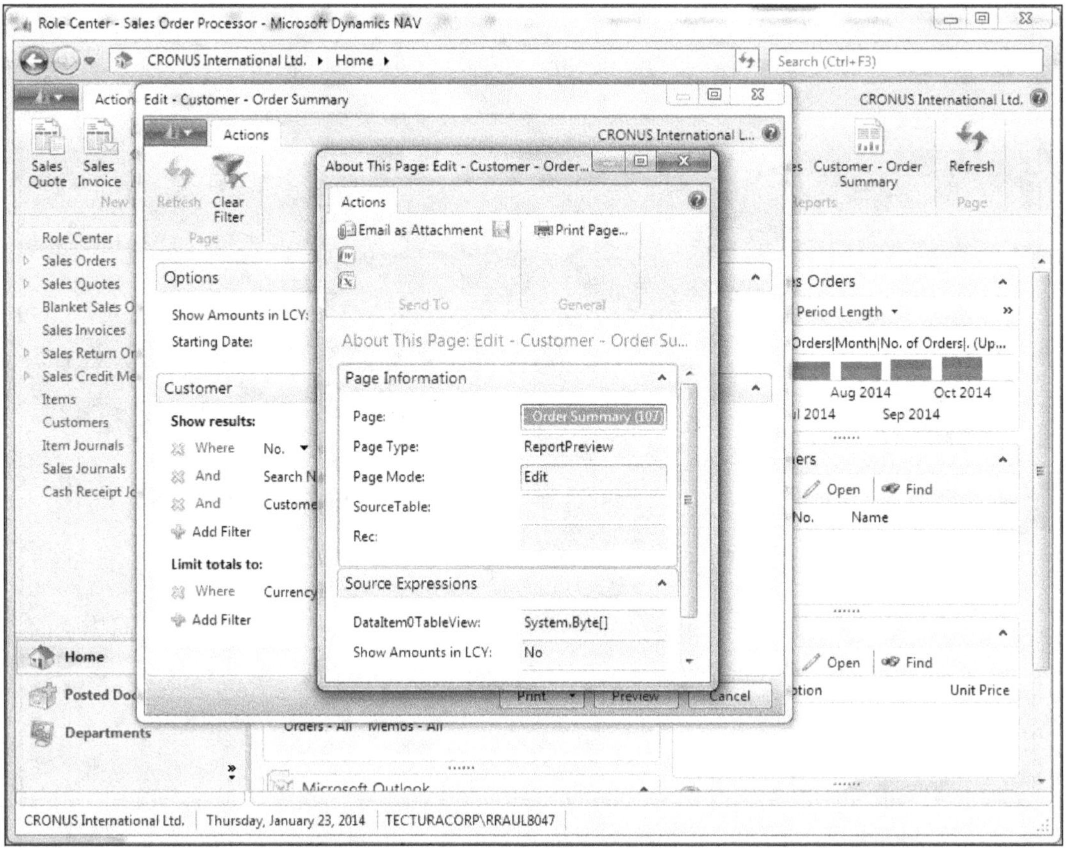

> If the About This Page shortcut is not working, use the shortcut *Ctrl* + *Alt* + *F1* to open a new window.

See also

- *Assigning a role to a user*
- *Creating a new role*
- *Using security filters*

Killing a user session

In Microsoft Dynamics NAV 2013, user sessions are controlled by client services. The NAV administration client provides plenty of options to manage user sessions; however, some time is needed to kill a particular session. With the help of this recipe, we will add a small code on the NAV standard session page to kill the session.

How to do it...

1. To start, open **Object Designer** and open page **9506, Session List** in the design mode.
2. To edit actions, navigate to **View** | **Page Actions** (*Ctrl* + *Alt* + *F4*).
3. Under the action group **Session**, add a new action with name `Kill Session`.
4. Set the following properties for the `Kill Session` action:

Property	Value
`Image`	`Delete`
`Promoted`	`Yes`
`PromotedCategory`	`Category4`
`PromotedIsBig`	`Yes`

5. Let's add the following code to the `OnAction` trigger of the `Kill Session` action.

```
IF CONFIRM ('Are you sure?') THEN
  STOPSESSION("Session ID")
```

6. It's time to save and close the page.

How it works...

As NAV provides a standard page for active sessions, we will use the same to take advantage of the default features. After setting a newly created action, we can see our action, as shown in the following screenshot:

To avoid an error during the killing session, we execute a confirmation dialog box before killing the selected session. This reduces the chance of killing the wrong session. However, the administrator who is killing the session should take care to avoid partial data posting. `STOPSESSION` is a standard NAV function to end/kill a session.

See also

- The *Configuring a NAV Server Instance* recipe in *Chapter 12, NAV Server Administration*

8
Leveraging Microsoft Office

In this chapter, we will learn:

- Sending data to Microsoft Word
- Managing stylesheets
- Sending e-mail from NAV through SMTP
- Exporting data using the Excel Buffer
- Creating data connection from Excel to NAV
- Showing data in Excel using PowerPivot
- Creating an InfoPath form for the NAV data
- Creating charts with Visio

Introduction

Microsoft Office is a related suite of applications. Just as the Dynamics platform encompasses multiple products, so does the Office product line. The three most popular programs are Word, Excel, and Outlook, which serve as word processor, spreadsheet application, and e-mail manager, respectively. NAV does not offer the same functionality that these applications provide, and integrating with them can open up many new possibilities for the users of the software.

Office also comes with other, lesser-known, programs that are used by many companies. We will also examine three of these products. The first is using stylesheets and sending data to Excel and InfoPath, which is used to generate XML-based forms for users to enter and view data. We will also learn about SMTP for sending mail. Finally, we will take a look at how to create charts in Visio. With all of these products working together as one, you will easily be able to see how to get your data to the people who need it.

Sending data to Microsoft Word

Creating attractive Word documents from NAV is a challenging task. This recipe will not show you how to create a document that looks exactly like your report from NAV, but it will introduce you to the basics of sending data to the application.

Getting ready

Microsoft Word must be installed on the client machine.

How to do it...

1. Create a new codeunit from **Object Designer**.
2. Then add the following global variables:

Name	Type	SubType	Length
`WordApp`	`Automation`	`'Microsoft Word 14.0 Object Library'. Application`	
`WordDoc`	`Automation`	`'Microsoft Word 14.0 Object Library'.Document`	
`WordAppSelection`	`Automation`	`'Microsoft Word 14.0 Object Library'.Selection`	
`WordFont`	`Automation`	`'Microsoft Word 14.0 Object Library'.Font`	
`CompanyInformation`	`Record`	`Company Information`	
`ExportedPicture`	`Text`		`250`
`NewLine`	`Char`		

3. At this stage, save an uncompiled version of the codeunit and close it.
4. Export the codeunit to a text file.
5. Open the file and remove all the events that were added by the automation variables.
6. It's time to save and close the text file.

7. Import the text file into NAV and compile the object.
8. Write the following code in the `OnRun` trigger of the codeunit:

```
NewLine := 13;
ExportedPicture := 'D:\Temp\CompanyInformationPicture.bmp';

CompanyInformation.GET;
CompanyInformation.CALCFIELDS(Picture);
CompanyInformation.Picture.EXPORT(ExportedPicture);
CREATE(WordApp,FALSE,TRUE);

WordDoc := WordApp.Documents.Add;
WordDoc.Activate;

WordAppSelection := WordApp.Selection;
WordDoc.Shapes.AddPicture(ExportedPicture);
WordFont := WordAppSelection.Font;
WordFont.Size(40);
WordFont.Name('Arial');
WordAppSelection.TypeText('Big Text' + FORMAT(NewLine));
WordFont.Size(20);
WordFont.Name('Courier New');
WordAppSelection.TypeText('Medium Text' + FORMAT(NewLine));
WordFont.Size(10);
WordFont.Name('Times New Roman');
WordAppSelection.TypeText('Small Text' + FORMAT(NewLine));
WordApp.Visible := TRUE;
```

9. Save and close the codeunit.

How it works...

This recipe requires an odd step in which you have to manipulate the object from a text file and not within **Object Designer**. When you add automation variables to your object, regardless of whether or not you set the `WithEvents` property, the events are added to the code. The `WithEvents` property just lets you see them when you are coding.

Unfortunately, NAV has a limit on just how long these event names can be, and many of them are similarly named. When they are added to NAV, the application truncates the end of the event name, which can result in duplicate events being defined. This throws an error when you compile the object. If you want to use these events in your NAV code, you will have to write your own .NET wrapper class with names that are not as long.

Now we can move to the actual code. To start, we export the logo from **Company Information**. Ideally, we would place this on a shared drive, or use an image that is not stored in NAV, because the `ENVIRON` command is no longer supported in the RTC.

Next, we create an instance of the Microsoft Word application. We then create a new blank document and activate it. Using the `Shape.AddPicture` method from the Word Document object, we can insert the logo that we exported from **Company Information**.

We can also manipulate text just as we would if we were using the application manually. By changing the font size and name, the `TypeText` method will alter the way it displays the text on the screen. If you were trying to duplicate a NAV report, you could set the font name to Helvetica and the font size to seven.

There's more...

For detailed reading on the Microsoft Word Object Model you can visit the following MSDN site:

`http://msdn.microsoft.com/en-us/library/kw65a0we(v=vs.100).aspx`

See also

- *Managing stylesheets*

Managing stylesheets

In this recipe we will set a stylesheet for a specific page.

Getting ready

Export the Excel stylesheet for page `22` from the older version of NAV which has stylesheet tools.

How to do it...

1. To start, open the `RoleTailored client`. In the RTC **Search** box, type `Manage Style Sheets`, and choose the related link.
2. In the **Show** field, choose **Style sheet for a specific page**.
3. In the **Page No.** field, type 22.

4. From the **Style Sheet** assist edit option, select your customized stylesheet.
5. Provide **Name** and choose Microsoft Excel as **Send-to Program**.
6. Click on **OK**.

How it works...

Microsoft Dynamics NAV 2013 provides an option to export page data into Word and Excel. Datasheet styles created in Word and Excel are predefined for all of the pages in the system. NAV 2013 provides options to manage stylesheets where we can import old stylesheets or export current stylesheets and customize them. For the older version of NAV, Microsoft has provided a stylesheet tool to customize or develop your own stylesheets; unfortunately, this tool is not supported in NAV 2013.

The **Manage Style Sheet** window helps to import and export stylesheets, as well as to view the list of available stylesheets. Changes made on the stylesheets are applicable to all users.

Sending an e-mail from NAV through SMTP

NAV 2013 supports **Simple Mail Transfer Protocol** (**SMTP**), which makes mail sending easy and independent. Through SMTP, NAV will send mail directly to the exchange server. In the older version, when we used to send it through Outlook, it consisted of a more complex code. This recipe will show you how to configure and use that SMTP code.

Getting ready

1. Open the `RoleTailored client`; in the RTC `Search` box type `SMTP`, and choose the related link.
2. Provide the SMTP server address and the server port.
3. Choose authentication type set by your IT department and, if required, provide credentials.

How to do it...

1. Start the development by creating a new codeunit from **Object Designer**.
2. Add the following global variables:

Name	Type	SubType
`SMTPMailSetup`	`Record`	`SMTP Mail Setup`
`SMTP`	`Codeunit`	`SMTP Mail`

3. Write the following code in the `OnRun` trigger of the codeunit:

```
IF SMTPMailSetup.GET THEN BEGIN
  SMTP.CreateMessage('Rakesh Raul','YourE-mail@microsoft.com',
'Someone@somewhere.com','E-mail Subject', 'E-mail Body', FALSE);
  SMTP.Send;
End;
```

4. It's time to save and close the codeunit.

How it works...

SMTP is the preferred way of sending e-mails with NAV. The code behind this functionality, and more specifically the `CreateMessage` function, is located in the codeunit `400` (`SMTP Mail`). This function uses the `'Microsoft Navision Mail'.SmtpMessage` automation to create a message for us based on the input parameters. These parameters are `Sender Name`, `Sender E-mail Address`, `Recipient E-mail Addresses`, `Subject`, `Body`, and `HTML Formatted`. We must manually call the `Send` function in the codeunit if we want to actually send the message.

There's more...

For more details on the Microsoft Outlook object model you can visit the following MSDN site:

`http://msdn.microsoft.com/en-us/library/ms268893(v=vs.110).aspx`

Sending an HTML-formatted e-mail

Many CRM applications or other programs send e-mails out automatically. Anything that is customer-facing should look professional. That is not to say that simple text e-mails are bad, just that HTML-formatted e-mails are more dynamic and more likely to get the customer's attention.

The following is a sample code which can be used to send an HTML-formatted e-mail:

```
IF SMTPMailSetup.GET THEN BEGIN
  SMTP.CreateMessage('Rakesh Raul','YourE-mail@YourCompany.com',
'Someone@Somewhere.com','E-mail Subject', '', TRUE);
  SMTP.AppendBody('<b><h2>Thank You!</h2></b><br><br>');
  SMTP.AppendBody('Your message has been received,<br><br>');
  SMTP.AppendBody('Administrator');
  SMTP.Send;
END;
```

By passing a value of `TRUE` as the last parameter to the `CreateMessage` function, we tell the system to format the e-mail for HTML. We can then use the `AppendBody` function to add lines to our message. These could be read from an external file, stored in NAV, or hardcoded as we have done here.

Exporting data using the Excel Buffer

NAV contains a wrapper object that allows you to export data to Microsoft Excel. This recipe will show you how to use it in its most common form—exporting a report to Excel.

Getting ready

Microsoft Excel must be installed on the client machine.

How to do it...

1. Create a new processing-only report based on the `Customer` table.
2. Add values in the `No.`, `Name`, and `Balance` fields.
3. Add the following global variables:

Name	Type	SubType
ExcelBuf	Record	Excel Buffer

4. Let's set the property `Temporary` of the `ExcelBuf` variable to `Yes`.
5. Now add a function named `MakeExcelInfo`.
6. Add the following code to the function:

```
ExcelBuf.SetUseInfoSheet;
ExcelBuf.AddInfoColumn(FORMAT('Company Name'),FALSE,'',TRUE,FALSE,
FALSE,'',ExcelBuf."Cell Type"::Text);
ExcelBuf.AddInfoColumn(COMPANYNAME,FALSE,'',FALSE,FALSE,
FALSE,'',ExcelBuf."Cell Type"::Text);

ExcelBuf.NewRow;
ExcelBuf.AddInfoColumn(FORMAT('Report Name'), FALSE,'',TRUE,FALSE,
FALSE,'',ExcelBuf."Cell Type"::Text);
ExcelBuf.AddInfoColumn(FORMAT('Print Report to Excel'),
FALSE,'',FALSE,FALSE,FALSE,'',ExcelBuf."Cell Type"::Text);

ExcelBuf.NewRow;
ExcelBuf.AddInfoColumn(FORMAT('Report Name'), FALSE,'',TRUE,FALSE,
FALSE,'',ExcelBuf."Cell Type"::Text);
ExcelBuf.AddInfoColumn(FORMAT('Print Report to Excel'),
FALSE,'',FALSE,FALSE,FALSE,'',ExcelBuf."Cell Type"::Text);

ExcelBuf.NewRow;
ExcelBuf.AddInfoColumn(FORMAT('Report No.'),
FALSE,'',TRUE,FALSE,FALSE,'',ExcelBuf."Cell Type"::Text);
```

```
ExcelBuf.AddInfoColumn(REPORT::"Print Report to Excel",
FALSE,'',FALSE,FALSE,FALSE,'',ExcelBuf."Cell Type"::Text);

ExcelBuf.NewRow;
ExcelBuf.AddInfoColumn(FORMAT('User Id'),
FALSE,'',TRUE,FALSE,FALSE,'',ExcelBuf."Cell Type"::Text);
ExcelBuf.AddInfoColumn(USERID,FALSE,'',FALSE,FALSE,FALSE,'',
ExcelBuf."Cell Type"::Text);

ExcelBuf.NewRow;
ExcelBuf.AddInfoColumn(FORMAT('Date / Time'), FALSE,'',TRUE,FALSE,
FALSE,'',ExcelBuf."Cell Type"::Text);
ExcelBuf.AddInfoColumn(TODAY,FALSE,'',FALSE,FALSE,FALSE,'',
ExcelBuf."Cell Type"::Text);
ExcelBuf.AddInfoColumn(TIME,FALSE,'',FALSE,FALSE,FALSE,'',ExcelBuf
."Cell Type"::Text);

ExcelBuf.NewRow;
ExcelBuf.AddInfoColumn(FORMAT('Filters'),FALSE,'',
TRUE,FALSE,FALSE,'',ExcelBuf."Cell Type"::Text);
ExcelBuf.AddInfoColumn(Customer.GETFILTERS,FALSE,'',
FALSE,FALSE,FALSE,'',ExcelBuf."Cell Type"::Text);
ExcelBuf.ClearNewRow;
MakeExcelDataHeader;
```

7. Add a function called `MakeExcelDataHeader`.
8. Add the following code to the function:

```
ExcelBuf.NewRow;
ExcelBuf.AddColumn(Customer.FIELDCAPTION("No."),FALSE,'',
TRUE,FALSE,TRUE,'@',ExcelBuf."Cell Type"::Text);
ExcelBuf.AddColumn(Customer.FIELDCAPTION(Name),FALSE,'',
TRUE,FALSE,TRUE,'',ExcelBuf."Cell Type"::Text);
ExcelBuf.AddColumn(Customer.FIELDCAPTION(Balance),FALSE,
'',TRUE,FALSE,TRUE,'',ExcelBuf."Cell Type"::Text);
```

9. Add a function called `MakeExcelDataBody`.
10. Add the following code to the function:

```
ExcelBuf.NewRow;
ExcelBuf.AddColumn(Customer."No.",FALSE,'',FALSE,FALSE,FALSE,'',
ExcelBuf."Cell Type"::Text);
ExcelBuf.AddColumn(Customer.Name,FALSE,'',FALSE,FALSE,FALSE,'',
ExcelBuf."Cell Type"::Text);
ExcelBuf.AddColumn(Customer.Balance,FALSE,'',FALSE,FALSE,FALSE,'#,
##0',ExcelBuf."Cell Type"::Number);
```

11. Add a function called `CreateExcelBook`.
12. Add the following code to the function:

    ```
    ExcelBuf.CreateBookAndOpenExcel('Data','',COMPANYNAME,USERID);
    ERROR('');
    ```

13. Create a new page action `Send Data To Excel`.
14. Add the following code to the `OnPreDataItem` trigger for the `Customer` data item:

    ```
    MakeExcelInfo;
    ```

15. Add the following code to the `OnAfterGetRecord` trigger for the `Customer` data item:

    ```
    MakeExcelDataBody;
    ```

16. Add the following code to the `OnPostReport` trigger:

    ```
    CreateExcelbook;
    ```

17. It's time to save and close the report.

How it works...

Sending data to Excel requires a record variable that refers to the Excel Buffer table. This table contains several functions that we will use throughout our code to communicate with the Excel program.

We will use four functions in this page and go through each of them one-by-one. The first function is named `MakeExcelInfo` and it contains a series of calls to the `AddInfoColumn` and `NewRow` functions in the Excel Buffer table. This function replicates what you see in the `Header` section of most reports, that is, the name of the report, the date and time when it was created, who it was created by, and any filters that may have been used.

The `AddInfoColumn` parameters deal with formatting of the text that will be entered in the cell. In order, the parameters are: `Value`, `IsFormula`, `CommentText`, `IsBold`, `IsItalics`, `IsUnderline`, `NumFormat`, and `CellType`.

At the end of our function, we make a call to `MakeExcelDataHeader`, which adds our column headings to the first row of a new sheet in the Excel Workbook.

There is a similar function, `MakeExcelDataBody`, which adds our actual data to the sheet.

Finally, we have a function called `CreateBookAndOpenExcel`, which loads the data from the Excel Buffer and displays the Excel worksheet.

Now that we have these functions, we need to use them in our report. When thinking about what each one does and how the report flows from start to finish, it becomes obvious when we should use them. The header information about the report is displayed in the `Header` section of the `Customer` record, so we can use the `MakeExcelInfo` function in the `OnPreDataItem` trigger. We retrieve data from the database in the `OnAfterGetRecord` trigger, so here is where we should add the data to the Excel file. Lastly, we don't want to view the Excel file until the report is completely generated, so we place the call to the `CreateBookAndOpenExcel` function in the `OnPostReport` trigger; it will not only create our Excel file but also display it on screen.

When you run the report, you should see a document like the one shown in the following screenshot:

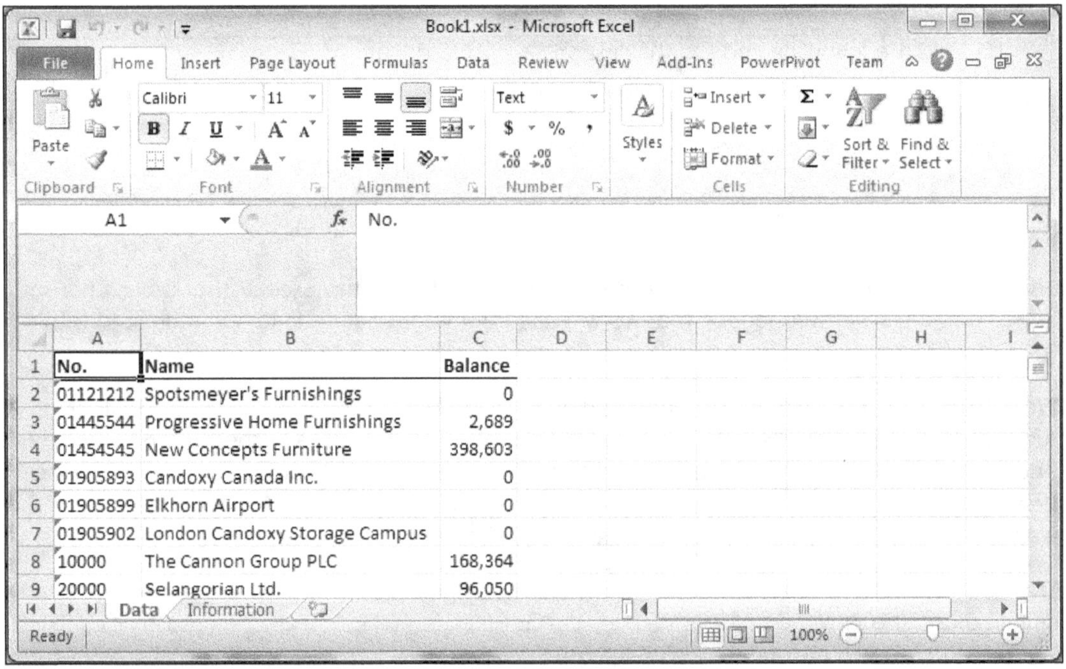

There's more...

Although the Excel Buffer table will provide for most of your needs, you can also write your own Excel automations.

> For more information on the Microsoft Excel Object Model, visit the following MSDN site:
>
> `http://msdn.microsoft.com/en-us/library/wss56bz7(v=vs.110).aspx`

See also

- The *Using a temporary table* recipe in *Chapter 3, Working with Tables, Records, and Queries*
- The *Using an RDLC report* recipe in *Chapter 5, Report Design*

Creating data connection from Excel to NAV

Instead of copying and pasting data from NAV into Excel, you can easily create an external connection to the NAV database.

Getting ready

Microsoft Excel must be installed on the client machine.

How to do it...

1. To start, open Microsoft Excel and select the **Data** tab.
2. From the **Get External Data** section of the menu, navigate to **From Other Sources** | **From SQL Server**:

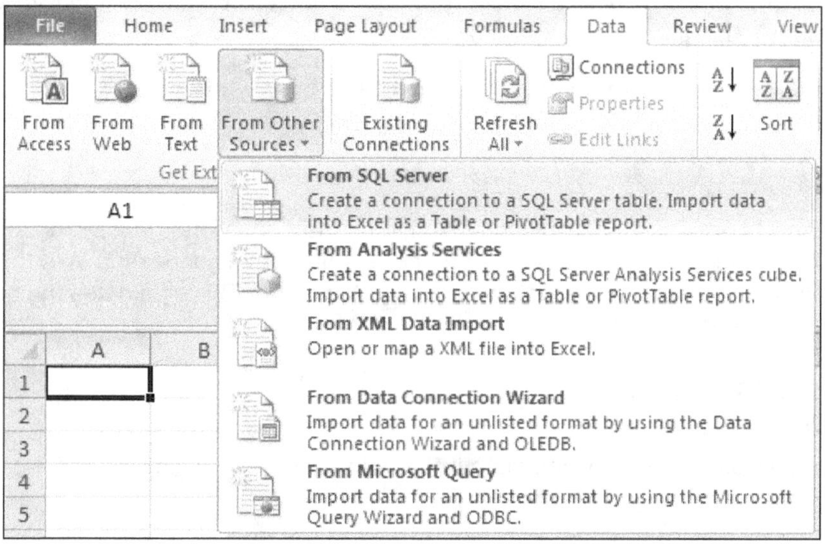

3. In the data connection wizard, enter the name of the SQL Server and your login credentials:

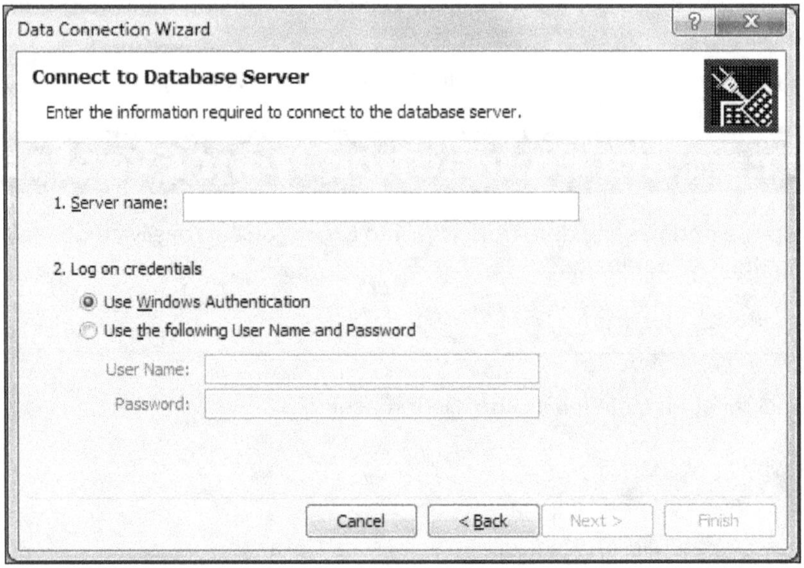

4. Click on **Next**.
5. In the next window, select the database and table you wish to view in Excel.
6. Click on **Finish**.
7. It may take a moment for the data to load into the workbook.

How it works...

Microsoft Excel maintains an active connection to the database when you set up an external data connection. When you save and close a file with a connection in it, the data is automatically reloaded the next time you open the document. This eliminates the need to log in to NAV to copy and paste data.

There's more...

The following MSDN article provides more information about managing your connections in Microsoft Excel:

`http://msdn.microsoft.com/en-us/library/bb545041%28office.11%29.aspx`

See also

- *Exporting data using the Excel Buffer*
- *Showing data in Excel using PowerPivot*

Showing data in Excel using PowerPivot

PowerPivot is a free add-in to the Excel 2010 version. It extends the capabilities of the PivotTable data by introducing the ability to import data from multiple sources. In this recipe, we will design a basic report on NAV database using PowerPivot.

Getting ready

Microsoft Excel must be installed on the client machine with PowerPivot add-in.

How to do it...

1. Start Microsoft Office Excel and select the **PowerPivot Window** action from the ribbon:

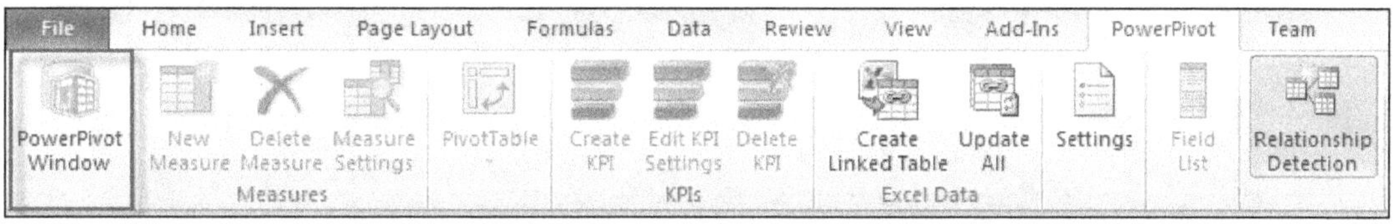

2. From the PowerPivot window, navigate to **From Database** | **From SQL Server**:

3. Provide the connection name and select SQL Server where NAV database is attached.
4. Provide the **Log on to the server** credentials.

5. Select a NAV database from the drop-down list provided by the **Database name** textbox.
6. Click on the **Advance** button; in the advance window, change the provider to **.Net Framework Data Provider For SQL Server**.
7. Click on **Next** and choose **Select** from a list of tables and **Views** to choose the data to import. You will then be directed to a window to select tables and views, as shown in the following screenshot:

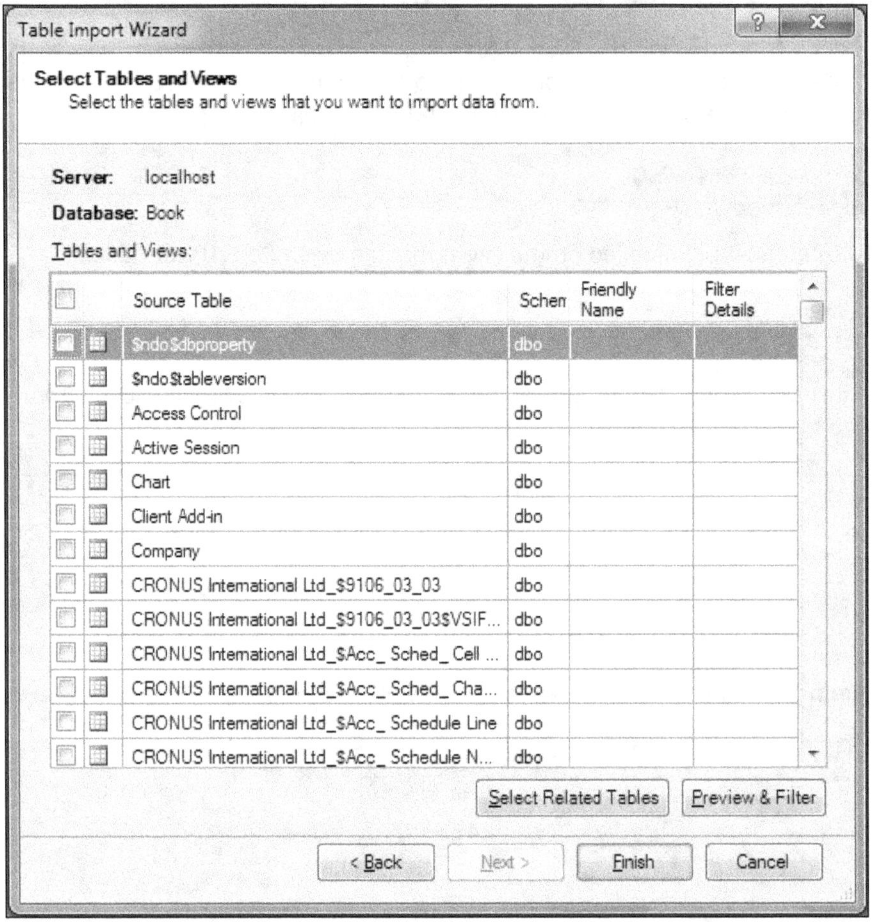

8. From the table list, select the `Item Sales Invoice Header`, `Sales Invoice Line`, and `Salesperson Purchaser` tables, and then click on **Finish**.
9. PowerPivot will import data and provide import status. Click on **Close**.

10. You will get three tables with data. If you choose **Diagram**, the view screen might look something like the one shown in the following screenshot:

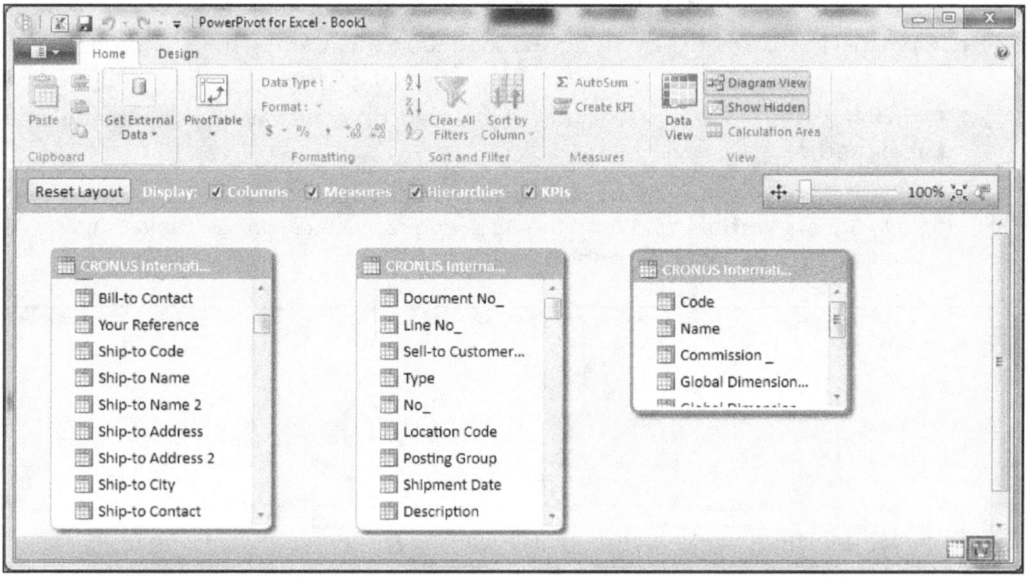

11. From the **Design** menu, select the **Create Relationship** action.
12. Set the first relationship of `[Sales Invoice Header].[No.]` with `[Sales Invoice Line].[Document No.]`.
13. Set the second relationship of `[Sales Invoice Header].[Salesperson Code]` with `[Salesperson Purchase].[Code]`.
14. Now from the **Grid** view go to the `Sales Invoice Header` table and add a new column `Invoice Amount` at the end of the table.
15. Add the following code to the `Invoice Amount` column:

```
=CALCULATE(Sum('CRONUS International Ltd_Sales Invoice
Line'[Amount]))
```

16. Right-click on the `Sales Invoice Line` table, and from the context menu select **Hide from Client Tools**:

17. On the **Home** tab, select the **PivotTable** action.
18. In the **Create PivotTable** dialog, select the **New Worksheet** option. It will create a new worksheet with the Pivot table options window.
19. From the `Item Sales Invoice Header` table's fields drag the `Invoice Amount` field into the `Values` and `Bill-to City` fields in the **Row Labels** section.
20. From the `Salesperson Purchaser` table field, drag the `Name` field to the **Column Labels** section.
21. Finally, from the `Sales Invoice Header` table fields, drag the `Bill-to City` field to **Slicers Vertical**, and from the `Salesperson Purchaser` table drag the `Name` field to the **Slicers Horizontal** section:

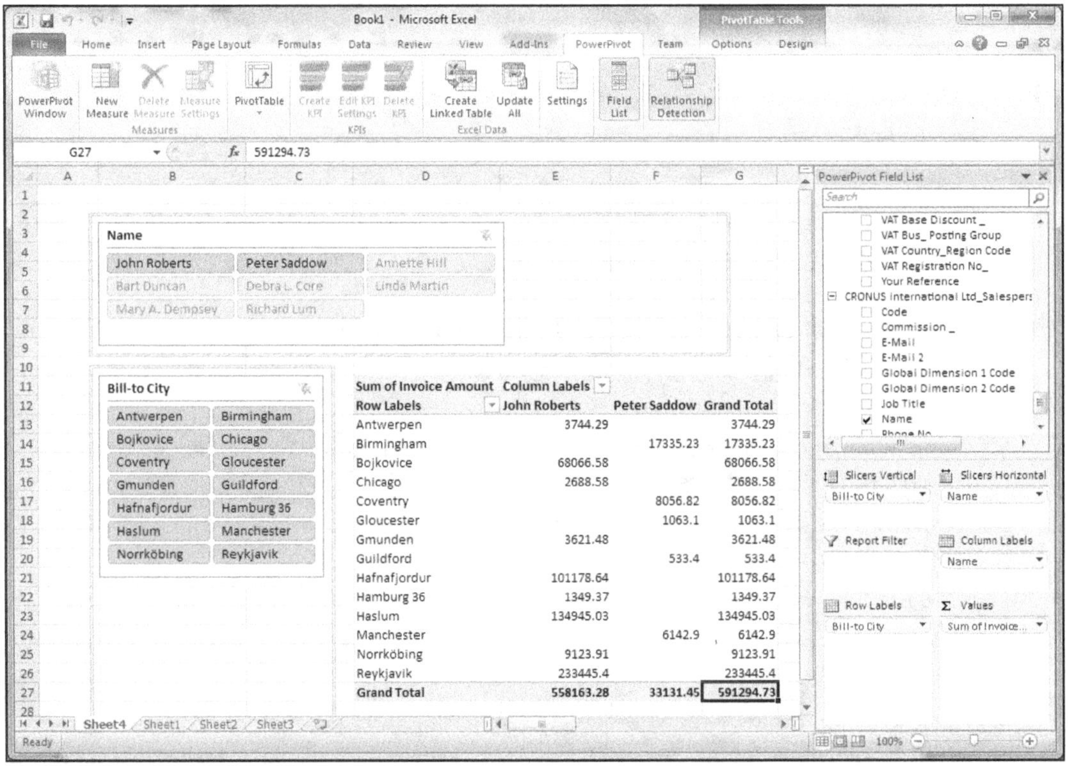

How it works...

PowerPivot allows end users to analyze data with complete freedom of applying filters and selecting desired fields. In this recipe we are designing very basic reports on the `Item` and `Location` tables. The process of designing a new PowerPivot report can de divided into four steps.

In the first step we have to set the connection details to connect the desired server and database. In our case, we are using the NAV database. While connecting to the database, we need to select an appropriate provider as per our system configuration. In our case, we choose .NET provider.

The second step is to select tables involved in our report. You must have noticed that there is an option to autoselect related tables; unfortunately, this option does not work for NAV databases, as NAV does not maintain a standard way of defining the primary and forging keys.

In the third and the last step of designing, we set relationships or carry out additional calculations on the PowerPivot tables. PowerPivot provides a wide range of functions to do addition calculations. We have used the function `CALCULATE` and table relations to bring invoice amount values from the `line` table to the `header` table.

To end the designing phase, we have selected the **PivotTable** action; this does not mean that we cannot make any further change to our design. Design of PowerPivot can be changed anytime.

Finally, we can analyze data from the Pivot table. By simply adding fields to report/filter/slicer section, we can carry out data analysis.

There's more...

The following Microsoft article provides more information about PowerPivot:

`http://www.microsoft.com/en-us/bi/powerpivot.aspx`

PowerPivot is available in 32 and 64 bit versions, so you need to find which version of Excel you are using. You will find the Excel version from the **About Microsoft Excel** section by navigating to **File** | **Help**.

To download PowerPivot visit the following URL:

`http://www.microsoft.com/en-us/download/details.aspx?id=7609`

See also

- *Exporting data using the Excel Buffer*
- *Creating data connection from Excel to NAV*

Creating an InfoPath form for the NAV data

Microsoft InfoPath allows you to create forms to view and enter data outside of the NAV application. There is no programming involved, other than having an existing NAV page exposed as a web service.

Getting ready

Microsoft InfoPath must be installed on the client machine.

How to do it...

1. Create a web service as described in the *Creating web services* recipe in *Chapter 10, Integration*.
2. By navigating to **File** | **New** in InfoPath, select **Web Service** and click on **Design Form**:

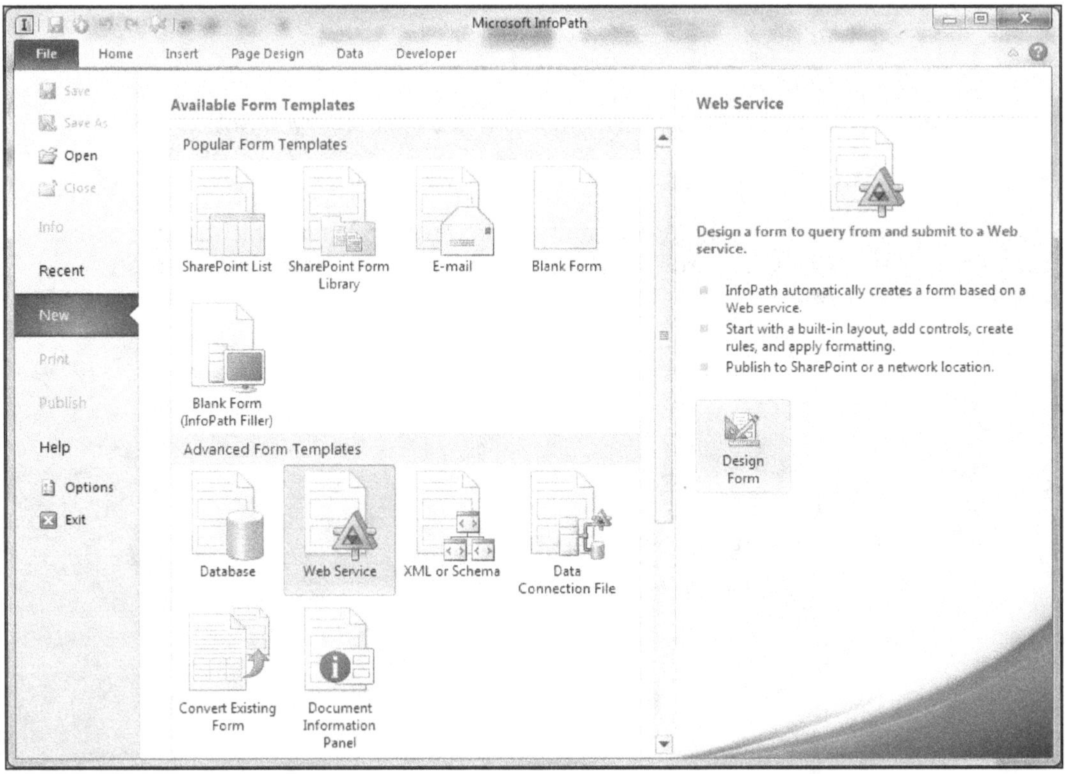

3. Select **Receive Data**.
4. From the **Dynamics NAV Web Server** page, go to the following address and find the web service:

   `http://localhost:7047/DynamicsNAV70/WS/services`

5. In this case we will be using `http://localhost:7047/DynamicsNAV70/WS/Page/CustomerList`, but this could be different on your system.
6. Enter this address in the **Data Connection Wizard** window.
7. Click on **Next**.
8. Select **Read Multiple**.
9. Click on **Next** and finally on **Finish**.
10. You should now have a design template that looks like the following screenshot:

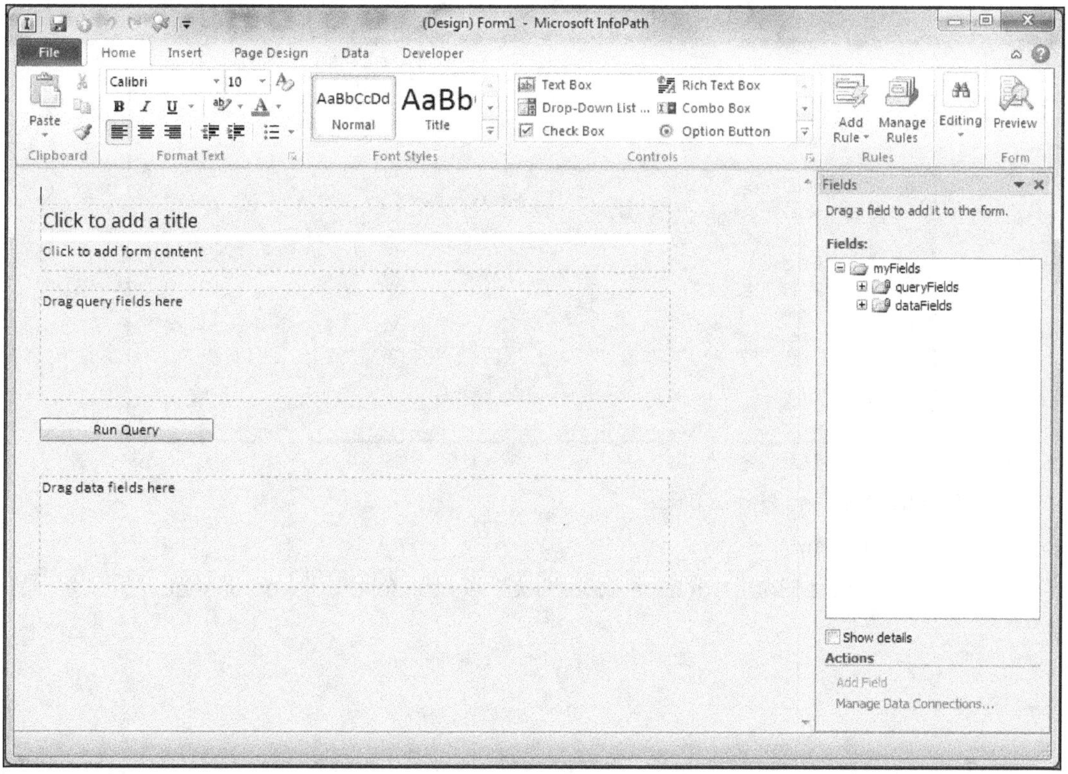

11. Change the title to `Customer List`.
12. From the **queryFields** node in the data source tree view on the right-hand side of the screen, drag the **Field** node into the **Drag query fields here** box on the form.
13. Select **Drop Down List Box**.
14. Drag the **Criteria** and **Set Size** nodes to the same area on the form.
15. Click on the box labelled **Drag data fields here**.
16. From the **Control Tool** box, go to the **Containers** section and choose **Repeating Table**.
17. Drill down in the **Data Fields** node and select **CustomerList**.
18. Click on **Next**.

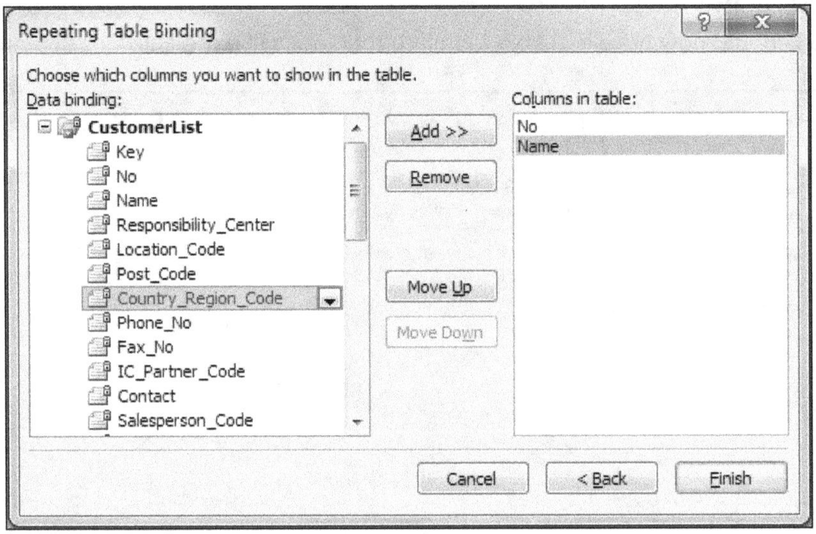

19. Add the **No.** and **Name** fields.
20. Click on **Finish**.
21. Your completed InfoPath form should look like the following screenshot:

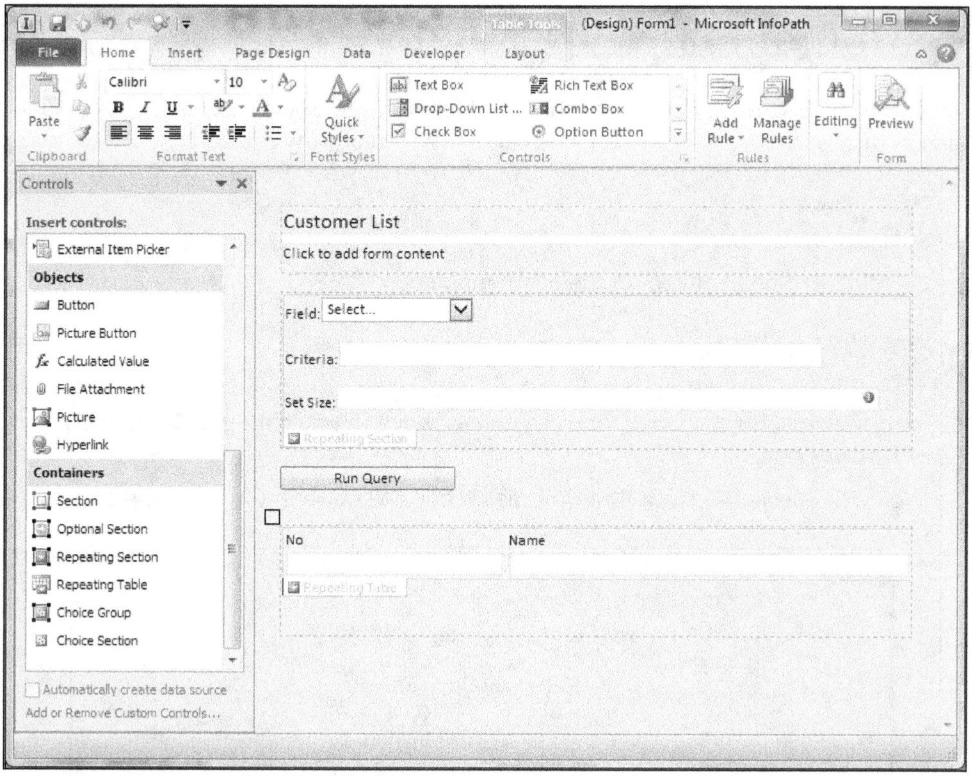

How it works...

To view the form, click on **Preview** in the InfoPath toolbar. Just like NAV, you can select your filter fields, but you must select **Run Query** in order to retrieve the data. The data will be presented in a list format at the bottom of the page.

There's more...

The most common use of InfoPath forms is to add them to a forms library in SharePoint. Although this example is used only for viewing data, you can also create forms to enter and modify data in NAV.

See also

- The *Consuming web services* recipe in *Chapter 10, Integration*

Creating charts with Visio

Visio is another Microsoft Office Suite product which helps to present data in a graphical manner. In this recipe, we will create PivotDiagram based on NAV data.

Getting ready

Microsoft Visio must be installed on the client machine.

How to do it...

1. Start Microsoft Office Visio and create a new file by navigating to **Business** | **PivotDiagram**.
2. You will receive the **Data Selector** dialog box as shown in the following screenshot:

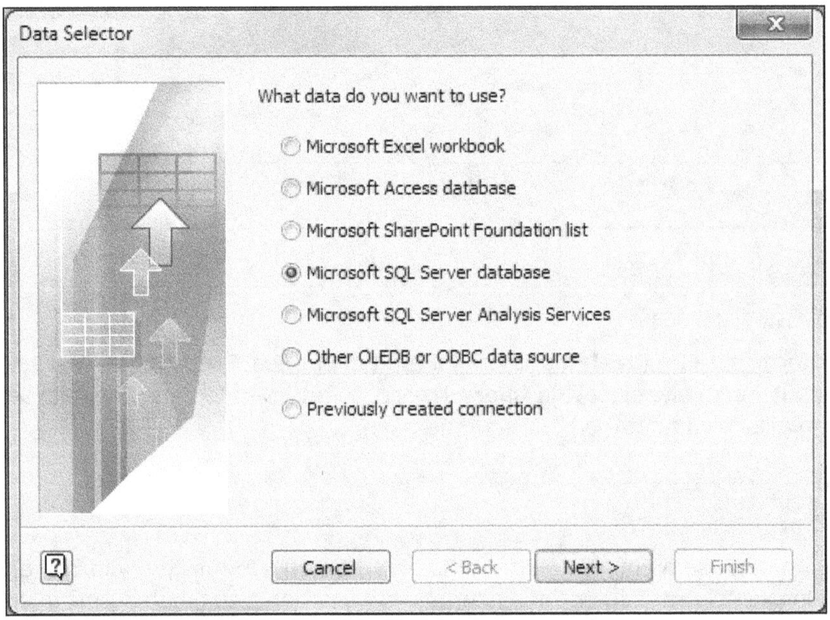

3. Select the option **Microsoft SQL Server database** and click on **Next**.
4. Provide the server name and login credentials, and then click on **Next**.
5. Select NAV database and the `Item Ledger Entry` table, and then click on **Finish**.
6. From the **Select Data Connection** dialog box, click on **Next** to choose the table fields.

7. To choose a column, click on **Select Columns** and select the **Item No., Location Code,** and **Quantity** fields, then click on **Finish**:

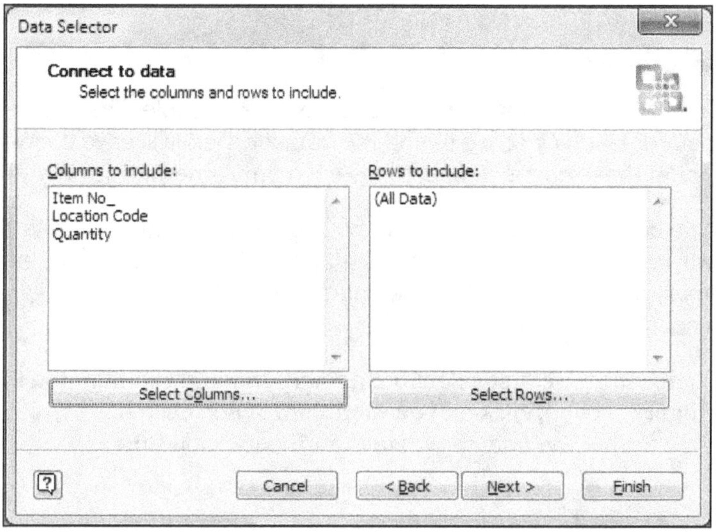

8. Visio will import data and add three shapes to page with the **PivotDiagram** option window:

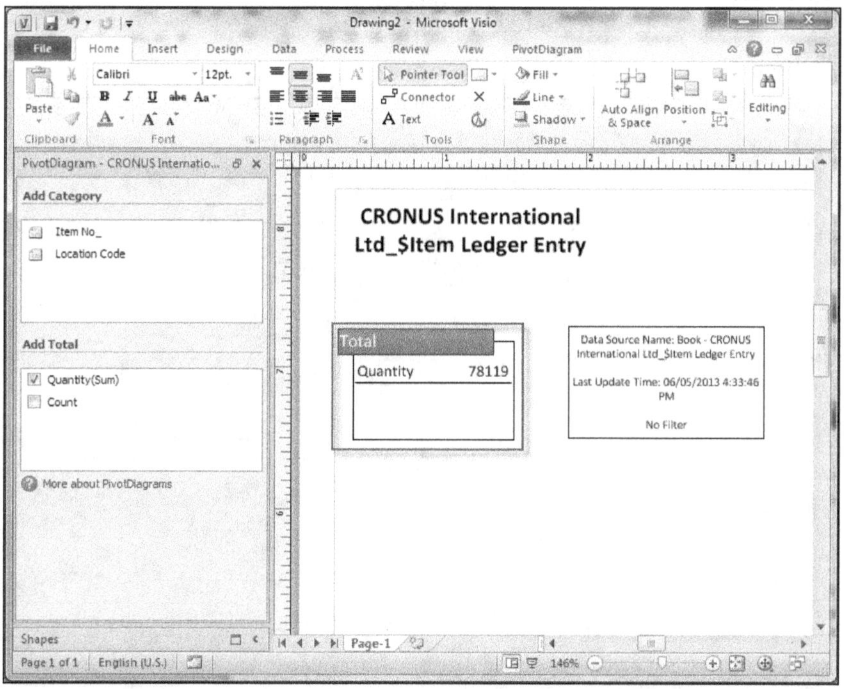

9. Select a primary shape and from the **Add Category** area, select **Location code**.
10. Select the **Blue** location and from the **Add Category** area, select **Item No**.

How it works...

Creating charts in Visio is very easy and similar to Excel PivotTable. First we create a connection with our dataset. Once we define the dataset, Visio will save connection information and offer these connection settings each time a new file is created.

After setting up the connection, it's time to select the specific data column to analyze. Once we finish, Visio will generate a page with three shapes, a legend about the data source, a title box, and the primary shape that imports the dataset. This Primary shape aggregates all the data in the data source.

To see the data by location, we first select the primary shape. Then from the **PivotDiagram** option's **Add Category** section, click on **Location Code**. Each child box corresponds to a location. To analyze further, we add item details for the location **Blue**.

There's more...

We may want to refer to these Visio diagrams again in future; we can refresh the data to reflect the changes in the underlying data sources. In the ribbon from the **PivotDiagram** tab, click on the **Refresh** button, as shown in the following screenshot. The data only updates in one direction. From the SQL data source to diagram, any change in the Visio diagram does not affect data source.

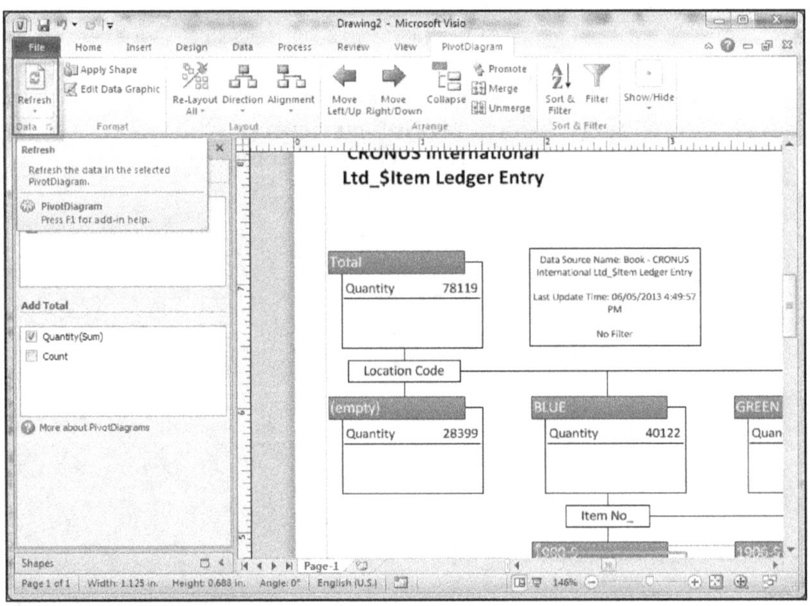

We can even add themes to our diagram. To find out more about Visio, visit the following URL:

`http://office.microsoft.com/en-in/visio-help/basic-tasks-in-visio-HA102749197.aspx`

See also

- *Showing data in Excel using PowerPivot*

9
OS Interaction

In this chapter, we will cover:

- Using HYPERLINK to open external files
- Working with environmental variables
- Using SHELL to run external applications
- Browsing for a file
- Browsing for a folder
- Checking file and folder access permissions
- Querying the registry
- Zipping folders and files within NAV

Introduction

When it comes to the operating system, we don't need to interact with device drivers or create multidimensional graphics for users; most of the time we just need to search the filesystem to access files or folders.

Windows provides multiple ways to interact with it. In this chapter, we will be using those functions to not only read the filesystem but also to check the user's environment, query the registry, or check for specific administrator permissions. These can all be performed within NAV, although many require a little outside help from a built-in or a custom automation control.

Using HYPERLINK to open external files

To open files externally, we use a hyperlink in most of the application or programming languages because it opens a file with the appropriate application. Let's see how we can use a hyperlink in NAV.

How to do it...

1. Create a new codeunit from **Object Designer**.
2. Then add the following global variables:

Name	Type
Selection	Integer

3. Write the following code in the `OnRun` trigger of the codeunit:

```
Selection := STRMENU('Image,Website');
IF Selection = 1 THEN
 HYPERLINK('C:\Users\Public\Pictures\SamplePictures\Penguins.jpg')
ELSE
 HYPERLINK('HTTP://www.mibuso.com');
```

4. It's time to save and close the codeunit.

How it works...

On execution of the codeunit, the system presents a simple selection menu where we need to choose between an image and a website. For both the options, we have provided the file location as a parameter to the `HYPERLINK` function. `HYPERLINK` visits the file location and loads that pointer using the default program on the current machine.

If we choose **Image**, the penguins' image that ships with Microsoft Windows 7 will load in the default program we have set to open pictures in our windows, usually **Windows Photo Viewer**.

If we choose **Website**, the Mibuso website will open in our default Internet browser, typically Internet Explorer.

There's more...

For Microsoft NAV 2013, we need to use HYPERLINK with shared drives. This is because the HYPERLINK command is running on the NAV service tier, not on the local computer or client. This example is for the system having a service tier and an RTC client on the same machine (thus the link to a file on the C:), but changing the parameter to a shared file on the network should work fine.

See also

- *Using SHELL to run external applications*
- *Browsing for a file*
- *Checking file and folder access permissions*

Working with environmental variables

The older version of Microsoft Dynamics NAV (version before 2013) has a built-in function called ENVIRON that allows us to collect OS environmental information; unfortunately, it is not compatible with the RoleTailored client. In this recipe, we will build a simple C# class that will help us to achieve the output given by the ENVIRON function.

How to do it...

1. To start, create a new Class Library project in Visual Studio.
2. In the newly created class, create a new file with the following code:

```
using System;
using System.Collections.Generic;
using System.Linq;
using System.Text;
using System.Management;
using System.Runtime.InteropServices;

namespace RemoteSystemInfo
{
    [ClassInterface(ClassInterfaceType.AutoDual)]
    [ProgId("RemoteSystemInfo")]
    [ComVisible(true)]
    public class RemoteSystemInfo
    {
        public string GetSysInfo(string machine, string variable)
        {
```

```
            ManagementObjectSearcher query = null;
            ManagementObjectCollection queryCollection = null;

            ConnectionOptions opt = new ConnectionOptions();
            opt.Impersonation = ImpersonationLevel.Impersonate;
            opt.EnablePrivileges = true;

            try
            {
                ManagementPath p = new ManagementPath(@"\\" +
                  machine + @"\root\cimv2");
                ManagementScope msc = new ManagementScope(p, opt);
                SelectQuery q = new SelectQuery("Win32_
                  Environment");
                query = new ManagementObjectSearcher(msc, q,
                  null);
                queryCollection = query.Get();

                foreach (ManagementBaseObject envVar in
                  queryCollection)
                {
                    if (envVar["Name"].ToString() == variable)
                    {
                        return envVar["VariableValue"].ToString();
                    }
                }
            }
            catch (ManagementException e)
            {
                throw new ManagementException("Management
                  Exception: " + e.Message);
            }
            catch (System.UnauthorizedAccessException e)
            {
                throw new ManagementException("Access Exception: "
                  + e.Message);
            }
            return "";
        }
    }
}
```

3. Set the properties of the program according to the *Writing your own automation using C#* recipe from *Chapter 10, Integration*.

4. Save, compile, and close the project.
5. Now in NAV, create a new codeunit from **Object Designer**.
6. Then add the following global variables:

Name	Type	Subtype	Length
RemoteSystemInfo	Automation	'RemoteSystemInfo'. RemoteSystemInfo	
Machine	Text		30
EnvVarName	Text		30

7. Add the following code to the `OnRun` trigger:

```
Machine := 'Your Machine NAME';
EnvVarName := 'TEMP';

CREATE(RemoteSystemInfo, FALSE, TRUE);
MESSAGE('%1', RemoteSystemInfo.GetSysInfo(Machine, EnvVarName));
```

8. Finally, save and close the codeunit.

How it works...

In the first part of the recipe, we have created a C# class to create an environmental function for NAV 2013. The second part is to use that function in the NAV C/AL code.

The NAV `CREATE` function takes three parameters. The first parameter is the variable of which we want to create an instance. The second parameter will instruct the system to create a new instance of the variable or using already created one, and its default value is `FALSE`; if we set it to `TRUE`, the system will create a new instance on every execution. The third and final parameter of the `CREATE` function tells the system to create the instance of the automation on the client (`TRUE`) and not the server (`FALSE`). As the code executes on the client machine, it can query the environment variables and easily return the correct result; just pass the appropriate values to the `GetSysInfo` function. In Windows 7, in order to see all of the options available to the `ENVIRON` command, simply right-click on **My Computer** and go to **Properties**:

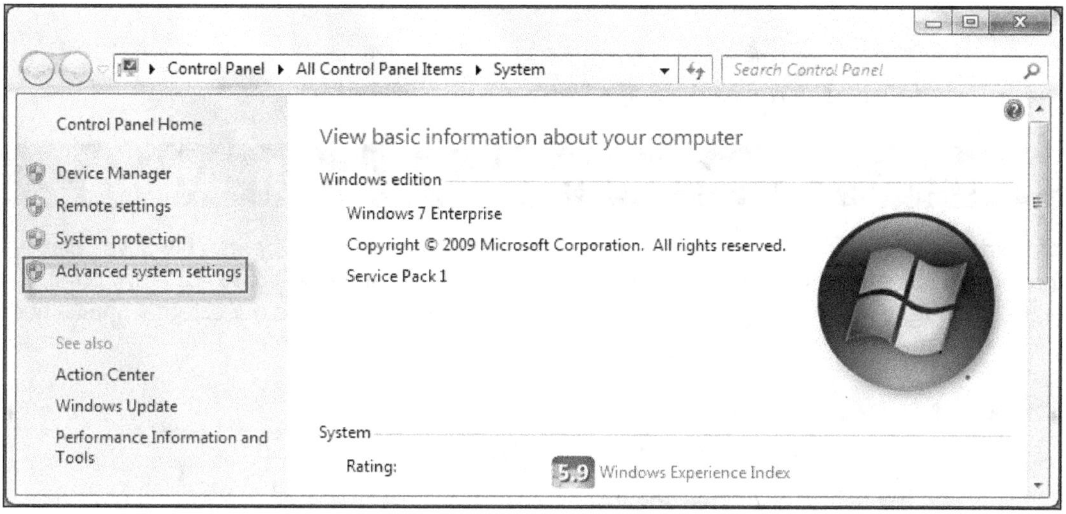

Click on **Advanced system settings**, then the **Advanced** tab, and finally on the **Environment Variables** button. You will find them in the **System variables** section of the window, as shown in the following screenshot:

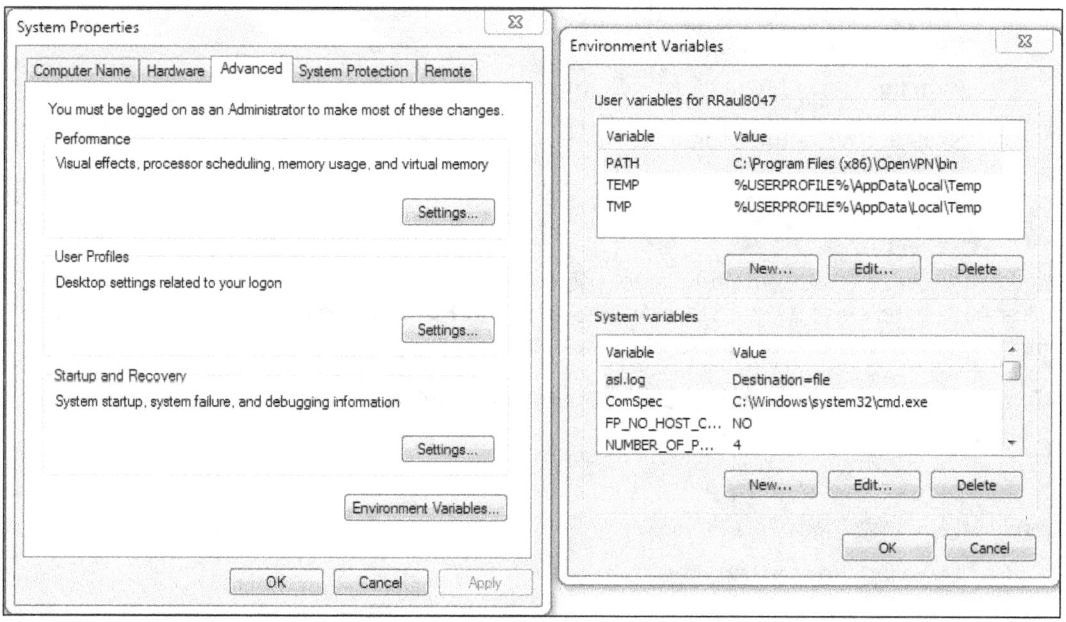

See also

- *Using SHELL to run external applications*

Using SHELL to run external applications

Opening an external program from NAV will not be a day-to-day activity for any NAV developer; however, this recipe can still be handy for a client with a special request to execute any other application from NAV. In the following recipe, we have taken Notepad as our external application.

How to do it...

1. Create a new codeunit from **Object Designer**.
2. Add the following global variables:

Name	Type	SubType
`WshShell`	`Automation`	`'Windows Script Host Object Model'.WshShell`

3. Write the following code in the `OnRun` trigger of the codeunit:

```
CREATE(WshShell,FALSE,TRUE);
WshShell.Run('C:\Windows\notepad.exe');
```

4. Save and close the codeunit.

How it works...

As the standard `SHELL` command is not compatible with NAV `RoleTailored client`, we are using the class `WshShell` of **Windows Script Host Object Model library**. It provides multiple commands that are close to the standard shell command.

After creating an instance of our automation on the client machine, we have used the `run` command to execute our `Notepad.exe` file.

See also

- *Querying the registry*

Browsing for a file

In the first recipe of this chapter, we saw how to use `HYPERLINK` to open an external file in an appropriate application; in this recipe, we will see how to use an NAV out of the box codeunit to select a file using a dialog box.

How to do it...

1. First create a new codeunit from **Object Designer** and follow the steps.
2. Then add the following global variables:

Name	Type	Subtype	Length
FileMgt	Codeunit	File Management	
SelectedFile	Text		255

3. Next, write the following code in the `OnRun` trigger of the codeunit:

```
SelectedFile := FileMgt.OpenFileDialog('NAV File Browser','*.
txt','');
MESSAGE('You selected %1', SelectedFile);
```

4. Finally, save and close the codeunit.

How it works...

To carry out file handling activities, NAV provides a codeunit `419` (`File Management`). It uses `.NET` interoperability, which allows using the function of the `.NET` library. The `OpenFileDialog` function of this codeunit allows us to open a simple dialog box in Open mode. This function takes three parameters.

The first is the title of the dialog box or window. Next is the default filename to look for. The third parameter is the filter to show specific type of files:

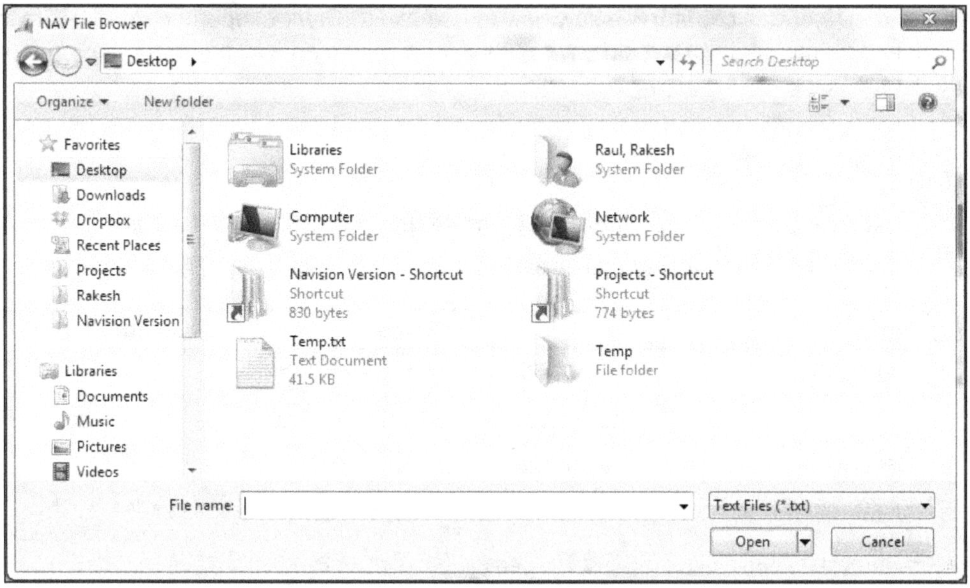

If we want to open a dialog box with a custom file type, we will have to enter a filter. A sample filter is provided as follows:

```
Text Files (*.txt)|*.txt|All Files (*.*)|*.*
```

There's more...

In the previous recipe, we saw how to use codeunit `419` to choose a file; the same codeunit contains another function that will help to save the file. The syntax for saving the file will be as follows:

```
FileMgt.SaveFileDialog('NAV File Browser',FileName,'');
```

See also

- *Using HYPERLINK to open external files*
- *Checking file and folder access permissions*
- *Browsing for a folder*

Browsing for a folder

We have seen how to browse a folder using the `File Management` codeunit. Unfortunately, we do not have any function that will help us to browse folders. To overcome this, we will use automation control that should be already installed on your Windows.

How to do it...

1. Create a new codeunit from **Object Designer**.
2. Add the following global variables:

Name	Type	Subtype	Length
MSShell	Automation	'Microsoft Shell Controls And Automation'.Shell	
Folder	Automation	'Microsoft Shell Controls And Automation'.Folder3	
FilesInFolder	Automation	'Microsoft Shell Controls And Automation'.FolderItems3	
CurrentFile	Automation	'Microsoft Shell Controls And Automation'.FolderItem2	
SelectedFolder	Text		1024

3. Write the following code in the `OnRun` trigger of the codeunit:

```
CREATE(MSShell, FALSE, TRUE);
Folder := MSShell.BrowseForFolder(0, 'NAV Folder Browser', 0);
FilesInFolder := Folder.Items();
CurrentFile := FilesInFolder.Item();
SelectedFolder := FORMAT(CurrentFile.Path);

MESSAGE('Selected Folder: %1\Contains %2 files',
SelectedFolder, FilesInFolder.Count());
```

4. Finally, save and close the codeunit.

How it works...

This recipe is based on Microsoft shell control and automation package.

> For a list of the objects found in this package, you can search MSDN or go to
> `http://msdn.microsoft.com/en-us/library/bb776890%28VS.85%29.aspx`

The main purpose of code is to get the folder name and address; nevertheless, let's go through the code and see what we are doing. First, we create an instance of our `MSShell` variable. The function `BrowseForFolder` of `MSShell` is used to launch the dialog box:

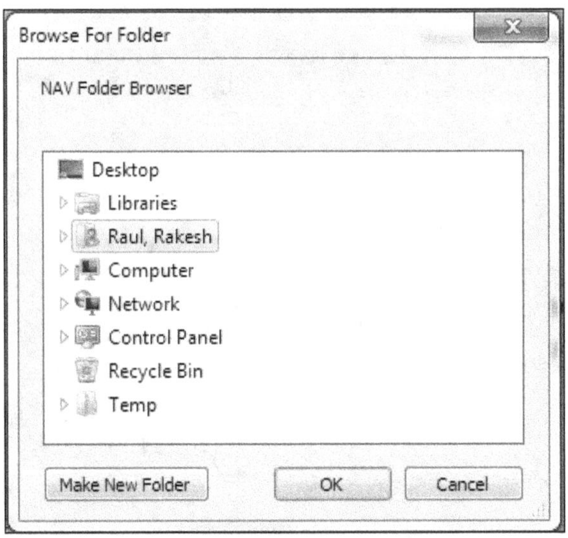

As this function returns only a folder object, we have to take it a step further. We retrieve a list of the files contained in that folder and stored in the `FilesInFolder` variable. Then we can access the first item in this list. This file has a path, and we can store that as our selected folder.

There's more...

There is another way to get the folder/directory name. In the codeunit `419 (File Management)`, you will find the function `GetDirectoryName`. This function takes one parameter, that is, `FileName`. So, to get the folder name, we have to first use the *Browsing for a file* recipe with this function. The following recipe is demonstrating the complete code:

1. First create a new codeunit from **Object Designer** and follow the steps.
2. Then add the following global variables:

Name	Type	Subtype	Length
FileMgt	Codeunit	File Management	
SelectedFile	Text		255

3. Now, write the following code in the `OnRun` trigger of the codeunit:

```
SelectedFile := FileMgt.OpenFileDialog('NAV File Browser','*.
txt','');
DirectoryName:=FileMgt.GetDirectoryName(SelectedFile);
MESSAGE('You selected %1', DirectoryName);
```

4. Finally, save and close the codeunit.

See also

- *Browsing for a file*
- *Checking file and folder access permissions*

Checking file and folder access permissions

In every organization, we have multiple departments and sections; every department and section has their own role and permission matrix to access the filesystem. If we are accessing files and folders that are under access control it is very important to check access rights to our file which will be accessed by the system. We can carry out this activity manually and set the rule. Still, let's take a look at this recipe to check the access permission by code.

How to do it...

1. Create a new `Class Library` project in Visual Studio and follow the steps.
2. Create a new file with the following code:

```
using System;
using System.Collections.Generic;
using System.Linq;
using System.Text;
using System.Security.Permissions;
using System.Runtime.InteropServices;

namespace FolderAccess
{
    [ClassInterface(ClassInterfaceType.AutoDual)]
    [ProgId("FolderAccess")]
    [ComVisible(true)]
    public class FolderAccess
    {
        public bool TestFolderAccess(string folder, string access)
        {
            System.Security.Permissions.FileIOPermissionAccess
              accessLevel;
            switch (access.ToUpper())
            {
                case "NOACCESS": accessLevel =
                  FileIOPermissionAccess.NoAccess; break;
                case "READ": accessLevel =
                  FileIOPermissionAccess.Read; break;
                case "WRITE": accessLevel =
                  FileIOPermissionAccess.Write; break;
                case "APPEND": accessLevel =
                  FileIOPermissionAccess.Append; break;
                case "PATHDISCOVERY": accessLevel =
                  FileIOPermissionAccess.PathDiscovery; break;
                case "ALLACCESS": accessLevel =
                  FileIOPermissionAccess.AllAccess; break;
                default: return false;
            }

            FileIOPermission permission = new
              FileIOPermission(accessLevel, folder);
            try
            {
                permission.Demand();
```

```
                }
                catch (Exception ex)
                {
                    return false;
                }

                return true;
            }
        }
    }
```

3. Set the properties of the program according to the *Writing your own automation using C#* recipe from *Chapter 10, Integration*.
4. Save, compile, and close the project.
5. Create a new codeunit from **Object Designer**.
6. Add the following global variable:

Name	Type	Subtype
`FolderAccess`	`Automation`	`'FolderAccess'.FolderAccess`

7. Add the following code to the `OnRun` trigger:

```
CREATE(FolderAccess, FALSE, TRUE);
MESSAGE('Access: %1',
FolderAccess.TestFolderAccess('C:\', 'WRITE'));
```

8. Save and close the codeunit.

How it works...

First, we have created a C# class to test the folder access. Our function `TestFolderAccess` takes in two parameters: the path or the folder to check, and the type of permission to check for. To get the access level, we used the `FileIOPermission` class. If we don't have access permission, the function will throw the exception; in this case, we return `FALSE`, else in all other cases, we return `TRUE`.

See also

- *Browsing for a file*
- *Browsing for a folder*

Querying the registry

You must be thinking, "Why do we need to query the registry with NAV?" Just take this recipe as an option.

How to do it...

1. Let's create a new `Class Library` project in Visual Studio.
2. Create a new file in the class with the following code:

```
using System;
using System.Collections.Generic;
using System.Linq;
using System.Text;
using System.Runtime.InteropServices;
using Microsoft.Win32;

namespace RegistryQuery
{
     [ClassInterface(ClassInterfaceType.AutoDual)]
     [ProgId("RegistryQuery")]
     [ComVisible(true)]
     public class RegistryQuery
     {
          public string GetKeyValue(string key, string name)
          {
               RegistryKey regKey = Registry.Users.OpenSubKey(key);
               if (regKey == null)
               {
                    return "Key not found!";
               }
               else
               {
                    object value = regKey.GetValue(name);
                    if (value != null)
                    {
                         return value.ToString();
                    }
                    else
                    {
                         return "Name not found!";
                    }
               }
          }
     }
}
```

3. Set the properties of the program according to the *Writing your own automation using C#* recipe from *Chapter 10, Integration*.
4. Save, compile, and close the project.
5. Now create a new codeunit from **Object Designer**.
6. Add the following global variable:

Name	Type	Subtype
FolderAccess	Automation	'RegistryQuery'. RegistryQuery

7. Add the following code to the `OnRun` trigger:

```
CREATE(RegistryQuery, FALSE, TRUE);
MESSAGE('%1', RegistryQuery.GetKeyValue('.DEFAULT\Environment',
'TEMP'));
```

8. Finally, save and close the codeunit.

How it works...

We used the `HKEY_USERS` root of the registry in this recipe. By using the function `Registry.Users.OpenSubKey`, we accessed the subkey. If the key is not found, or is `null`, we return a suitable message. To access the other root folders, we have to pass an additional parameter.

Next, we try to access the names stored in the key. Again, if we are unable to find the key that is equal to the second parameter of our function, we return `null`. If we do find it, we return its value, as shown in the following screenshot:

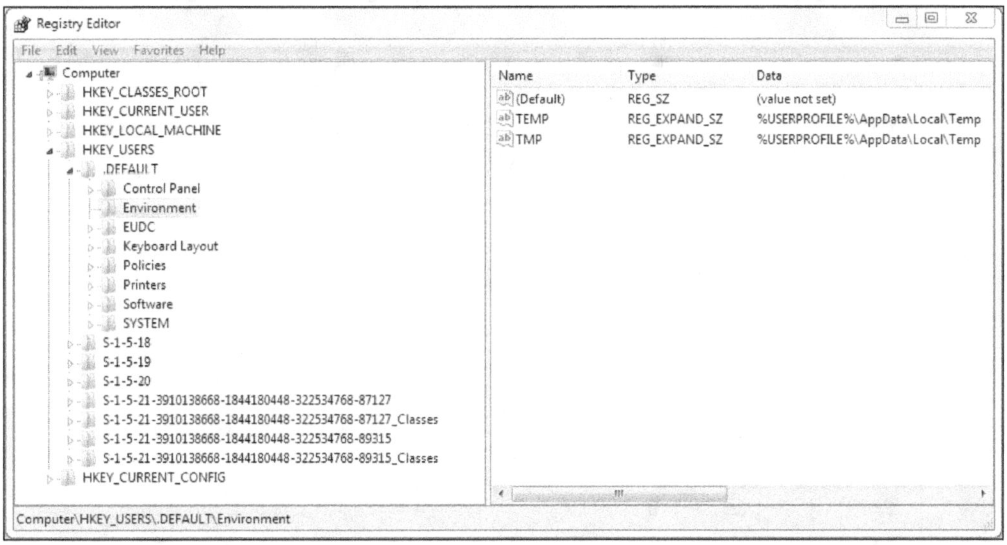

There's more...

To perform other actions on the registry, we can use the `CreateSubKey` and `DeleteSubKey` functions, but we need to be very careful while playing with the registry. One mistake in modification of the registry can cause an entire system crash.

> For more information about the registry, you can view the following MSDN article:
> `http://msdn.microsoft.com/en-us/library/h5e7chcf.aspx`

See also

- *Working with environment variables*

Zipping folders and files within NAV

Zipping files or folders by code is not a common task; nevertheless, let's see how we can do it!

How to do it...

1. Create a new codeunit from **Object Designer**.
2. Add the following global variables:

Name	Type	Subtype
`ZipFile`	`File`	
`MSShell`	`Automation`	`'Microsoft Shell Controls And Automation'.Shell`
`ZipFolder`	`Automation`	`'Microsoft Shell Controls And Automation'.Folder`

3. Write the following code in the `OnRun` trigger of the codeunit:

```
ZipFile.CREATE('C:\Users\Public\Pictures\Sample Pictures\Pictures.
zip');

CREATE(MSShell, FALSE, TRUE);

ZipFolder := MSShell.NameSpace('C:\Users\Public\Pictures\Sample
Pictures\Pictures.zip');

ZipFolder.CopyHere('C:\Users\Public\Pictures\Sample Pictures\
Desert.jpg');
```

4. Finally, save and close the codeunit.

How it works...

`ZipFile` is only a folder with compressed contents, so creating this file or folder is the same as creating a text file using the `CREATE` function. We assigned the namespace of the `MSShell` object to `Zipfile`, which means that the action done on the `MSShell` variable will be actually done on our file.

After creating `ZipFolder`, we will simply move our file into it by using the `CopyHere` function. The parameter of this function is the file that we want to copy in the `ZipFolder`.

10

Integration

In this chapter, we will cover the following recipes:

- Sharing information through XMLports
- Writing to and reading from a file using the C/AL code
- Creating web services
- Consuming web services
- Sending data through FTP
- Printing a report in a PDF, Excel, and Word format
- Writing your own automation using C#
- Using ADO to access outside data

Introduction

Business depends on multiple applications. Until now, all these applications were hosted in-house, on the company's own server, which integrated applications by exchanging a flat file or directly accessing the database. In the last few years, technologies have taken a big leap and introduced numerous ways of managing business applications; cloud computing is one of them.

Microsoft has made sure that Dynamics NAV will continue to meet its customer's integration needs for this new type of infrastructure. In this chapter, we will be taking a look at the different ways of integration with Microsoft Dynamics NAV.

This chapter will show you how to share information using XML or flat text files, creating and consuming web services, and loading files on an FTP server. These recipes will serve as a foundation for all your future integration efforts.

Sharing information through XMLports

Exporting or importing data is a common requirement for financial or ERP applications. There are a number of formats in which data can be asked, but when there is no manual intervention with data, or that data has to be used by two different applications, then it is mostly asked in a delimited, fixed length or XML format. **Extensible Markup Language** (**XML**) is a format for creating structured computer documents. XMLports are object types in Microsoft Dynamics NAV that help to create these types of documents.

How to do it...

1. Let's get started by creating a new XMLport from **Object Designer**.
2. Add the following variables to XMLport designer:

Node Name	Node Type	Source Type	Data Source
Root	Element	Text	<Root>
Customer	Element	Table	<Customer>(Customer)
No	Element	Field	<Customer>::No.
Name	Element	Field	<Customer>::Name

3. XMLport designer should look similar to the following screenshot:

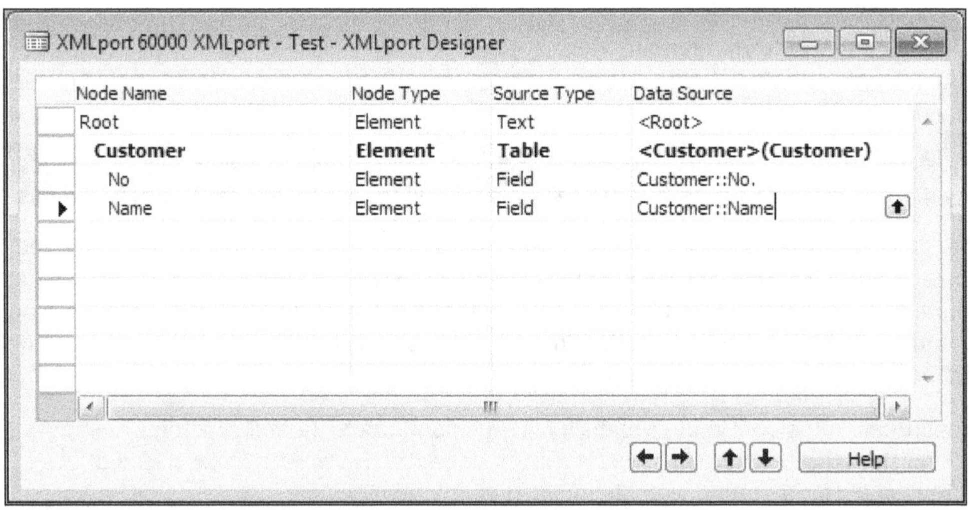

4. Now save and close the XMLport.

How it works...

XMLports are similar to discontinued NAV integration object type dataports. Developing XMLports is a bit different from developing dataports. The following screenshot displays a portion of an output file, which will help in understanding the XMLport structure:


```
  <?xml version="1.0" encoding="UTF-16"?>
- <Root>
  - <Customer>
      <No>01121212</No>
      <Name>Spotsmeyer's Furnishings</Name>
    </Customer>
  - <Customer>
      <No>01445544</No>
      <Name>Progressive Home Furnishings</Name>
    </Customer>
  - <Customer>
      <No>01454545</No>
      <Name>New Concepts Furniture</Name>
    </Customer>
  - <Customer>
      <No>01905893</No>
      <Name>Candoxy Canada Inc.</Name>
    </Customer>
  - <Customer>
      <No>01905899</No>
      <Name>Elkhorn Airport</Name>
    </Customer>
  - <Customer>
      <No>01905902</No>
      <Name>London Candoxy Storage Campus</Name>
    </Customer>
```


XML is a tree-like structure made up of nodes. Every file has to start with a parent/root node. Under the root node, we define a table from which we want to read the data, and finally we define fields we want to use from that table. In this recipe, we have used a customer table.

In our output file, we can see that each value is surrounded by a node with the name of the field, and a set of fields is surrounded by a parent node, which is just our table named `Customer`.

There's more...

XMLports are not only made to export/import XML files, but we can even work with text files of a fixed length and delimited formats. To achieve this, we have to change the `Format` property of XMLport to `Fixed Text` or `Variable Text`. Along with this, we have the `FieldStartDelimiter`, `FieldEndDelimiter`, and `FieldSeparator` properties that help to read multiple file formats.

Exporting Sales Invoices in the CSV format

In the previous recipe, we took the first step by creating a very basic XMLport to export data from a single table. Now let's take another step. Here we will export the sales data, but this time it will be in the **CSV** (**Comma Separated Values**) format.

1. Let's get started by creating a new XMLport from **Object Designer**.
2. Go to the XMLport's properties from **View** | **Properties** (*Shift* + *F4*).
3. Set the properties mentioned in the following table:

Property	Value
Direction	Export
Format	Variable Text
FieldDelimiter	<None>
Table Separator	<NewLine>

4. Add the following variables to the XMLport designer:

Node Name	Node Type	Source Type	Data Source
Root	Element	Text	<Root>
PurchaseHeader	Element	Table	<Purchase Header>(Purchase Header)
PH_DocType	Element	Field	Purchase Header::Document Type
PH_No	Element	Field	Purchase Header::No.
PH_Vendor	Element	Field	Purchase Header::Buy-from Vendor No.
PH_OrderDate	Element	Field	Purchase Header::Order Date
PH_PostingDate	Element	Field	Purchase Header::Posting Date
PurchaseLine	Element	Table	<Purchase Line>(Purchase Line)
PL_DocType	Element	Field	Purchase Line::Document Type
PL_DocNo	Element	Field	Purchase Line::Document No.
PL_LineNo	Element	Field	Purchase Line::Line No.
PL_Type	Element	Field	Purchase Line::Type
PL_No	Element	Field	Purchase Line::No.
PL_UOM	Element	Field	Purchase Line::Unit of Measure
PL_Quantity	Element	Field	Purchase Line::Quantity
PL_LineAmt	Element	Field	Purchase Line::Line Amount

5. After indenting all nodes, XMLport designer should look similar to the following screenshot:

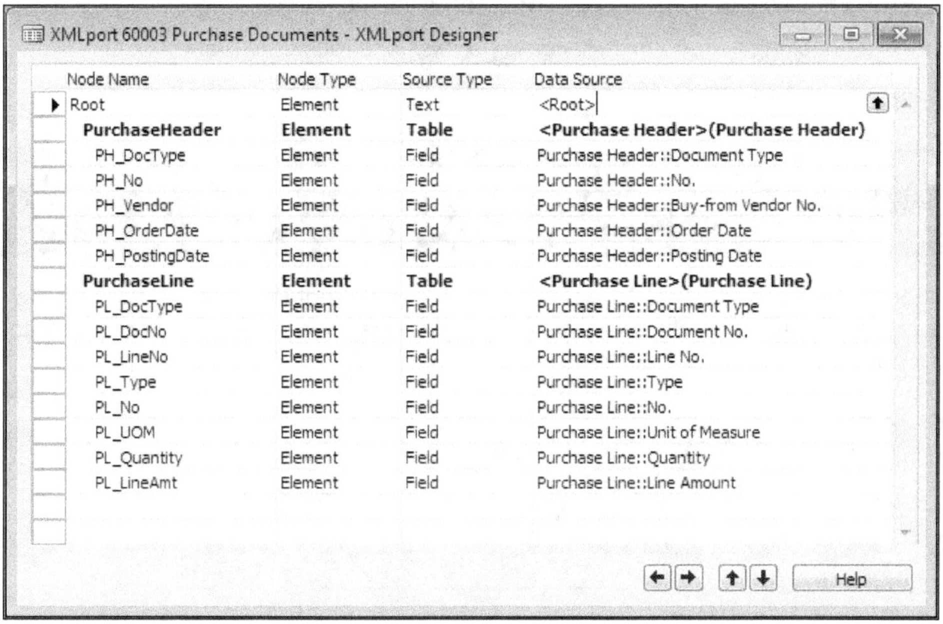

6. Now set the following property for the `PurchaseHeader` node:

Property	Value
SourceTableView	SORTING(Document Type,No.)

7. Set the following property for the `PurchaseLine` node:

Property	Value
SourceTableView	SORTING(Document Type,Document No.,Line No.)

8. Now save and close XMLport.

On execution of the preceding recipe, the system will show a dialog box to save the output file.

While setting a value of the XMLport's `TableSeparator` property, we keep one space before `<NewLine>`. This change will not help in exporting data, but if we use the same dataport to import the file, the system needs to differentiate between a record and a table separator, and this time our setting will help.

See also

- The *Browsing for a file* recipe in *Chapter 9, OS Interaction*
- The *Checking file and folder access permissions* recipe in *Chapter 9, OS Interaction*
- *Sending data through FTP*

Writing to and reading from a file using the C/AL code

Even though the XMLport takes care of the file integration requirements, sometimes we may want to perform this activity by using the C/AL code. This recipe will demonstrate how to read or write from a file using the C/AL code.

How to do it...

1. Let's start by creating a new codeunit from **Object Designer**.
2. Add the following global variables:

Name	Type	Length
StremOut	OutStrem	
FileOut	File	
StremIn	InStrem	
FileIn	File	
TextLine	Text	250

3. Add the following code in the `OnRun` trigger:

```
IF NOT FileOut.CREATE('D:\NAVFile.txt') THEN
  IF NOT FileOut.OPEN('D:\NAVFile.txt') THEN
    ERROR('Unable to write to file!');
FileOut.CREATEOUTSTREAM(StreamOut);
StreamOut.WRITETEXT('Line 1');
StreamOut.WRITETEXT();
StreamOut.WRITETEXT('Line 2');
StreamOut.WRITETEXT();
FileOut.CLOSE;
IF NOT FileIn.OPEN('D:\NAVFile.txt') THEN
  ERROR('Unable to read file!');
```

```
FileIn.CREATEINSTREAM(StreamIn);
WHILE NOT StreamIn.EOS DO BEGIN
  StreamIn.READTEXT(TextLine);
  MESSAGE('%1', TextLine);
END;
FileIn.CLOSE;
```

4. Save and close the codeunit.

How it works...

In this recipe, we are first creating a new file using the `CREATE` function. If the system fails to create that file, we consider that there may be a file present with the same name in that location. Then we try to open that file; if we fail in this attempt as well, we generate an error message as we do not have any file to work with.

As we are writing data to a file, we have to use `OutStream`. Actually, the activity of sending data to a file is done by the stream object's `WRITETEXT` function. This function does not send a carriage return; that's why we are using the `WRITETEXT` function with a blank parameter. After we finish writing to the file, we close the file.

The process of reading from a file is very similar to writing. Instead of using an `OutStream` variable, we use an `InStream` variable. It has the **EOS** (**End of Stream**) function. The `EOS` function returns the `True` value when we reach the end of the file. Until we reach the end of the file, we can retrieve data using the `READTEXT` function. The parameter of the `READTEXT` function is of the `text` datatype, which stores the line of text. In our code, we use the `MESSAGE` function to display the line read by our code.

See also

- *Sharing information through XMLports*

Creating web services

The web services allow sharing of an application's functionalities to an external system and its users. It also takes proper authorization before sharing any information. In Microsoft Dynamics NAV, creating a web service is an easy task; we can expose pages, codeunits, and queries as web services.

How to do it...

1. Start Microsoft Dynamics NAV RoleTailored `client` and follow the steps.
2. Either search for `Web Service` in NAV's search, or from the `Department` menu, visit the following path:
3. `CRONUS International Ltd.` | `Departments` | `Administration` | `IT Administration` | `General` | `Web Services.`
4. Create a new web service using the following record:

Object Type	Object ID	Service Name	Published
Page	22	Customer List	Yes

5. Close the page.

How it works...

We can publish two types of web services, `SOAP` and `OData`. The `SOAP` web service provides flexibility for building an operation-centric service. We can publish a page or a codeunit as SOAP services. The `OData` web service is designed for querying tabular data. We can publish a page or a query object as OData services. The SOAP services allow us to create, read, update, and delete operations using the `Page` object, whereas OData services only support the read-only operations.

Creating a web service requires us to expose a page, codeunit, or query object type, provide a service name, and check the published field. At this time, the system does not have any idea about the service type. The system chooses the service type when we execute or use it. NAV provides the configuration of web services from the Microsoft Dynamics NAV administrator console. Here we specify the ports for both the service types, and we also have an option to enable or disable the service.

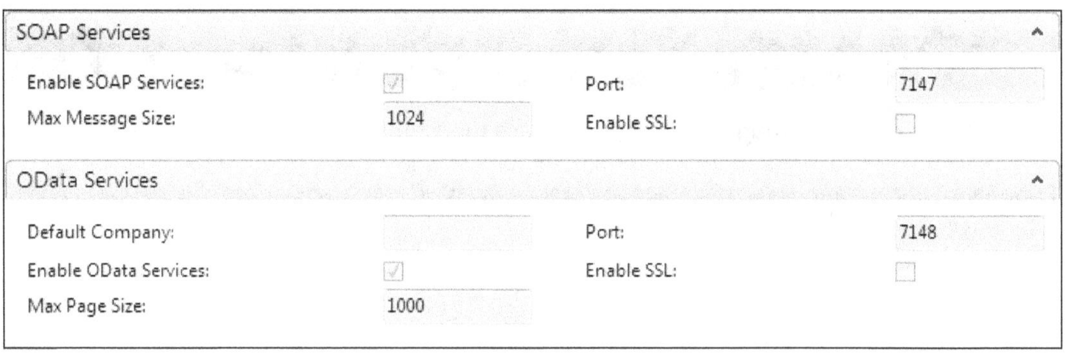

To verify the web service, start Windows Internet Explorer and provide an address in the following format:

```
http://<Server>:<WebServicePort>/<ServerInstance>/WS/<CompanyName>/
services
```

Our service type depends on the value mentioned for `WebservicePort` in the previous address format.

See also

- The *Creating an InfoPath form for the NAV data* recipe in *Chapter 8, Leveraging Microsoft Office*
- *Consuming web services*

Consuming web services

Microsoft Dynamics NAV provides an easy interface to create web services, which allow us to expose the NAV data with business logic and proper authentication. Now, let's see how to use these web services.

How to do it...

1. Let's get started by creating a new codeunit from **Object Designer**.
2. Add the function name as `GetCustomer`.
3. The function should take the following parameter:

Name	DataType	Length
CustNo	Code	20

4. Add the following local variable to the function:

Name	DataType	Subtype
Customer	Record	Customer

5. The function should return a text variable of length 50.
6. Add the following code to the function:

```
IF Customer.GET(CustNo) THEN
  EXIT(Customer.Name)
ELSE
  EXIT('Not Found!');
```

7. Save and close the codeunit.
8. Search for the `Web Services` page in `RoleTailored client`.
9. In the `Web Services` page, choose `New`.
10. Create a new web service with our codeunit ID, and in the service name, enter `ConsumeWS`.
11. Finally, mark the checkbox in the `Published` column.
12. Create a new `Console Application` project in Visual Studio.
13. In **Solution Explorer**, right-click on the **Reference** node and choose **Add Service Reference**.
14. In the **Add Service Reference** window, choose the **Advance** button.
15. In the **Service Reference Settings** window, choose **Add Web Reference**. Then enter `http://localhost:7047/DynamicsNAV70/WS/Services` (this may be different depending on the web server, service name, and NAV company name) and click on the green button with an arrow.

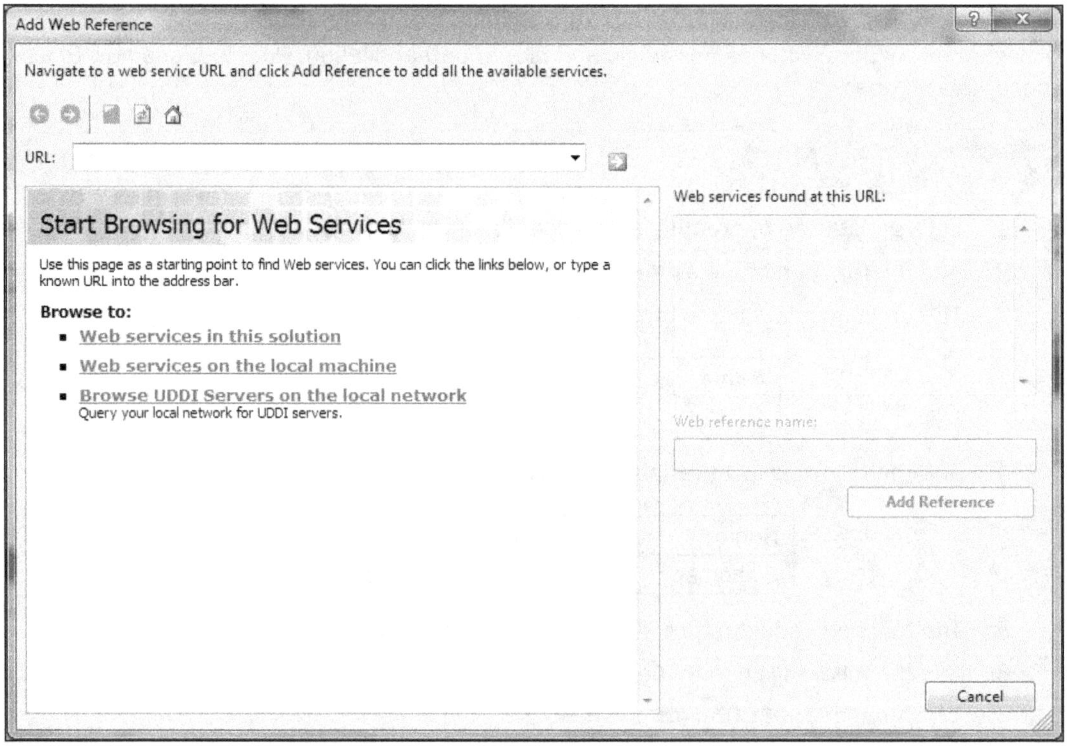

16. When the `ConsumeWS` service is displayed, choose **View Service**. Then enter `WebService` in **Web reference name:** and choose **Add Reference**.

17. Add the following code to the program:

```
using System;
using System.Collections.Generic;
using System.Linq;
using System.Text;
namespace ConsumeWebService
{
  using WebService;
  public class ConsumeWebService
  {
    public static void Main(string[] args)
    {
      ConsumeWS ws = new ConsumeWS();
      ws.UseDefaultCredentials = true;
      Console.WriteLine(ws.GetCustomer("10000"));
      Console.ReadLine();
    }
  }
}
```

18. Compile, save, and close the program.

How it works...

In the previous recipe, we had created a codeunit that returns the name of a customer if executed successfully, else it returns a text saying `Not Found`. Then we published this codeunit as a web service to make it available for external applications.

In the .NET program, we need to provide the right reference of our web service, otherwise we will not be able to build our application with the code provided in the previous recipe.

To use our web service in the .NET program, we have provided its reference. The `using WebService` line tells the program to use the functions from our web service. Then we created an instance of our service `ConsumeWS` and used the default credentials. Now we can call the functions of our page or of the codeunit. As we have created the `GetCustomer` function in our codeunit, we are using that function for finding `Customer No. 10000`.

See also

- The *Creating an InfoPath form for the NAV data* recipe in *Chapter 8, Leveraging Microsoft Office*
- *Creating web services*

Sending data through FTP

Sometimes, our client may ask us to upload a datafile on the FTP server. We can use the Windows built-in client to develop our FTP upload program.

Getting ready

Make sure we have an active FTP server and logon credentials.

How to do it...

1. Let's start by creating a new codeunit from **Object Designer**.
2. Add a function name `FTP` that takes in the following parameters:

Name	DataType	Length
UserName	Text	50
Password	Text	50
ServerName	Text	50
FileToMove	Text	250

3. Then add the following local variables to the function:

Name	Type	Length
BatchFileName	Text	250
BatchFile	File	
BatchfileStream	OutStream	
BatchFileData	Text	250

4. Now add the following code to the function:

```
BatchFileData := 'D:\Temp\navFTP.dat';
BatchFileName := 'D:\Temp\navFTP.bat';
BatchFile.CREATE(BatchFileName);
BatchFile.CREATEOUTSTREAM(BatchfileStream);
BatchfileStream.WRITETEXT('@echo off');
BatchfileStream.WRITETEXT;
BatchfileStream.WRITETEXT('echo user ' +UserName + ' >>
  ' + BatchFileData);
BatchfileStream.WRITETEXT;
BatchfileStream.WRITETEXT('echo ' +Password + ' >>
  ' + BatchFileData);
BatchfileStream.WRITETEXT;
```

```
BatchfileStream.WRITETEXT('echo bin >> ' +BatchFileData);
BatchfileStream.WRITETEXT;
BatchfileStream.WRITETEXT('echo put ' +FileToMove + ' >>
  ' + BatchFileData);
BatchfileStream.WRITETEXT;
BatchfileStream.WRITETEXT('echo quit >> ' +BatchFileData);
BatchfileStream.WRITETEXT;
BatchfileStream.WRITETEXT('FTP -n -s:' +BatchFileData +
  ' ' + ServerName);
BatchfileStream.WRITETEXT;
BatchfileStream.WRITETEXT('del ' + BatchFileData);
BatchfileStream.WRITETEXT;
BatchFile.CLOSE;
CREATE(WshShell,FALSE,TRUE);
WshShell.Run(BatchFileName);
```

5. Write the following code in the `OnRun` trigger of the codeunit:

```
FTP('YourUserName', 'YourPassword', 'YourServer', 'YourFile');
```

6. Save and close the codeunit.

How it works...

File Transfer Protocol (**FTP**) is a way of sending data from one filesystem to another. Windows provides a command-line utility to upload a file on FTP. Even though it is very basic, it works well for our integration requirement.

We have created two files: a batch file and a data file. A batch file instructs the FTP program and transfers the data file. Let's go through every line.

To enhance the security, we have added the first line, `@echo off`. It will not display any command of our program on the screen. On the next two lines, we have applied the same principle to secure our username and password. We are instructing the batch file for sending text to an actual file, hence we are adding `>>BatchFileData` at the end of all the lines. Next, we are setting the transfer type as binary and sending the file.

There's more...

For a list of available options or parameters that can be used with the FTP program, type `ftp ?` in the command prompt.

With the default settings of NAV, you may get the following error on execution of this recipe:

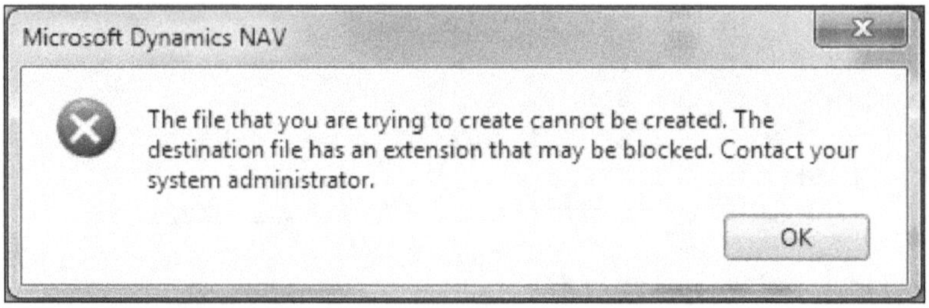

You are receiving this error because of Navision's service configuration. Open `CustomSettings.Config` from your server instance; the default path for this is `C:\Program Files\Microsoft Dynamics NAV\70\Service\Your Instance name`. You need to remove the file extension "bat" value from the default value of the key `ClientServicesProhibitedFileTypes`.

See also

- *Sharing information through XMLports*

Printing a report in a PDF, Excel, and Word format

Sharing recorded information is very important in our day-to-day activities; having the same format for the shared information is very important. If clients want to send a purchase order to a vendor, they will prefer to do so in a PDF format, or if the management wants to do some further analysis on a report's data, it will prefer Excel. Let's see how to do this.

How to do it...

1. Let's create a new codeunit from **Object Designer**.
2. Add the following global variables:

Name	Type	Subtype	Length
FileName	Text		250
Customer	Rec	Customer	

3. Add the following code in the `OnRun` trigger:

```
Customer.setrange(City,' London');
//Export to PDF
FileName := 'C:\NAVReports\CuatomerList.pdf';
```

```
REPORT.SAVEASPDF(101, FileName,Customer);
//Export to Excel
FileName := 'C:\NAVReports\CustomerList.xls';
REPORT.SAVEASPDF(101, FileName,Customer);
//Export to Word
FileName := 'C:\NAVReports\CustomerList.doc';
REPORT.SAVEASPDF(101, FileName,Customer);
```

4. Save and close the codeunit.

How it works...

Saving the report in a PDF, Excel, or Word format is a very simple activity. NAV provides a built-in function for each file type, which takes three parameters. The first parameter is a report object. The second parameter is the name and location of the file. The last parameter is an optional parameter; it is used for filtering a record set on which the report is getting generated. In our example, we have taken the report `101` (`Customer-List`) and we have applied a filter on the city `London`.

See also

- The *Browsing for a file* recipe in *Chapter 9, OS Interaction*

Writing your own automation using C#

C/AL provides almost everything to meet our client's requirements. Sometimes though, we may need to extend the scope of C/AL to take care of some complex requirements. In this recipe, we will see an example of how to develop a basic .NET application, and more importantly, how to use it within NAV.

How to do it...

1. Let's get started by creating a new `Class Library` project in Visual Studio and follow the steps.
2. Create a new file with the following code:

```
using System;
using System.Collections.Generic;
using System.Linq;
using System.Text;
using System.Runtime.InteropServices;
namespace NAVAdd
{
```

```
    [ClassInterface(ClassInterfaceType.AutoDual)]
    [ProgId("NAVAdd")]
    [ComVisible(true)]
    public class NAVAdd
    {
      public int Add(int a, int b)
      {
        return a + b;
      }
    }
  }
```

3. View the properties for the project.
4. Then on the **Application** tab, set the **Assembly** name to **NAVAdd**.
5. After that, on the **Build*** tab, set the **Register for COM interop** property to true (checked):

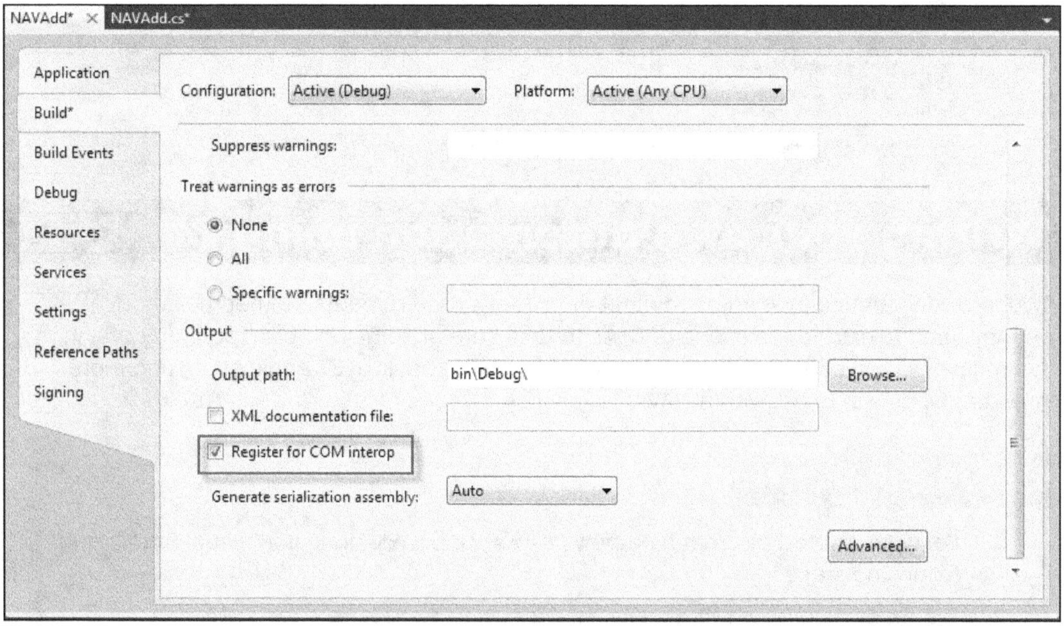

6. Save and compile your objects.
7. Create a new codeunit from **Object Designer**.

8. Add the following global variable:

Name	DataType	Subtype
NAVAdd	Automation	'NAVAdd'.NAVAdd

9. Add the following code in the `OnRun` trigger:

```
CREATE(NavAdd,FALSE,TRUE);
MESSAGE('%1', NavAdd.Add(2, 3));
```

10. Save and close the codeunit.

How it works...

In our Visual Studio program, we are setting the `ClassInterfaceType.AutoDual` value to call the `CalssInterface` attribute, which will register a program automatically. The second attribute `ProgID` is the name of our program. Finally, to instruct the system about class registration, we are using the last attribute, `COMVisible`.

Now, we set some properties of our program. To register our class as `Automation`, we need to select the `Register for COM interop` property. As soon as we compile this program, we can see that our `NAVAdd` is available in the `Automation` list.

See also

- The *Querying the registry* recipe in *Chapter 9, OS Interaction*

Using ADO to access outside data

ActiveX Data Object (**ADO**) is a set of COM objects used for accessing data sources. ADO allows developers to write programs to access data without knowing what a database structure is, or how the database is implemented. Let's see how to use ADO in C/AL programing.

How to do it...

1. Let's get started by creating a new codeunit from **Object Designer**.
2. Create a function named `CreateConnectionString`.

3. Add the following parameters to the function:

Name	DataType	Length
ServerName	Text	50
DatabaseName	Text	50
UserName	Text	50
Password	Text	50

4. Set the function's return value of type `text` with length `1024`.
5. Add the following code to the function:

```
EXIT(
  'Driver={SQL Server};' + 'Server=' + ServerName + ';'
  +'Database=' + DatabaseName + ';' + 'Uid=' + UserName
  +';' + 'Pwd=' + Password + ';');
```

6. Add the following global variables:

Name	DataType	Subtype	Length
ADOConnection	Automation	'Microsoft ActiveX Data Objects 6.0 Library'.Connection	
ADORecordSet	Automation	'Microsoft ActiveX Data Objects 6.0 Library'.Recordset	
SQLString	Text		250

7. Write the following code in the `OnRun` trigger of the codeunit:

```
CREATE(ADOConnection,FALSE,TRUE);
ADOConnection.ConnectionString :=
  CreateConnectionString('localhost', 'Book', 'Super',
  'rrsaw0201');
ADOConnection.Open;
SQLString:=  'SELECT * FROM [CRONUS International
  Ltd_$Customer] WHERE [No_] = ''10000''';
CREATE(ADORecordSet,FALSE,TRUE);
ADORecordSet:=ADOConnection.Execute(SQLString);
ADORecordSet.MoveFirst;
REPEAT
  MESSAGE(FORMAT(ADORecordSet.Fields.Item('Name').Value));
  ADORecordSet.MoveNext;
UNTIL ADORecordSet.EOF;
ADORecordSet.Close;
ADOConnection.Close;
```

8. Save and close the codeunit.

How it works...

First of all, we are setting up the connection string, which carries the server, database, and logon information. Once we open the connection, we can send our query to the database. In this recipe, we are selecting the customer information from the `Customer` table with a filter for `Customer No. 10000`.

To view the query result, we open the record set. Even though we know there will be only one record, we loop through the record set, just to understand how to play with multiple records. For looping, we use the simple `REPEAT UNTIL` loop till the end of the record set. Finally, to read data from each field, we use the `Fields.Item(FieldName)` syntax. To send the cursor to the next record, we use the `MoveNext` function.

11
Working with the SQL Server

In this chapter, we will cover the following seven recipes:

- Creating a basic SQL query
- Understanding SIFT
- Using the SQL profiler
- Displaying data from a SQL view in NAV
- Identifying Blocked and Blocking sessions from SQL
- Setting up a backup plan
- Maintaining the transaction logfiles

Introduction

NAV was introduced with a proprietary database management system. All the information was stored in a flat file, which is called as **FDB** (**Financial Database**). With new versions, Microsoft added a second option, that is, SQL Server. FDB was supported until Version 2009 R2. From NAV 2013, SQL Server is the only database option for NAV.

With the SQL Server, we get better options to maintain, secure, optimize, and analyze the data; these options make the SQL Server a very important part of the NAV system. Considering this, Microsoft added a mandatory certification for every partner on SQL Server implementation and maintenance.

In this chapter we will learn some of the basic activities, which all developers need to know while developing NAV 2013.

Creating a basic SQL query

Let's write a very simple query to retrieve data from a table.

How to do it...

1. Open **Microsoft SQL Server Management Studio** and connect to the server that holds the NAV database.
2. Click on the **New Query** option.
3. Then, select the NAV database in the database dropdown.

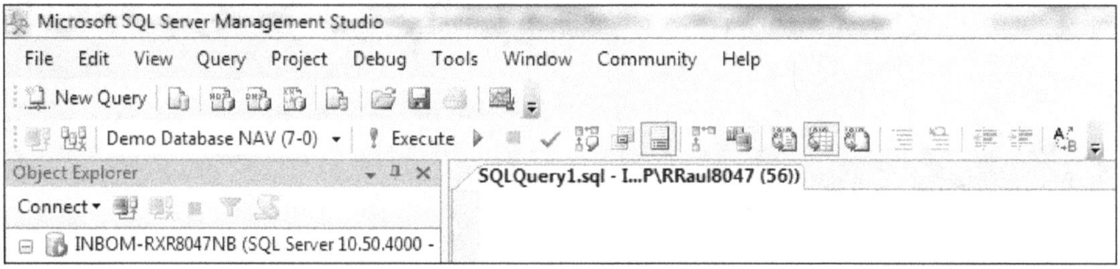

4. Enter the following code in the query window:

```
SELECT [No_], [Name], [Address], [City], [County], [Post
  Code]
FROM [CRONUS International Ltd_$Customer]
WHERE [No_] = '10000'
```

5. Press *F5* to run the query. The result should be identical to the following screenshot:

	No_	Name	Address	City	County	Post Code
1	10000	The Cannon Group PLC	192 Market Square	Birmingham		B27 4KT

How it works...

This query is just a simple question, which has three parts: what (fields of table), from (table), and condition (filters). Using the `SELECT` keyword, we are telling the system the names of the fields we want to retrieve. Most of the time, the NAV field names contain reserved keywords or spaces. To let the system know the exact field name, we have enclosed the field names with brackets, `[]`. For example, we store the customer number field as `No.` in NAV, whereas in our query we have referenced it by `No_`.

After choosing the fields, we are telling our query which table these fields belong to. In our case, it is the `customer` table. In the case of the NAV table, we have a slightly different naming convention maintained in the SQL Server. The table name format is `Company$Table`. In NAV, we have a table property called `DataPerCompany`. If we set this property to `No`, the table will not contain the company's name as prefix. At the same time, our data for all the companies will be stored in a single table. We do have such tables in NAV, for example, `Users`.

Finally, we are applying our condition to filter data. To do so, we are using the `WHERE` clause, and applying a filter on customer number `'10000'`.

Let's see the equivalent C/AL code for this query:

```
CustomerRec.SETRANGE("No.", '10000');
IF CustomerRec.FINDFIRST THEN;
```

There's more...

The SQL queries can be used to retrieve, insert, modify, or delete data from multiple tables. Let's take a look at these options:

- Adding/inserting data:

  ```
  INSERT INTO [CRONUS International Ltd_$Customer]
  ([No_],[Name],[Address],[City],[Post Code],[County])
  VALUES ('98456','Rakesh Raul','104 Airoli',
  'Navi Mumbai','400708','IN')
  ```

- Editing/modifying data:

  ```
  UPDATE [CRONUS International Ltd_$Customer]
  SET [Name] = 'Rakesh Raul'
  WHERE [No_] = '10000'
  ```

- Deleting data:

  ```
  DELETE [CRONUS International Ltd_$Customer]
  WHERE [No_] = '10000'
  ```

It is not suggested to manipulate NAV data using SQL Server as it does not contain business logic written in a NAV application. The NAV C/AL code is a powerful language, which can help you to take care of any complex activity, including business logic.

See also

- The *Retrieving data using FIND and GET Statements* recipe in *Chapter 3, Working with Tables, Records, and Query*
- The *Advanced Filtering* recipe in *Chapter 3, Working with Tables, Records, and Query*

Understanding SIFT

SIFT stands for **Sum Index Field Technology**; it keeps track of data of type decimal and helps to complete complex calculations quickly. Let's see how it works.

How to do it...

1. Design `Table 379 Detailed Cust. Ledg. Entry-keys.`
2. Click on **View** | **Keys** from the menu.

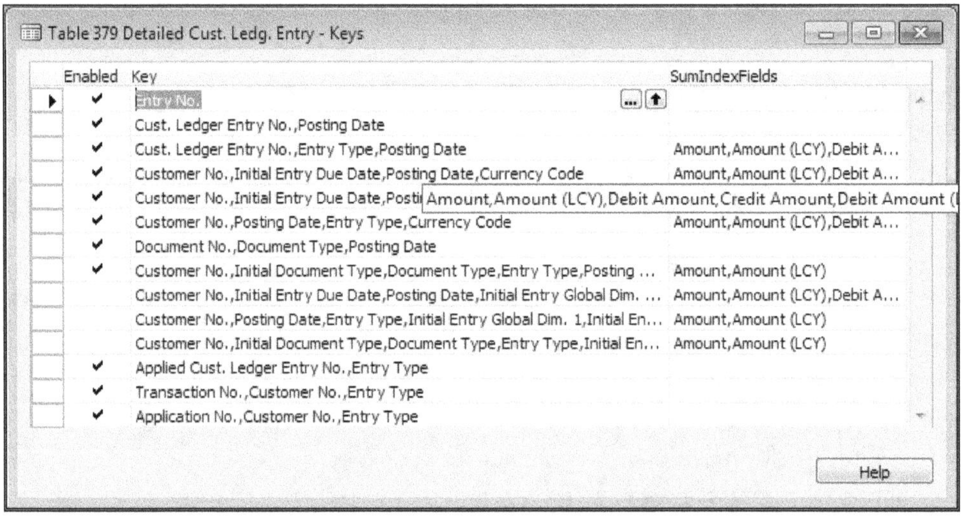

3. The selected key has a value in the `SumIndexFields` column. Go to **Properties** of the selected keys. The property, `MaintainSIFTIndex`, tells the SQL Server to store the total of `SumIndexFields`.

How it works...

Initially, SIFT values were stored in actual tables. Later, it was identified that inserting multiple entries in the SIFT table on every transaction puts an extra load on the system performance. To reduce this load from NAV 5 SP1, these values are stored in `View` and called **VSIFT**. In this example, we will focus on VSIFT.

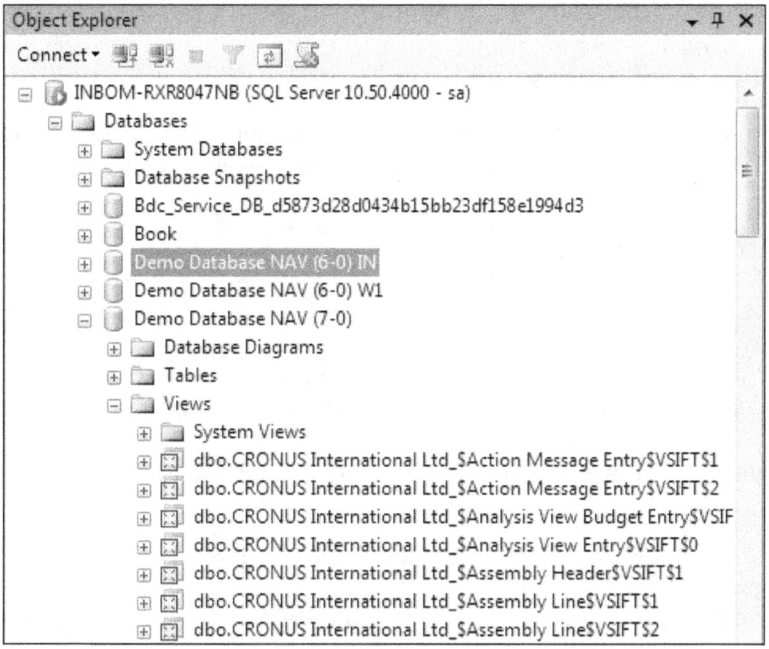

Let's take a look at the fourth key `Customer No., Initial Entry Due Date, Posting Date, Currency Code`. In the NAV key, the count starts at zero; that's why we said the fourth key. The VSIFT view name format is very similar to the table naming convention. Additionally, it contains the key number, `Company$Table$VSIFT$Key_Number`.

Right click on the `CRONUS International Ltd_$Detailed Cust_ Ledg_ Entry$VSIFT$4` view and go to **Script View As** | **CREATE To** | **New Query Editor Window**. You should see a code similar to the following code:

```
CREATE VIEW [dbo].[CRONUS International Ltd_$Detailed Cust_ Ledg_
  Entry$VSIFT$4]
WITH SCHEMABINDING AS
SELECT [Customer No_],[Initial Entry Due Date],[Posting
  Date],COUNT_BIG(*) "$Cnt",SUM([Amount]) [SUM$Amount],SUM([Amount
  (LCY)]) [SUM$Amount (LCY)]
FROM dbo.[CRONUS International Ltd_$Detailed Cust_ Ledg_ Entry]
GROUP BY [Customer No_],[Initial Entry Due Date],[Posting Date]
```

VIEW is just a Select statement. If a table used in VIEW gets updated, the VIEW is also updated. VIEW does not store data, it just collects it. The whole process is optimized by the SQL Server for faster transactions.

We can retrieve the data from VIEW in the same way as tables. If we select the records from our view used in the previous recipe, we should see the following result:

	Customer No_	Initial Entry Due Date	Posting Date	$Cnt	SUM$Amount	SUM$Amount (LCY)
1	01445544	2015-01-31 00:00:00.000	2015-01-19 00:00:00.000	1	2688.58000000000000000000	1499.02000000000000000000
2	01454545	2015-01-31 00:00:00.000	2014-12-31 00:00:00.000	1	398602.67000000000000000000	222241.32000000000000000000
3	10000	2015-01-01 00:00:00.000	2014-12-31 00:00:00.000	2	76167.75000000000000000000	76167.75000000000000000000
4	10000	2015-01-01 00:00:00.000	2015-01-11 00:00:00.000	2	-76167.75000000000000000000	-76167.75000000000000000000
5	10000	2015-01-05 00:00:00.000	2014-12-31 00:00:00.000	1	67704.67000000000000000000	67704.67000000000000000000
6	10000	2015-01-05 00:00:00.000	2015-01-11 00:00:00.000	1	-67704.67000000000000000000	-67704.67000000000000000000
7	10000	2015-01-11 00:00:00.000	2015-01-11 00:00:00.000	7	-292.84000000000000000000	-292.84000000000000000000

To understand how records are formed in VIEW, let's look at record number three of the previous result.

```
SELECT [Customer No_],[Initial Entry Due Date],[Posting Date],
  [Amount],[Amount (LCY)]
FROM [CRONUS International Ltd_$Detailed Cust_ Ledg_ Entry]
WHERE [Customer No_] = '10000' AND
[Initial Entry Due Date] = '2015-01-01' AND
[Posting Date] = '2014-12-31'
```

We found two records, which form our VIEW record.

	Customer No_	Initial Entry Due Date	Posting Date	Amount	Amount (LCY)
1	10000	2015-01-01 00:00:00.000	2014-12-31 00:00:00.000	25389.25000000000000000000	25389.25000000000000000000
2	10000	2015-01-01 00:00:00.000	2014-12-31 00:00:00.000	50778.50000000000000000000	50778.50000000000000000000

Now, let's take a look at the C/AL code identical to our previous SQL query to get the sum of the Amount field.

```
DtlCustLedgEntry.SETCURRENTKEY(
  "Customer No.", "Initial Entry Due Date", "Posting Date");
DtlCustLedgEntry.SETRANGE("Customer No.", '10000');
DtlCustLedgEntry.SETRANGE("Initial Entry Due Date", 010115D);
DtlCustLedgEntry.SETRANGE("Posting Date", 123114D);
DtlCustLedgEntry.CALCSUMS(Amount);
```

See also

- The *Adding a FlowField* recipe in *Chapter 3, Working with Tables, Records, and Query*
- The *Creating a Sumindex Field* recipe in *Chapter 3, Working with Tables, Records, and Query*

Using the SQL profiler

The SQL profiler is a very helpful tool to monitor the T-SQL command sent through NAV by a specific user. Let's take a look at the basic configuration of this tool.

How to do it...

1. Go to **Start** | **All Programs** | **Microsoft SQL Server 2008 R2** | **Performance Tools** | **SQL Server Profiler**.

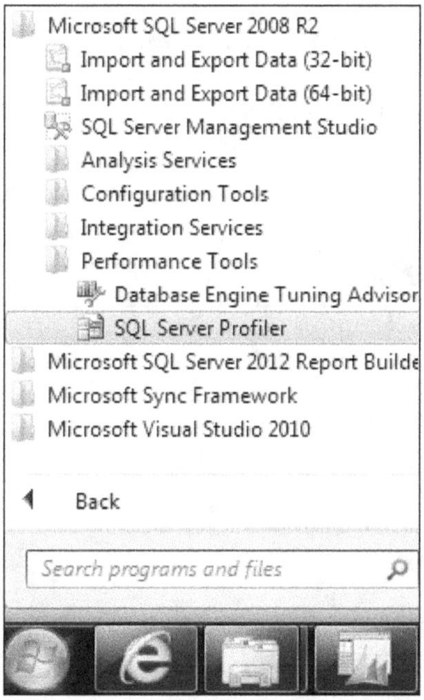

2. Click on **File** | **New Trace**. This should prompt a new window to connect to the SQL Server.

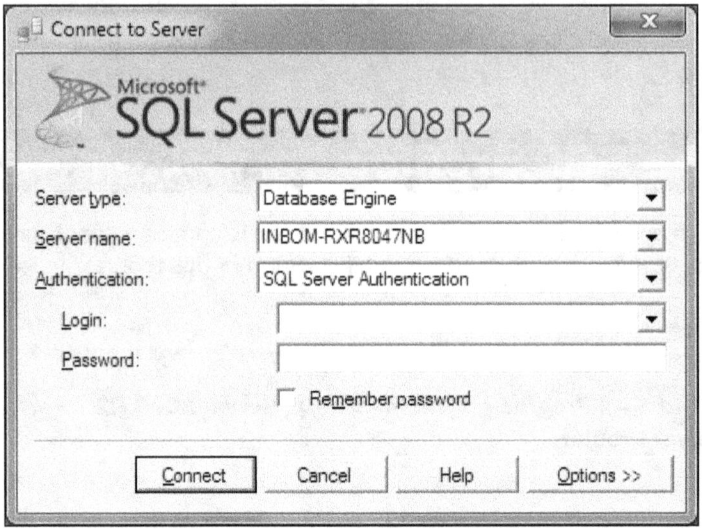

3. On successful connection to the SQL Server, the next window will be **Trace Properties**.

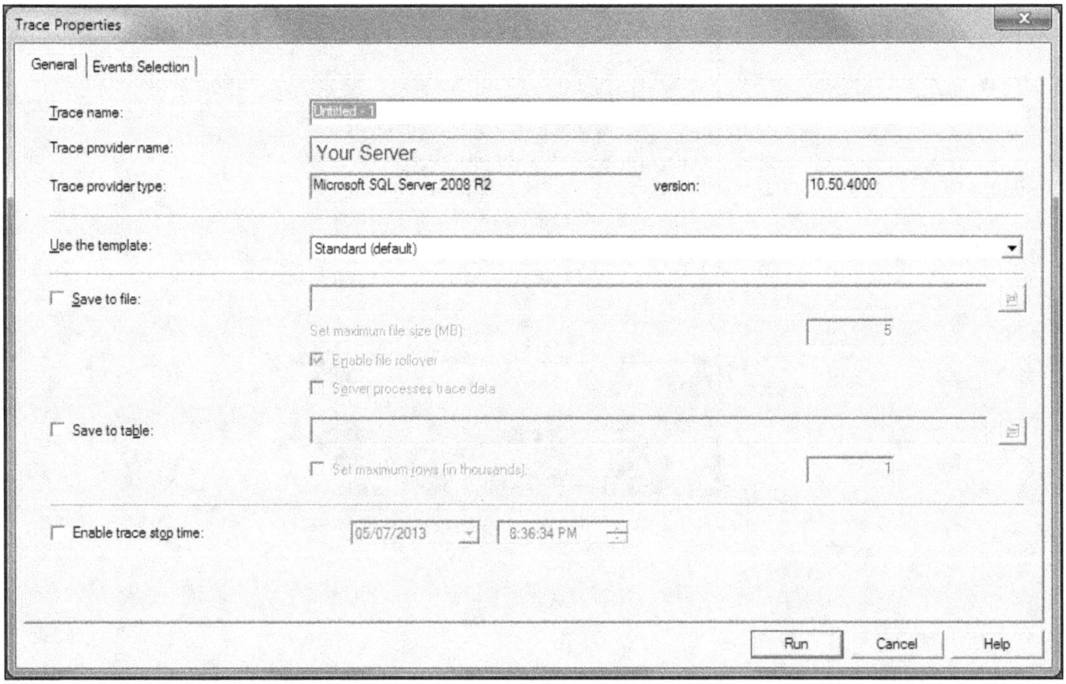

4. Provide a name to the trace and the saving details. Open the **Events Selection** tab to choose an event and a field, which needs to be recorded.

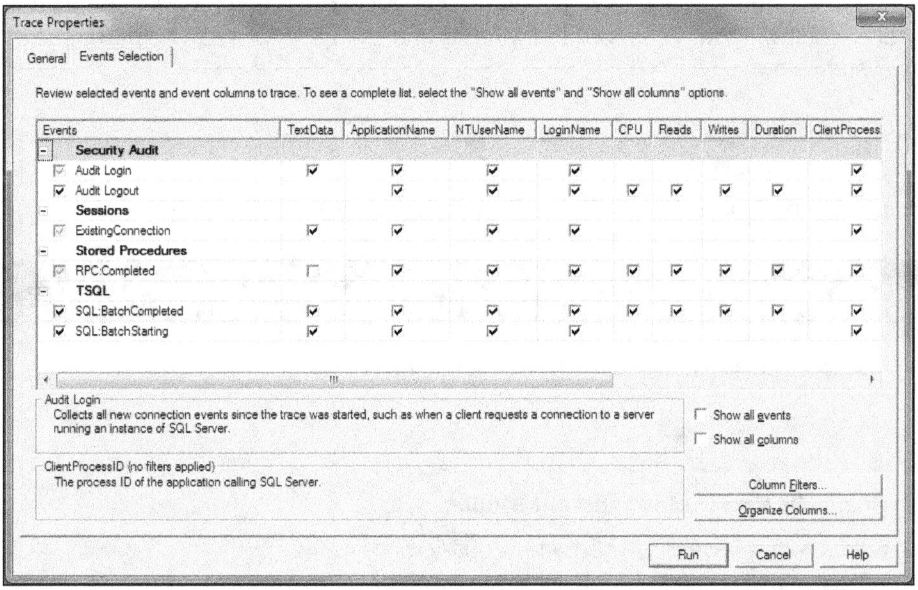

5. On completion of the setup, click on **Run**. This will begin the trace and we should get an output similar to the following window:

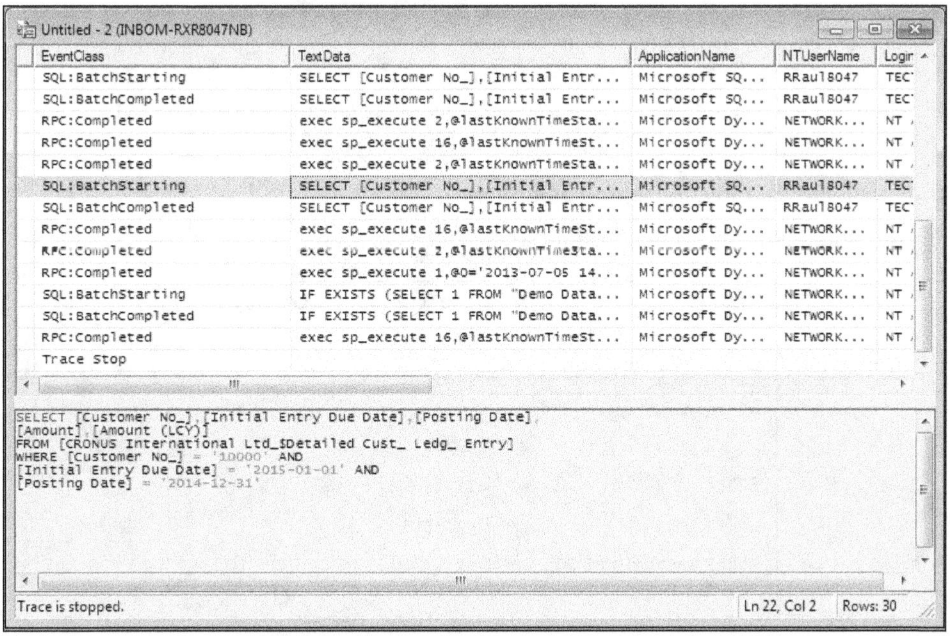

How it works...

We can see, username reads and writes on the database execution time and actual query in our trace result window. There are many fields and events, which can help to trace issues, such as system slowness.

See also

- *Identifying Blocked and Blocking sessions from SQL*

Displaying data from a SQL view in NAV

In this recipe we will see how to display data for a SQL view.

How to do it...

1. Open **SQL Server Management Studio**.
2. Select a database and open a new query window.
3. Copy the following code to the query window and execute it:

```
CREATE VIEW [Customer Ledger View] AS
SELECT "Customer No_","Initial Entry Due Date","Posting
  Date",
COUNT_BIG(*) "$Cnt", SUM("Amount") "SUM$Amount",
SUM("Amount (LCY)") "SUM$Amount (LCY)"
FROM [CRONUS International Ltd_$Detailed Cust_ Ledg_ Entry]
GROUP BY "Customer No_", "Initial Entry Due Date",
"Posting Date"
```

4. Create a new table in **Object Designer**.
5. Add the following fields to the table:

Name	DataType	Length
Customer No_	Code	20
Initial Entry Due Date	Date	
Posting Date	Date	
$Cnt	BigInteger	
SUM$Amount	Decimal	
SUM$Amount(LCY)	Decimal	

6. Add the following properties to the table:

Property	Value
`DataPerCompany`	`No`
`LinkedObject`	`Yes`
`LinkedInTransaction`	`No`

7. Save the table as `Customer Ledger View`.
8. On execution of the table, you should see the following data:

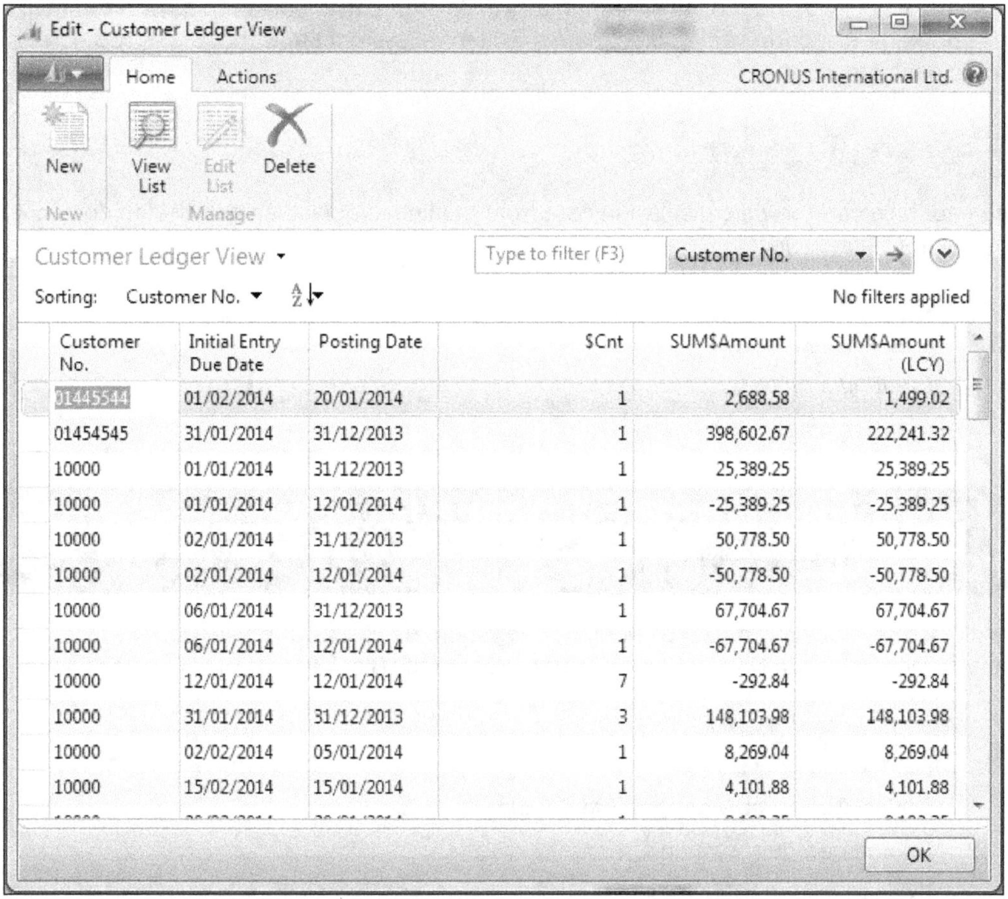

Customer No.	Initial Entry Due Date	Posting Date	$Cnt	SUM$Amount	SUM$Amount (LCY)
01445544	01/02/2014	20/01/2014	1	2,688.58	1,499.02
01454545	31/01/2014	31/12/2013	1	398,602.67	222,241.32
10000	01/01/2014	31/12/2013	1	25,389.25	25,389.25
10000	01/01/2014	12/01/2014	1	-25,389.25	-25,389.25
10000	02/01/2014	31/12/2013	1	50,778.50	50,778.50
10000	02/01/2014	12/01/2014	1	-50,778.50	-50,778.50
10000	06/01/2014	31/12/2013	1	67,704.67	67,704.67
10000	06/01/2014	12/01/2014	1	-67,704.67	-67,704.67
10000	12/01/2014	12/01/2014	7	-292.84	-292.84
10000	31/01/2014	31/12/2013	3	148,103.98	148,103.98
10000	02/02/2014	05/01/2014	1	8,269.04	8,269.04
10000	15/02/2014	15/01/2014	1	4,101.88	4,101.88

How it works...

To start with, we are making a copy of the VSIFT view from the `Customer Ledger Entry` table. Then we are careering the table exactly identical to our view.

Now, we have two different objects with the same structure. We are linking these two objects to each other. To do so, we are setting the table property `LinkedObject` to `Yes`. We have another property now to attend, `LinkedInTransaction`, which we need to set as `No`. Finally, we set the `DataPerCompany` property to `No`. As we are setting the `DataPerCompany` property to `No`, the table will not contain the company name as a prefix in the SQL Server. At the same time our data for all the companies will be stored in a single table. With the help of these properties and the same object name, we let the system know that these two objects refer to each other.

There's more...

We need to be careful while displaying data from the linked object, as permission does not apply to the linked objects.

See also

- *Creating a table*
- *Creating a basic SQL query*

Identifying Blocked and Blocking sessions from SQL

Deadlock does not allow a user to work in the system. Blocking other user actions is a common occurrence in NAV. In this recipe we will identify Blocked and Blocking sessions.

How to do it...

1. Open **SQL Server Management Studio**.
2. Open a new query window.
3. Execute the following code:

```
sp_who
```

4. The resulting window should be similar to the following screenshot:

	spid	ecid	status	loginame	hostname	blk	dbname	cmd	request_id
1	1	0	background	sa		0	NULL	RESOURCE MONITOR	0
2	2	0	background	sa		0	NULL	XE TIMER	0
3	3	0	background	sa		0	NULL	XE DISPATCHER	0
4	4	0	background	sa		0	NULL	LAZY WRITER	0
5	5	0	background	sa		0	NULL	LOG WRITER	0
6	6	0	background	sa		0	NULL	LOCK MONITOR	0
7	7	0	background	sa		0	master	SIGNAL HANDLER	0
8	8	0	sleeping	sa		0	master	TASK MANAGER	0
9	9	0	background	sa		0	master	TRACE QUEUE TASK	0
10	10	0	background	sa		0	master	BRKR EVENT HNDLR	0
11	11	0	background	sa		0	master	BRKR TASK	0
12	12	0	background	sa		0	master	TASK MANAGER	0
13	13	0	background	sa		0	master	CHECKPOINT	0

How it works...

The `sp_who` command returns a list of all the connections to the server by querying the `sys.sysprocesses` system table. The column `blk` will show the `spid` of the user who is blocking.

There's more...

We can find deadlocks by writing a query on the SQL Server. Let's take a look at the query:

```
SELECT
SP.[spid] AS [SPID],
CASE WHEN SP.[blocked] > 0 THEN 'Yes' ELSE '' END AS [Blocked],
SP.[blocked] AS [Blocked by SPID],
SP.[nt_username] AS [User ID],
SD.[name] AS [Database],
SP.[waittime],
SP.[status] as [Current Status],
SP.cmd AS [Current Command]
FROM
[master].[dbo].[sysprocesses] AS SP JOIN
[master].[dbo].[sysdatabases] AS SD ON
(SP.dbid = SD.dbid) LEFT OUTER JOIN
[master].[dbo].[sysprocesses] AS SP2 ON (SP.[blocked] =
SP2.[spid])
WHERE SP.[program_name] Like '%Dynamics NAV%'
ORDER BY SP.[waittime] DESC, SP.cmd DESC
```

The previous query will give us blocked user IDs as well as other details, which will help us find the root cause of the block. We can pass the `KILL spid` command on blocking the user IDs to resolve our deadlock. Before killing any user, please collect all the user activity information to avoid partial posting of data.

See also

- *Using the SQL profiler*

Setting up a backup plan

Taking a backup of the database is very important; mostly the customer ID department takes care of this activity. Still, it's better to have an idea of how to set up the backup plan.

How to do it...

1. Open **SQL Server Management Studio** and connect to your server. In the **Object Explorer** pane on the left-hand side, expand the tree to **Management Maintenance Plans**.
2. Right-click on the `Maintenance Plans` folder and select **Maintenance Plan Wizard**.

3. Click on **Next**.
4. In the next window, set the backup plan name and the to-change schedule. Then click on the **Change...** button.

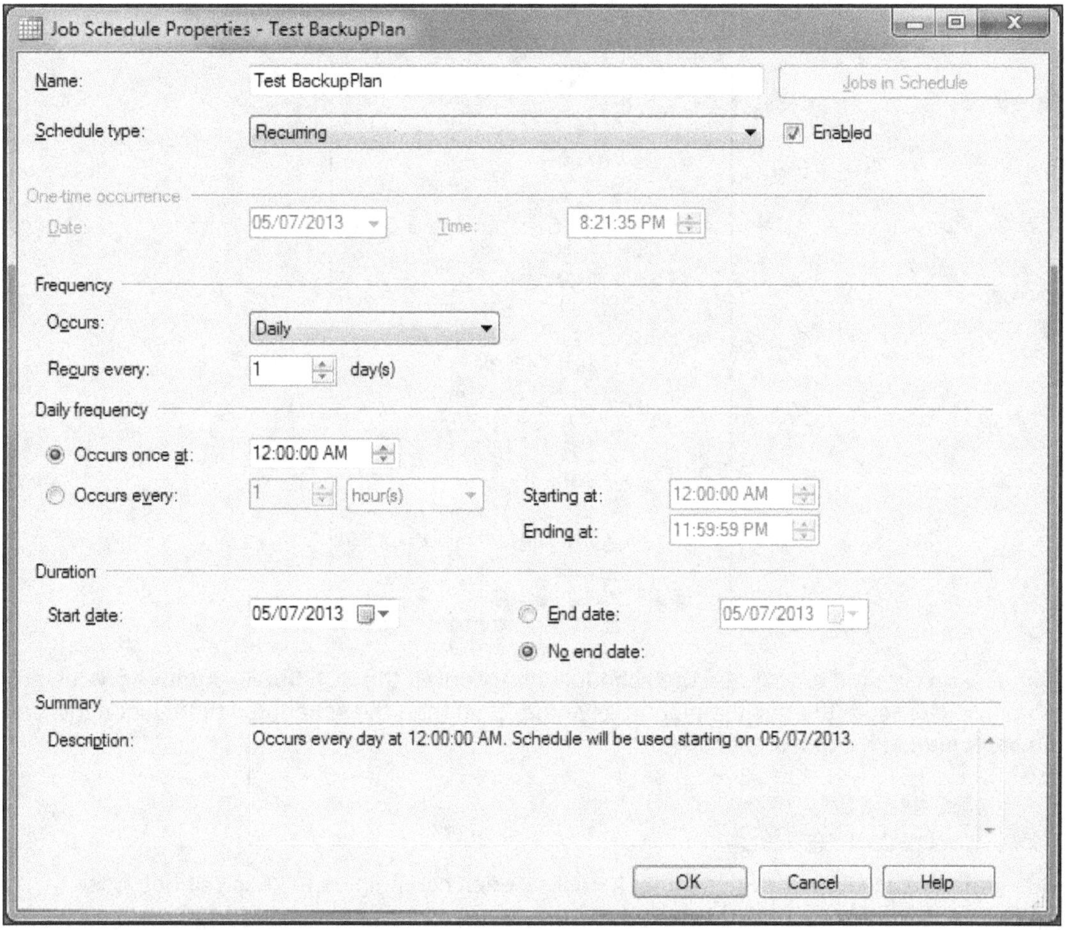

5. We have scheduled our backup to run every midnight.
6. Click **Ok** in the **Job Schedule Properties** window.
7. Then click on **Next**.
8. Select the **Back Up Database (Full)** option.
9. Click on **Next**.
10. Select the desired database.
11. Keep clicking on **Next** until you finish the wizard.

How it works...

On completion of the wizard, we should see our backup plan in the **Object Explorer** tree under `Maintenance Plans`.

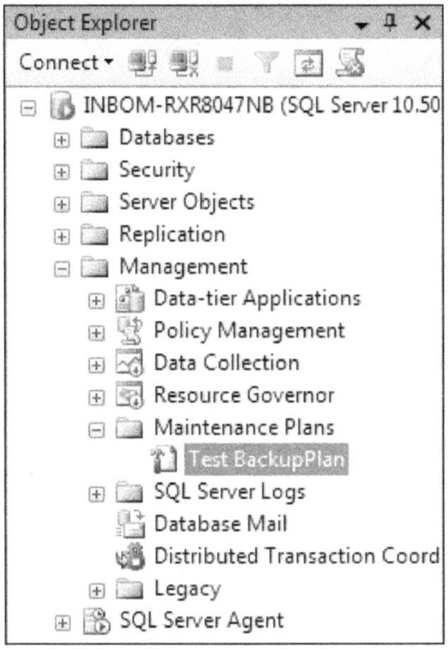

Our backup plan will execute on the scheduled time only if the **SQL Server Agent** services are running. To execute the backup plan at any other time than the scheduled time, just right-click on **back plan** and choose **execute**.

There's more...

SQL Maintenance Plan provides multiple tasks, which can help us to keep our database optimized. A few important tasks and their details are as follows:

- **Reorganize Index**: This task will defragment and compact indexes. It will help to improve index scanning performance. This task can be set on a monthly basis; if there is a high volume of data insertion, it can also be set on a weekly basis.
- **Rebuild Index**: This is equivalent to creating an index again. It will highly optimize the seek-and-scan performance of the index. This activity can take a longer time as well as lock the database tables.

See also

- *Creating a basic SQL query*

Maintaining the transaction logfiles

The transaction log is a record of all the transactions that have been performed on the database. If not properly maintained, the transaction logfile can become very large. If the size of the transaction logfile reaches its maximum limit or the disk hosting file is running out of space, the user will receive an error and the system will not allow us to create new transactions. In this recipe we will see how to shrink the transaction logfile.

Getting ready

Make a complete backup of the database and store it in an offline location.

How to do it...

1. Open **SQL Server Management Studio** and connect to the server that holds the NAV database.
2. Click on **New Query**.
3. Then select the NAV database in the database dropdown.
4. Enter the following code in the query window:

   ```
   BACKUP LOG <MyDatabase> WITH TRUNCATE_ONLY
   ```

5. Press *F5* to run the query.
6. Delete the previous SQL statement from the **Query** window and add the following code:

   ```
   DBCC SHRINKFILE (Logfilename, Newsize)
   ```

7. Press *F5* to run the query.

How it works...

The SQL Server database has three types of physical files, that is, primary datafile, secondary datafile, and transaction logfile. There can be only one primary datafile; the extension of a primary datafile is `.mdf`. We can have multiple secondary files; the maximum size of a secondary file can be configured. A secondary file extension is `.ndf`. Multiple transaction logfiles can be created; the file extension for this is `.ldf`.

The previous recipe is divided into two parts. In the first part, we are removing the committed transactions in the logfile, which will leave an empty logfile. At this point, the size of the file is the same. The `TRUNCATE_ONLY` command only removes the transactions, it does not modify the file size. To modify the file size, we are using the next command, that is, `DBCC SHRINKFILE`. As a parameter, we need to provide a logfile name, which is nothing but a database file with extension `.ldf` and the desired file size. It is suggested not to shrink the logfile completely, but to a size that you know will be used. If the file is completely shrunk, a new log added to the file can have fragmentation.

See also

- *Creating a basic SQL query*
- *Setting up a backup plan*
- The *Creating a new database* recipe in *Chapter 12, NAV Server Administrator*

12
NAV Server Administration

In this chapter, we will cover the following recipes:

- Creating a NAV Server Instance
- Configuring NAS to run Job Queue
- Creating a user on NAV
- Changing the NAV license
- Creating a new database
- Testing the NAV database

Introduction

The old NAV versions were based on two-tier architecture; that means client executable is directly talking to **relational database management system** (**RDBMS**) whereas NAV's current version is based on three tiers. In addition to client executable and RDBMS, we have one more tier, that is, **Microsoft Dynamics NAV Server**. This tier works as a middleman between the client and RDBMS. With this new tier, Microsoft has not only allowed us to distribute the user on multiple services for load management, but also opened a new way of integration, which even takes care of NAV business logic. With these advantages, we also have new responsibilities of implementing and maintaining the server tier.

The two-tier and three-tier architectures are shown in the following diagram:

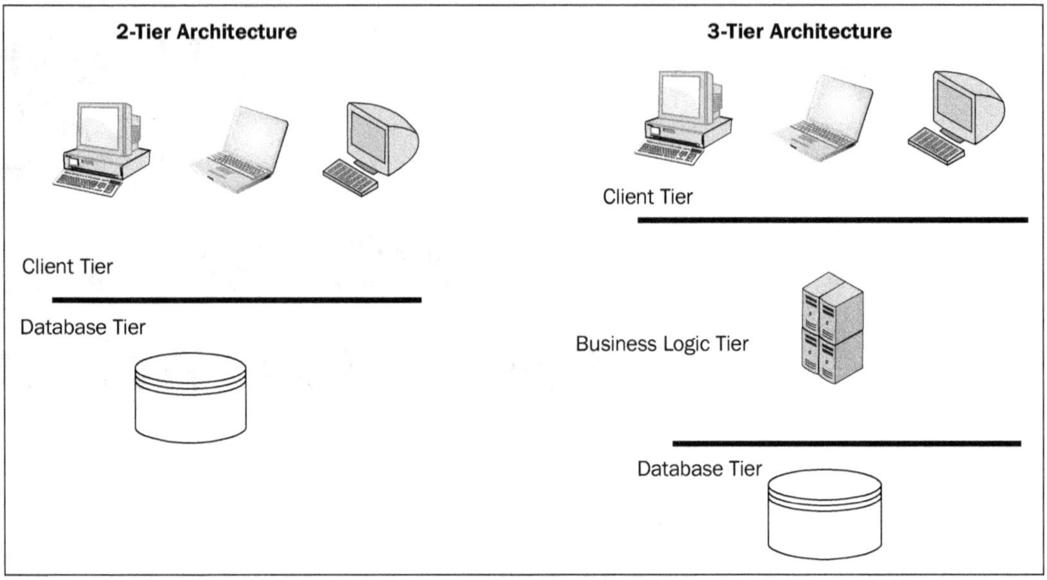

Administering NAV Server, creating and managing users and their permissions, and managing the license, database, and companies, are all done by the NAV administrator. Microsoft has provided different tools for all these administrative tasks.

Tool	Task
`Microsoft Dynamics NAV Administration`	To create and manage Microsoft Dynamics NAV Server Instance.
`Microsoft Dynamics NAV 2013 Administration Shell`	To administer NAV by command line.
`RoleTailored client`	To create and manage users, permissions, and profiles.
`Development Environment`	To manage the license, database, and companies.

In this chapter, we will look at six simple recipes to carry out these administrative tasks.

Creating a NAV Server Instance

NAV Server Instance is a service through which a NAV client interacts with the SQL Server database. When we install NAV Server on a machine it creates a single instance of NAV Server. In this recipe, we will see how to create an additional NAV Server Instance.

How to do it...

1. Open the **Microsoft Dynamics NAV Administration** tool. Your system will present the window as shown in the following screenshot:

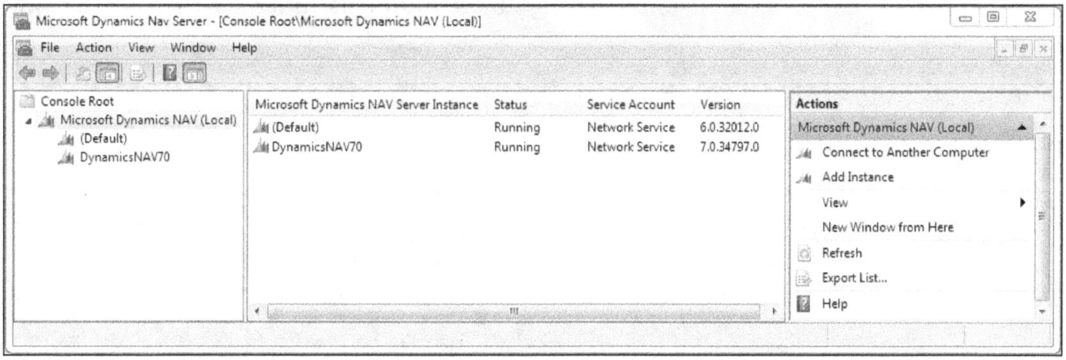

2. Right-click on **Microsoft Dynamics NAV (Local)** and choose **Add Instance**.

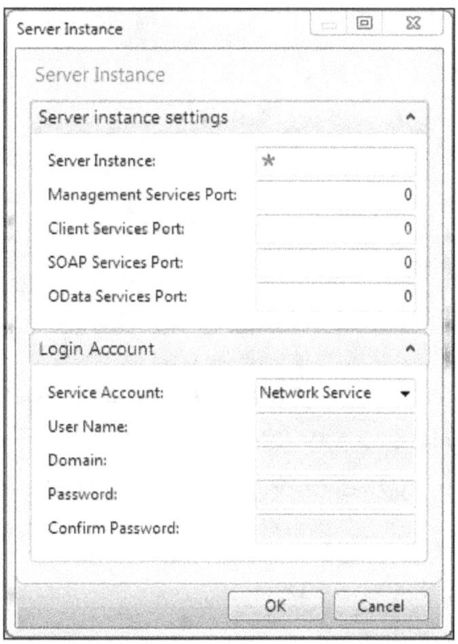

3. A new server instance will be created as shown in the previous screenshot. Select the newly created server instance from the left pane of **Microsoft NAV Server Administration** and update the following settings for that instance:

Setting	Value
Server Instance:	`DynamicsNAV70-Test`
Management Services Port:	`7145`
Client Services Port:	`7146`
SOAP Services Port:	`7147`
OData Services Port:	`7148`

4. From the left pane of the **Microsoft NAV Server Administration** tool, select the newly created instance.

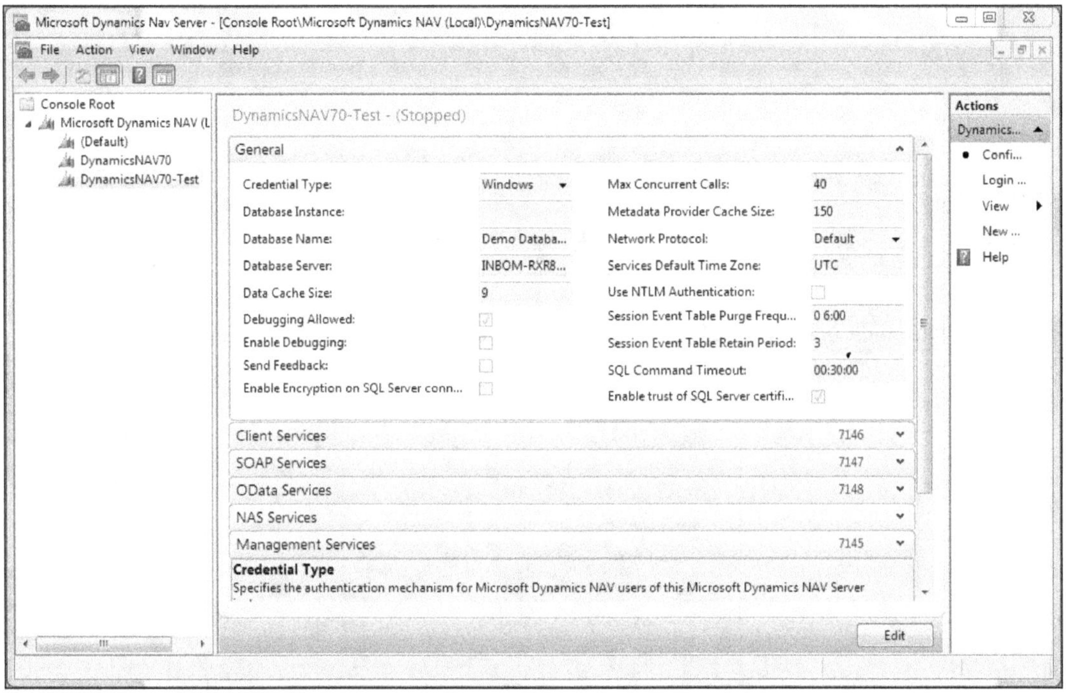

5. Navigate to **Edit** to select a NAV **Database Name** and **Database Server**.
6. Select **Microsoft Dynamics NAV (Local)** from the left pane.
7. From the center pane, right-click on the newly created server instance and choose **Start**.

8. Start the `RoleTailored client` and provide the following value as the server address to connect the newly created server, where `LocalHost` is your machine name hosting the NAV Server service. Refer to the following screenshot.

   `LocalHost:7146/DynamicsNAV70-Test`

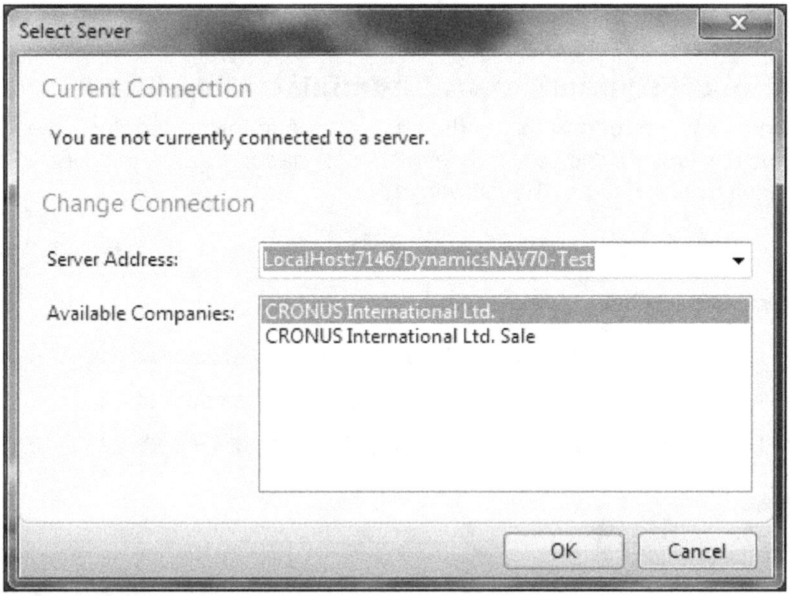

How it works...

Creating an additional NAV Server Instance using the **Microsoft Dynamics NAV Administration** tool is a very simple activity. We have already created a new instance by providing very minimal information. To create the NAV Server Instance, we first create the instance name; it is suggested we provide a name that gives us a quick hint about our database. Then, we provide a TCP port number on which our server will communicate. The valid range for a port number is from 1 to 65535. Then, we have an option to provide a specific logon account. By default, the value for these settings is `Network Service`; but it is suggested that on a production server, you use the valid domain account which is dedicated to running the service.

After the creation of the instance, your system will update all the settings with default values. These values are taken from the primary instance, which is created during the installation of the server. To just access the database, we only need to verify the **Database Name** and **Database Server** settings.

There's more...

Details of all the settings options are provided in the last section of the **Microsoft Dynamics NAV Administrator** tool. For more details, you can visit the following URL:

`http://msdn.microsoft.com/en-us/library/dd355055(v=nav.70).aspx`

Using Microsoft Dynamics NAV Administration Shell

Administration of NAV Server can be handled using the Administration Shell client. This client is just Windows Powershell. You can find detailed information about the tasks we can carry out using Administration Shell at the following URL:

`http://msdn.microsoft.com/en-us/library/jj672916(v=nav.70).aspx`

Let's take a look at a few basic commands:

- `Get-Command *NAVServer*`: Used to get the list of commands
- `Get-Help <cmd name>`: Used to get help about the commands
- `Get-Help Get-NAVServerInstance`: Used to get help about NAV Server Instance

See also

- *Configuring NAS to run Job Queue*
- *Changing the NAV license*

Configuring NAS to run Job Queue

Navision Application Server (**NAS**) is nothing but a faceless client that is running as service and Job Queue is the setup available in NAV to schedule multiple activities at designated dates and times. In this recipe, we will be configuring NAS to execute Job Queue activities.

How to do it...

1. Open the **Microsoft Dynamics NAV Administration** tool and choose **NAV Server Instance** to configure NAS.

2. Update the following settings for **NAS Services**. Refer to the following screenshot.

Setting	Value
Company:	`Your Company form NAV Database`
Startup Argument:	`JOBQUEUE`
Startup Codeunit:	`1`
Startup Method:	`NASHandler`

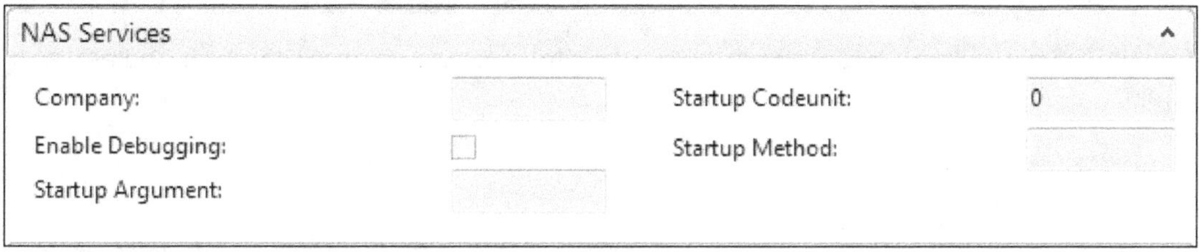

3. Save the settings and restart the instance.

How it works...

NAS is executed on the basis of which company we select; so to instruct our service which company to use, we have provided a company name for setting company. This means, for every company for which we want to execute NAS, we need to create a Navision Server Instance for that database and company. Beneath the **Company:** field, there is a selection available to activate the debugging of NAS services.

The next setting is **Startup Argument:**; here we specify the application configuration information. In our case, we provided the standard option, `JOBQUEUE`, to activate the Job Queue application. This property is basically depending on **Startup Codeunit:** and **Startup Method:** for its functioning.

Later, we have supplied the value for **Startup Codeunit:**, that is, `1` (`ApplicationManagement`). The last setting is **Startup Method:**. In this setting, we provide the method that we want to call from the codeunit mentioned in **Startup Codeunit:**. If we do not provide any value for this setting, it will execute the `OnRun` trigger of **Startup Codeunit:**.

There's more...

There is another way to run Job Queue from NAS without using codeunit `1`, `ApplicationManagement`. In the previous example, we are executing the `NASHandler` method of `codeunit 1`. If you follow that code, it is further going to `codeunit 44`, `NASManagement`, in the function `NASHandler`. From this function, with the help of Startup Argument, system executes Codeunit related to Job Queue.

So, we can directly execute `codeunit 450`, `Job Queue-NAS Startup`, with blank **Startup Argument:** and **Startup Method:** settings.

See also

- *Creating a NAV Server Instance*

Creating a user on NAV

Creating a user is a very important activity. In this recipe, we will create one user and assign it a role.

How to do it...

1. Start the `RoleTailored client` and navigate to **Departments** | **Administration** | **IT Administration** | **General** | **Users**.
2. From the list page, navigate to **Actions** | **New**. You will see a window similar to the one shown in the following screenshot:

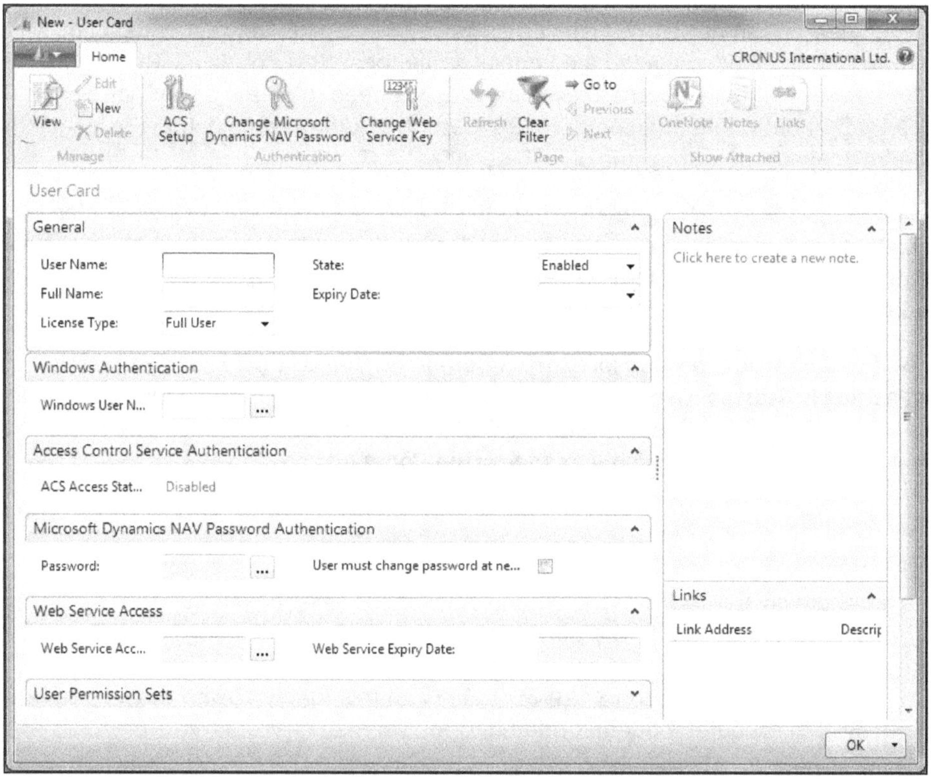

3. From the **Windows Authentication** fast tab, select the assist edit button in the **Windows User Name** field.
4. It will open a window to run a search for the windows user account.

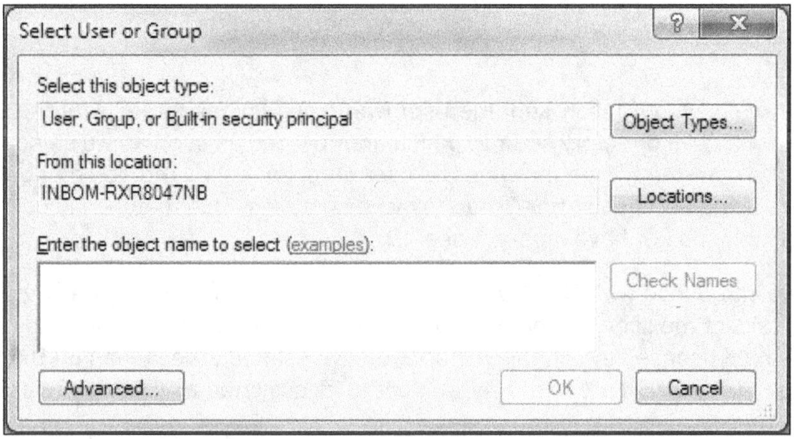

5. Enter the username and click on **Check Names**. Then, after getting the desired user account, click on **OK**.
6. In **License Type**, select **Full User**.
7. Set **State** as **Enabled**.
8. Provide **31/12/2013** as **Expiry Date**.
9. Go to the **User Permission Sets** fast tab and assign the **SUPER** role to the user.

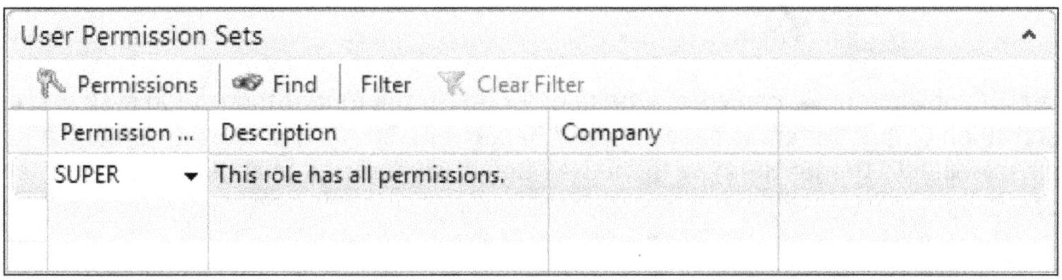

10. Click on **OK** to close the user creation page.

How it works...

The Microsoft Dynamics NAV 2013 supports four credential authorization systems: `Windows`, `UserName`, `NavUserPassword`, and `AccessControlService`. In this recipe, we are creating a user of type `Windows`. Fields not mentioned in this recipe are irrelevant for creating a `Windows` user.

In this recipe, we have purposely kept the **User Name:** field blank as we want the username derived from the active directory settings which are updated as soon as we select **Windows User Name**. We can simply type the windows user name including the domain; but in this recipe, we are using **Select User or Group** to avoid mistakes. This feature will help us find users for whom we do not have an exact user ID.

License Type, introduced with NAV 2013, is necessary at the time of purchasing a NAV license to provide details of the license type. Based on the purchase details, we need to configure the user with the right license type. In this recipe, we have selected the value **Full User**, which will allow the user to access all areas of NAV, subject to its assigned role and permissions.

The next two settings provide control over user access by allowing you to change users' status or providing an expiry date.

In the final setting, we have selected the role **Super**. Combination of the role **Super** and license type **Full User**, allows user to have access to the entire NAV application. There is the possibility of controlling user access based on the company selected. For this, we need to select a company corresponding to each role. If the column `Company` does not have a value entered for any role, that means the user has that particular role in all companies of the current database.

There's more...

In the NAV application, we can create the user for any of the four authorization systems, but the activation of that system is based on NAV Server settings. To activate any authorization system, select it in **Credential Type** in the NAV Server service and restart the server instance to apply the changes.

See also

- *Creating a NAV Server Instance*
- *Changing the NAV license*

Changing the NAV license

NAV system access and modules are controlled by a license. The client can add a number of concurrent users or modules with their existing license. In this recipe, we will see how to update the license and check license information from the `RoleTailored client`.

How to do it...

1. Open **Microsoft Dynamics NAV 2013 Development Environment**.
2. Navigate to **Tools** | **License Information**; it will open a window displaying current license information.

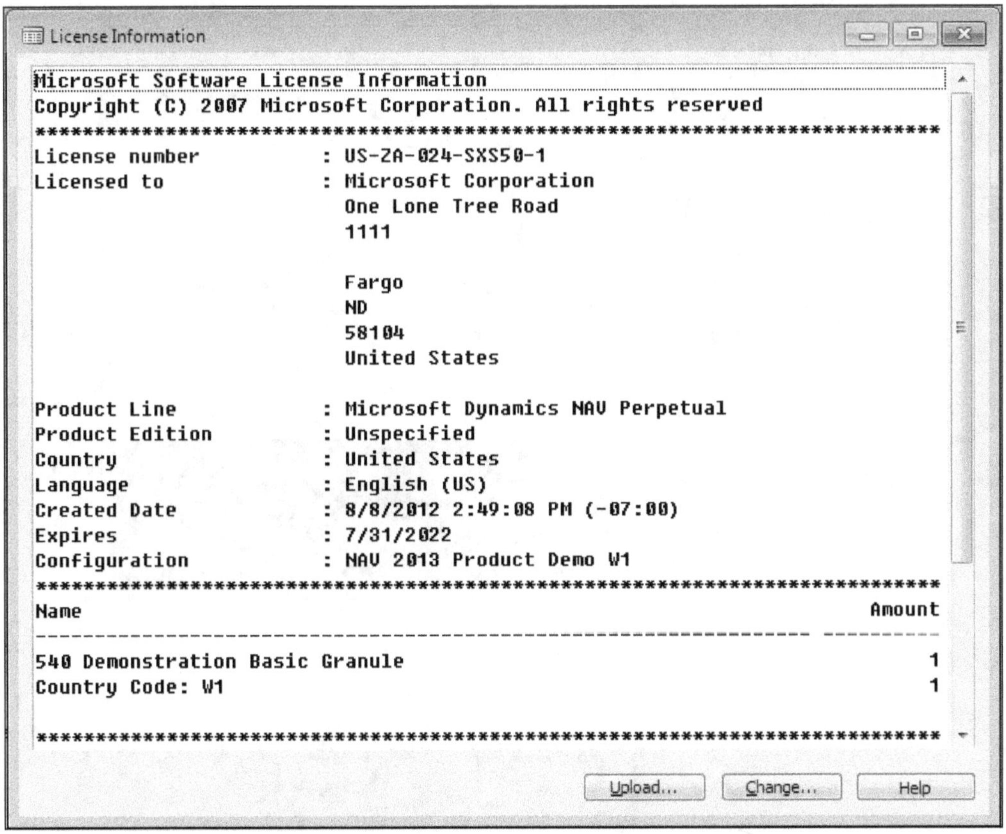

3. Click on **Upload...**, which will open the windows dialog box, and choose license file.
4. Restart the NAV Server Instance.

5. Start `RoleTailored client` and navigate to **Application Menu** | **Help** | **About Microsoft Dynamics NAV**.
6. From the **About Microsoft Dynamics NAV** window, select **View your license information**.

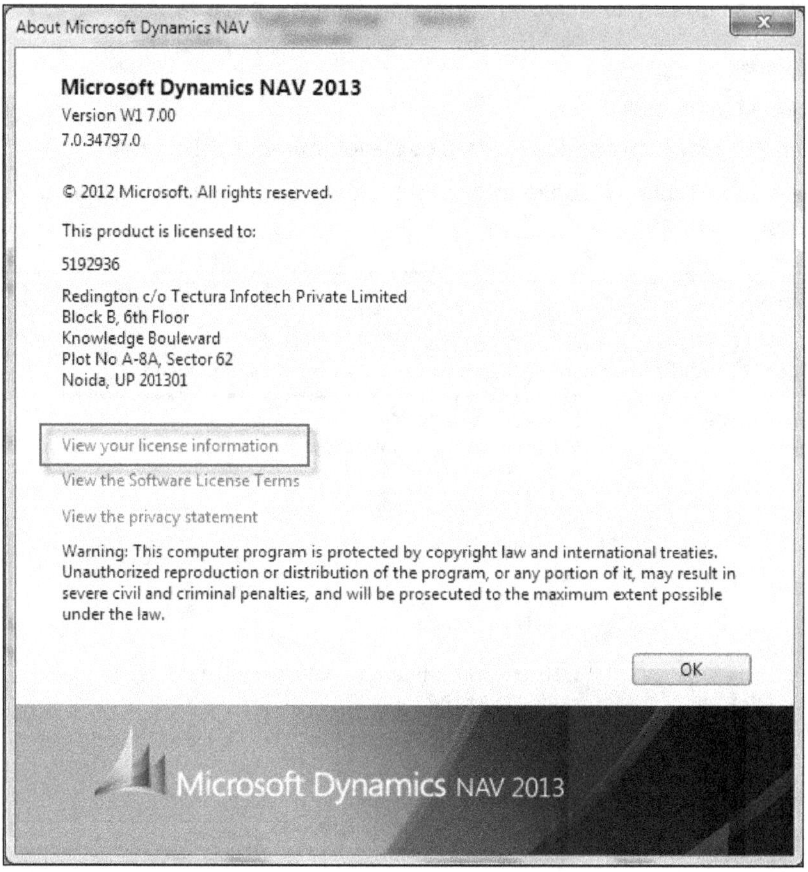

How it works...

With the purchase of additional concurrent users, new granule or NAV add-on solution, Microsoft provides a new license file which contains the permission set for the new purchase. Only after updating the license in the system can the user avail the benefit of these new features. In NAV 2013, any changes related to license can only be done from the development environment. In the **License Information** window, we see two buttons, that is, **Upload...** and **Change....** If we choose **Change...**, it will only change the license for the instance of the development environment. In this recipe, we choose **Upload...** as we want to apply that license on our NAV system.

The license will take effect only after restarting the NAV Server Instance. If you have multiple NAV Server Instance connected to a single database, all server instances need to restart to apply the new license.

There's more...

The license file carries a lot of important information, such as related NAV versions, number of users, and application granules. Almost all the information is encrypted; only very basic information is readable if the license file opens in Notepad. The same information can be viewed by the client after applying for the license. Microsoft provides one more file with the license file, which is not encrypted and provides detailed information about each and every object the user is allowed to use.

Sometimes, we may not have this file and want to know the details of allowed objects. This can be achieved by developing a simple report. Create a NAV report on a virtual table `2000000040`, **License Information** and add all the fields of this table to that report.

See also

- *Creating a NAV Server Instance*
- *Creating a user on NAV*
- *Creating a new database*

Creating a new database

Creating a new database is not a day-to-day activity, but knowing about it will be an advantage. In this recipe, we will create a new NAV database and take a look at a few very important settings.

How to do it...

1. Open **Microsoft Dynamics NAV 2013 Development Environment**.
2. Go to **File** | **Database** | **New** and provide your SQL server details and logon credentials. You will be presented with a **New Database** screen.

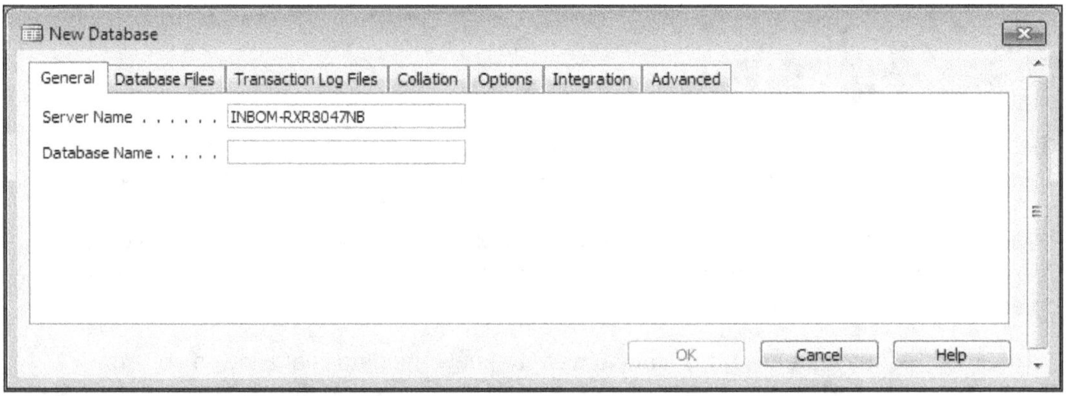

3. Provide the **Server Name** and **Database Name**. The database name needs to be unique among all the databases of that server.
4. Next, go to the **Database Files** tab and modify the default value of the `File Name` column to save the data file on the non-system drive.

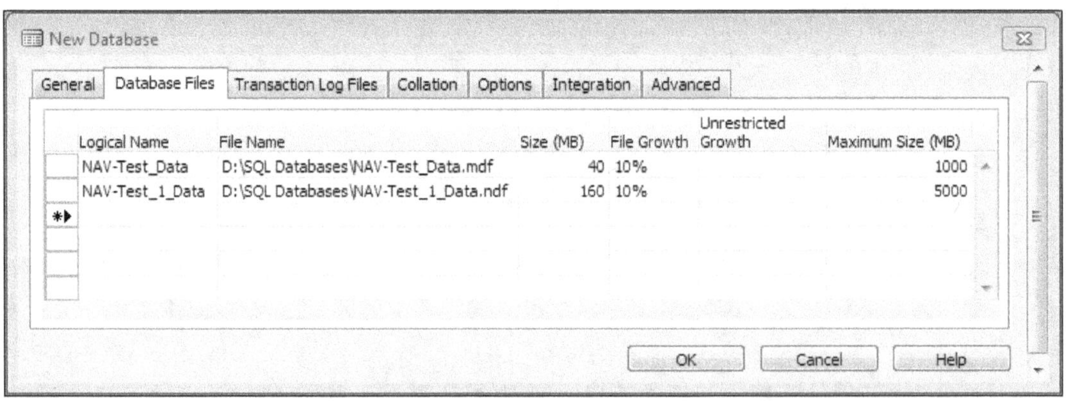

5. From the same tab, uncheck the column value of `Unrestricted Growth` and provide a `Maximum Size` value, as shown in the previous screenshot.
6. As you did previously, update the **Transaction Log File** tab.

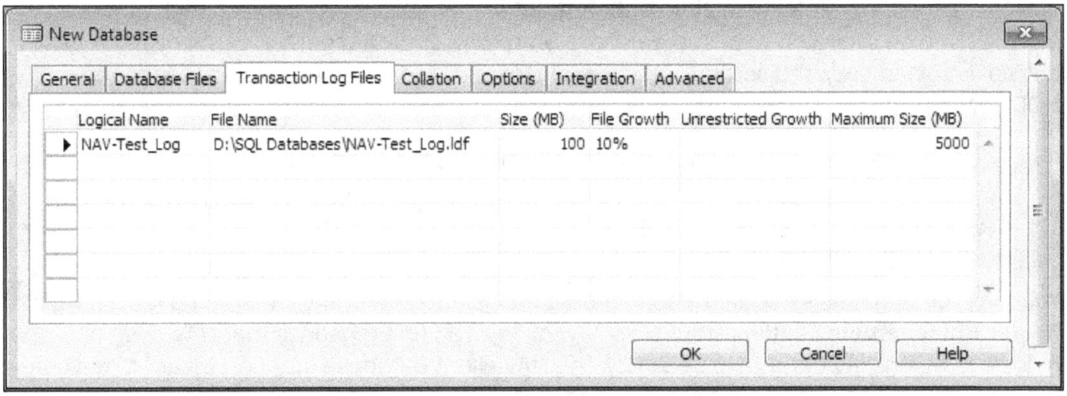

7. Next, open the **Options** tab and change **Recovery model.....** to **Simple**.

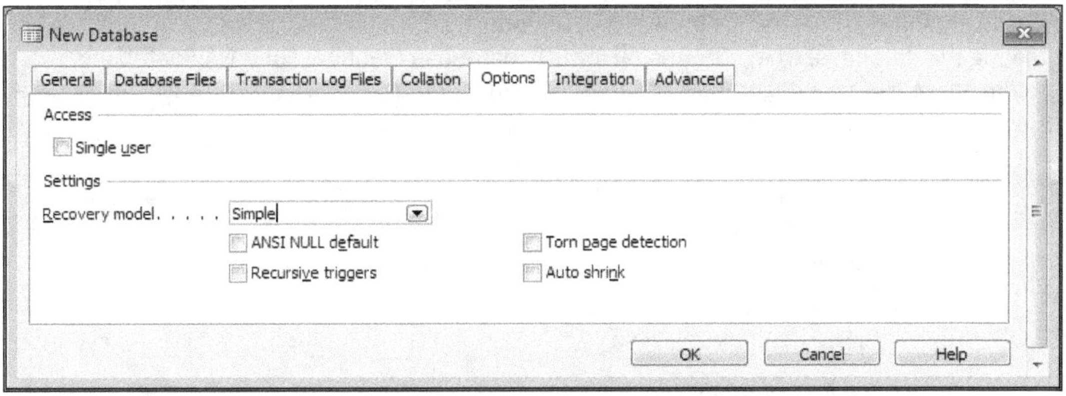

8. Finally, from the **Integration** tab, select the **Save license in database** option and click on **OK**.
9. Your system will open a dialog box. To select the NAV license file, provide a valid NAV license file to complete the database creation.

How it works...

From NAV 2013, we have only one database option, that is, Microsoft SQL Server. NAV development environment provides a simple wizard to create a SQL Server Database. This wizard starts by providing the database name. As soon as we provide the database name, the system updates the remaining settings with default values.

Next, we have provided a folder location to save the database files in a non-system location; this is always advisable to protect the database file from system crash and provide efficient HDD space management. The SQL server has a database logging system that keeps track of each and every transaction. The **Recovery Model.....** setting helps to let the SQL server know how to log the database's activities. **Bulk-logged** and **Full** will keep track of each and every activity done on related databases, whereas **Simple** will only keep track of important activity. It is advisable to keep the setting value **Simple** for test and temporary databases to save HDD space.

Finally, we updated the settings to upload the license to the database.

There's more...

You must be thinking, since we need to create a SQL database, why can't we do it from **SQL Server Management Studio** rather than NAV client. The first reason is that NAV does not recognize a non-NAV database. Secondly, the NAV client database creation wizard takes care of all NAV database-related settings and configurations.

While creating the previous database, we have seen that after providing the database name, the system updates all other settings with default values. All these values are very specific for NAV databases. For example, the system creates a secondary database file at the time of creating the database, which is unusual for SQL database creation. For a NAV database, the system saves all the configuration and metadata in a primary file, whereas transactional data is stored in a secondary file.

See also

- *Creating a NAV Server Instance*
- *Creating a user on NAV*
- *Changing the NAV License*
- *Testing the NAV database*

Testing the NAV database

For any system, consistency of data is very important. NAV provides tool to verify consistency. In this recipe, we will see how to run that tool.

How to do it...

1. Open **Microsoft Dynamics NAV 2013 Development Environment**.
2. Navigate to **File** | **Database** | **Test Database**. Your system will present a window similar to the one shown in the following screenshot:

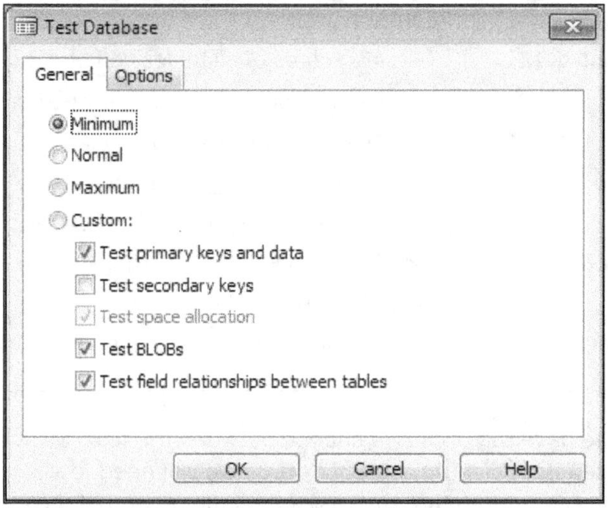

3. Select the option **Maximum** and then the second tab **Options**.
4. From the **Options** tab, select the option **File** and provide a location to save the logfile.

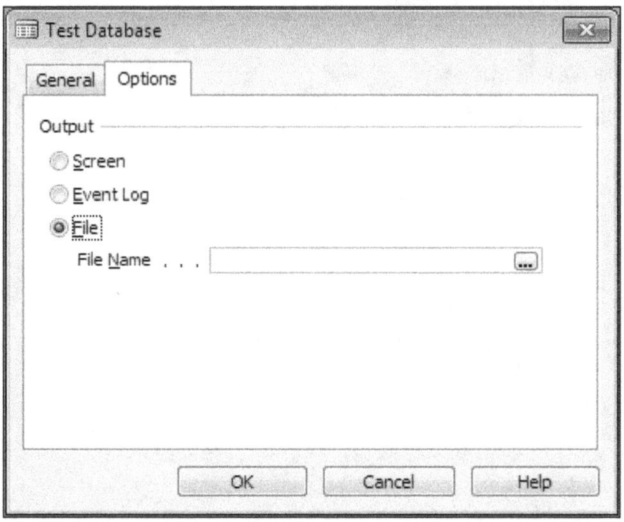

5. Click on **OK** to start the test.

How it works...

This tool verifies the consistency of data, so it is very important and viable to run this tool on a periodical basis. If we have huge data, then executing this tool on the **Maximum** setting will take a huge amount of time. Lets take a look at the task executed in the **Maximum** test.

Setting	Feature tested
Test primary keys and data	▸ All records of all tables can be read ▸ Record sorting order as per the primary key ▸ Field data and data type relation
Test secondary keys	▸ All secondary keys can be read ▸ Record sorting order as per secondary key
Test space allocation	Allocation of space to key sorting order management
Test BLOBs	All BLOBs fields can be read
Test field relationships between tables	All field relation can be read and data flow is correct

On the second tab, we have the option to choose between the test result output methods. In this recipe, we choose **File**, as in the case of **Screen** we will need to sit in front of our system to accept each and every error so that the test will continue, and in the case of **Event log**, we need to have windows system administration permission to read the log.

See also

- *Creating a NAV Server Instance*
- *Changing the NAV license*
- *Creating a new database*

Index

Symbols

D

E

F

G

H

I

J

K

L

M

N

O

P

T

U

V

W

X

Y

Z

[PACKT] enterprise
professional expertise distilled
PUBLISHING

Thank you for buying
Microsoft Dynamics NAV 7 Programming Cookbook

About Packt Publishing

Packt, pronounced 'packed', published its first book "*Mastering phpMyAdmin for Effective MySQL Management*" in April 2004 and subsequently continued to specialize in publishing highly focused books on specific technologies and solutions.

Our books and publications share the experiences of your fellow IT professionals in adapting and customizing today's systems, applications, and frameworks. Our solution-based books give you the knowledge and power to customize the software and technologies you're using to get the job done. Packt books are more specific and less general than the IT books you have seen in the past. Our unique business model allows us to bring you more focused information, giving you more of what you need to know, and less of what you don't.

Packt is a modern, yet unique publishing company, which focuses on producing quality, cutting-edge books for communities of developers, administrators, and newbies alike. For more information, please visit our website: `www.PacktPub.com`.

About Packt Enterprise

In 2010, Packt launched two new brands, Packt Enterprise and Packt Open Source, in order to continue its focus on specialization. This book is part of the Packt Enterprise brand, home to books published on enterprise software - software created by major vendors, including (but not limited to) IBM, Microsoft and Oracle, often for use in other corporations. Its titles will offer information relevant to a range of users of this software, including administrators, developers, architects, and end users.

Writing for Packt

We welcome all inquiries from people who are interested in authoring. Book proposals should be sent to `author@packtpub.com`. If your book idea is still at an early stage and you would like to discuss it first before writing a formal book proposal, contact us; one of our commissioning editors will get in touch with you.

We're not just looking for published authors; if you have strong technical skills but no writing experience, our experienced editors can help you develop a writing career, or simply get some additional reward for your expertise.

[PACKT] enterprise
professional expertise distilled
PUBLISHING

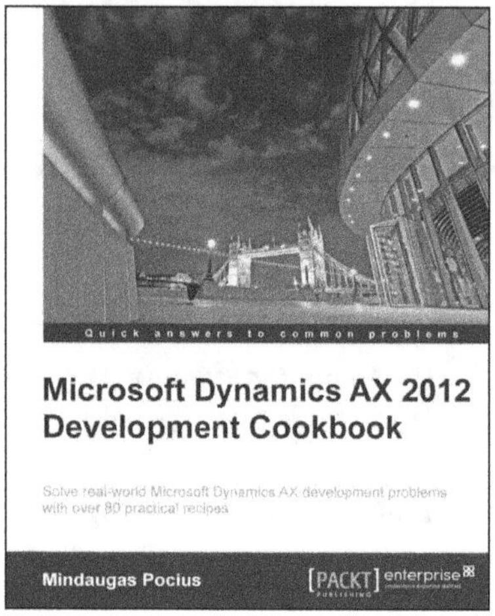

Microsoft Dynamics AX 2012 Development Cookbook

ISBN: 978-1-84968-464-4 Paperback: 372 pages

Solve real-world Microsoft Dynamics AX development problems with over 80 practical recipes

1. Develop powerful, successful Dynamics AX projects with efficient X++ code with this book and eBook
2. Proven recipes that can be reused in numerous successful Dynamics AX projects
3. Covers general ledger, accounts payable, accounts receivable, project modules and general functionality of Dynamics AX

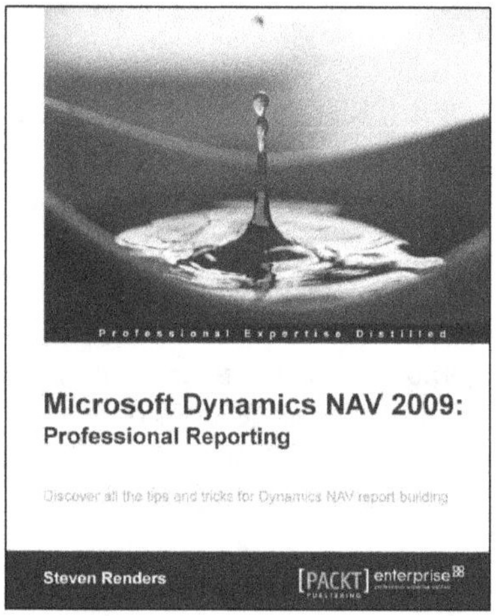

Microsoft Dynamics NAV 2009: Professional Reporting

ISBN: 978-1-84968-244-2 Paperback: 352 pages

Discover all the tips and tricks for Dynamics NAV report building

1. Get an overview of all the reporting possibilities, in and out of the box
2. Understand the new architecture and reporting features in Microsoft Dynamics NAV 2009 with this book and e-book
3. Full of illustrations, diagrams, and tips with clear step-by-step instructions and real-world examples

Please check **www.PacktPub.com** for information on our titles

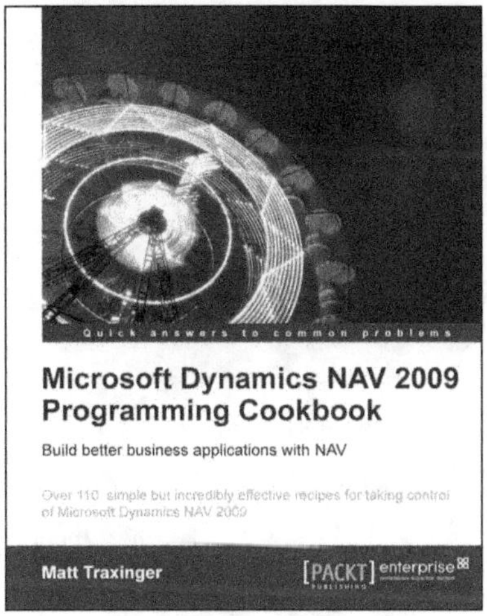

Microsoft Dynamics NAV 2009 Programming Cookbook

ISBN: 978-1-84968-094-3 Paperback: 356 pages

Over 110 simple but incredibly effective recipes for taking control of Microsoft Dynamics NAV 2009

1. Write NAV programs to do everything from finding data in a table to integration with an instant messenger client
2. Develop your own .NET code to perform tasks that NAV cannot handle on its own
3. Work with SQL Server to create better integration between NAV and other systems
4. Learn to use the new features of the NAV 2009 Role Tailored Client

---

Microsoft Dynamics AX 2009 Development Cookbook

ISBN: 978-1-84719-942-3 Paperback: 352 pages

Solve real-world Dynamics AX development problems with over 60 simple but incredibly effective recipes

1. Develop powerful, successful Dynamics AX projects with efficient X++ code
2. Proven AX recipes that can be implemented in various successful Dynamics AX projects
3. Covers general ledger, accounts payable, accounts receivable, project, CRM modules and general functionality of Dynamics AX
4. Step-by-step instructions and useful screenshots for easy learning

Please check **www.PacktPub.com** for information on our titles

www.ingramcontent.com/pod-product-compliance
Lightning Source LLC
LaVergne TN
LVHW080029210926
848481LV00011B/3140
* 9 7 8 1 8 4 9 6 8 9 1 0 6 *